17	NELSON'S MONUMENT	23	PARLIAMENT HOUSE	28	UNIVERSITY
18	GAS WORKS	24	GRASSMARKET	29	PLEASANCE
19	HOLYROOD PALACE	25	LAWNMARKET	30	ST MARY'S WYND
20	ST LEONARDS	26	HIGH STREET	31	YORK PLACE
21	ARTHUR'S SEAT	27	HIGH KIRK	32	PICARDY PLACE
22	**REGISTER HOUSE**		OF ST GILES	33	LEITH WALK

THE ASSOCIATION FOR SCOTTISH LITERARY STUDIES

NUMBER TWENTY-TWO

THE TAVERN SAGES

PLACE IN RETURN BOX to remove this checkout from your record.
TO AVOID FINES return on or before date due.

DATE DUE	DATE DUE	DATE DUE

MSU Is An Affirmative Action/Equal Opportunity Institution

THE ASSOCIATION FOR SCOTTISH LITERARY STUDIES

The Association for Scottish Literary Studies aims to promote the study, teaching and writing of Scottish literature, and to further the study of the languages of Scotland.

To these ends, the ASLS publishes works of Scottish literature (of which this volume is an example), literary criticism in *Scottish Literary Journal*, scholarly studies of language in *Scottish Language*, and in-depth reviews of Scottish books in *SLJ Supplements*. And it publishes *New Writing Scotland*, an annual anthology of new poetry, drama and short fiction, in Scots, English and Gaelic, by Scottish writers.

All these publications are available as a single 'package', in return for an annual subscription. Enquiries should be sent to: ASLS, c/o Department of English, University of Aberdeen, Aberdeen AB9 2UB.

ANNUAL VOLUMES

1971 James Hogg, *The Three Perils of Man*, ed. Douglas Gifford.
1972 *The Poems of John Davidson*, vol. I, ed. Andrew Turnbull.
1973 *The Poems of John Davidson*, vol. II, ed. Andrew Turnbull.
1974 Allan Ramsay and Robert Fergusson, *Poems*, ed. Alexander M. Kinghorn and Alexander Law.
1975 John Galt, *The Member*, ed. Ian A. Gordon.
1976 William Drummond of Hawthornden, *Poems and Prose*, ed. Robert H. MacDonald.
1977 John G. Lockhart, *Peter's Letters to his Kinsfolk*, ed. William Ruddick.
1978 John Galt, *Selected Short Stories*, ed. Ian A. Gordon.
1979 Andrew Fletcher of Saltoun, *Selected Political Writings and Speeches*, ed. David Daiches.
1980 *Scott on Himself*, ed. David Hewitt.
1981 *The Party-Coloured Mind*, ed. David Reid.
1982 James Hogg, *Selected Stories and Sketches*, ed. Douglas S. Mack.
1983 Sir Thomas Urquhart of Cromarty, *The Jewel*, ed. R.D.S. Jack and R.J. Lyall.
1984 John Galt, *Ringan Gilhaize*, ed. Patricia J. Wilson.
1985 Margaret Oliphant, *Selected Short Stories of the Supernatural*, ed. Margaret K. Gray.
1986 James Hogg, *Selected Poems and Songs*, ed. David Groves.
1987 Hugh MacDiarmid, *A Drunk Man Looks at the Thistle*, ed. Kenneth Buthlay.
1988 *The Book of Sandy Stewart*, ed. Roger Leitch.
1989 *The Comic Poems of William Tennant*, ed. Alexander Scott and Maurice Lindsay.
1990 Thomas Hamilton, *The Youth and Manhood of Cyril Thornton*, ed. Maurice Lindsay.
1991 *The Complete Poems of Edwin Muir*, ed. Peter Butter.
1992 *The Tavern Sages: Selections from the 'Noctes Ambrosianae'*, ed. J.H. Alexander.

THE ASSOCIATION FOR SCOTTISH LITERARY STUDIES

GENERAL EDITOR – C.J.M. MACLACHLAN

THE TAVERN SAGES

Selections from the *Noctes Ambrosianae*

edited by

J.H. Alexander

ABERDEEN

1992

First published in Great Britain, 1992
by The Association for Scottish Literary Studies
c/o Department of English
University of Aberdeen
Aberdeen AB9 2UB

ISBN 0 9488 7717 0

Introduction and Notes © 1992, J.H. Alexander

The Association for Scottish Literary Studies
acknowledges subsidy from the Scottish Arts Council
towards the publication of this volume.

Typeset by Roger Booth Associates, Newcastle upon Tyne
Printed in Great Britain by Bell and Bain Ltd, Glasgow

CONTENTS

INTRODUCTION

The *Noctes Ambrosianae* are a series of seventy-one largely imaginary conversations which appeared in *Blackwood's Edinburgh Magazine* between March 1822 and February 1835. Most of them are set in the actual tavern run by the Yorkshireman William Ambrose at 1 Gabriel's Road, and from No. 29 (November 1826) in his superior establishment, Ambrose's North British Hotel, Tavern, and Coffee-House at 15 Picardy Place. In summer, noctes are often held at the fictitious Buchanan Lodge (named after the Renaissance humanist George Buchanan), situated just outside Edinburgh overlooking the Firth of Forth.[1] The conversations—often lasting till dawn or beyond—are conceived of as being taken down in shorthand by Nathaniel Gurney of Norwich, ensconced in a convenient cupboard.[2]

In the *Noctes* the generally rather drab cultural life of the reigns of George IV and William IV managed to produce one of the major achievements of Scottish literature. (Like most Romantic masterpieces, the conversations have a distinctly serendipitous air about them.) The series as a whole has indeed many faults, which the present selection minimises but inevitably to some extent reflects: crassness, banality, tedium, repetitiveness, and nastiness are all evident from time to time. But the faults are outweighed, and in this selection reduced almost to insignificance, by precious virtues: endless variety; unbounded energy; a high degree of inventiveness in prose and verse; linguistic alertness and originality in English and Scots; passionate, frank, and often penetrating analyses of the literature and general culture of the late Romantic and pre-Victorian periods; hymns to human companionship and conviviality; and an unrivalled series of pictures of the peerless city of Edinburgh, both its ordinary life and those consecrated days when its potentially miraculous qualities are realised and celebrated. For the modern reader, all that is needed to participate fully in this mixture of wonder and fun, and to share in this unique close-up view of the 1820s and early 1830s, is some help with the topical allusions which come thick and fast for several pages at a time. This volume aims to present a broadly representative selection from the *Noctes*, and to provide sufficient explanatory material to fill in the context and elucidate the obscurities occasioned by the passing of seventeen decades.

The series falls into two parts. The early group, consisting of numbers 1 to 18 and number 20, were by various hands, chiefly those of Walter Scott's son-in-law John Gibson Lockhart, John Wilson (Professor of

Moral Philosophy at Edinburgh University from 1820), and William Maginn of Cork: there was a good deal of cooperation on individual numbers, and Blackwood himself played some part in assembling the often disparate material.[3] The later and larger group, numbers 19 and 21 to 71, were mostly Wilson's work: Maginn moved to London in 1823 and Lockhart (to become editor of the Tory *Quarterly Review*) in 1825, though Lockhart contributed a number of largely political noctes from the metropolis after his change of residence.[4]

The overall effect of each of the two main groups is distinctive. The early noctes tend to be fairly short (rarely more than twenty pages), and they are mostly very heterogeneous in subject matter. There is often a large dramatis personae, but the central characters of the whole series were established early. There is Christopher North, a fictionalised, aged and infirm version of Wilson: poetical, loquacious, sentimental; Timothy Tickler of Edinburgh's Southside, based on Wilson's uncle Robert Sym, who lived in George Square: old-fashioned, unpoetical, companionable, brusque; Odoherty, Maginn's alter ego: Irish; the under-characterised Dr Mordecai Mullion; and the Shepherd, or Hogg: only superficially a 'boozing buffoon', a complex embodiment of profoundly intuitive responses to experience, standing in a teasing and stimulating relationship with his original.[5]

The early noctes grew naturally out of the rest of Maga (as *Blackwood's* was familiarly known). The Tory publisher William Blackwood launched his new periodical, as the *Edinburgh Monthly Magazine*, in April 1817, in order to counter his Whig rival Archibald Constable's *Scots Magazine* and *Edinburgh Review*; but the dullness of his founding editors disappointed his expectations, and in October 1817 the renamed *Blackwood's Edinburgh Magazine* burst on the city and the world with Lockhart and Wilson as the publisher's coadjutors and principal contributors. The young men who between them wrote much of the new numbers were controversial, dogmatic, argumentative, clever, crude, very funny, very tedious, and most other things except sober and responsible: often they were several of these at the same time. They adopted an endless variety of pseudonyms (including North, Tickler, Odoherty, and Mullion), and signed contributions with each others' real or assumed names, or with the names of figures of intermittent fun such as Coleridge. They abused Wordsworth and Coleridge roundly in one number and praised them to the skies in the next. From one point of view this was sheer irresponsibility, and in Wilson's case the expression of temperamental instability. From another, it was a unique experiment in Romantic criticism, involving the reader in compulsive and often ironic debate.[6] It was certainly successful: Maga soon attained widespread fame and a circulation of between six and seven thousand; and scandalous: the early copies of the October 1817 number carried the Chaldee Manuscript, a mock-biblical satire on the discharge of the founding editors widening into a more general satire on Edinburgh society, initiated by Hogg and made considerably more outrageous by Lockhart and Wilson, which led to the first of a long series of lawsuits.[7]

It soon became clear that Maga was to be an intensely self-referential periodical, with a tendency for individual articles to coalesce into something larger than themselves. Articles in numbered series flourished, some abortive, some long-running, and tending to percolate beyond their own limits: for instance Lockhart's attacks (as 'Z') 'On The Cockney School of Poetry, No. I.' and 'No. II.' (*BM* 2.38–41, 194–201) are reinforced by his 'Letter from Z. to Mr Leigh Hunt' (*BM* 2.414–17). This coagulative tendency led in August and September 1819 to two overtly through-composed sequences: 'The True and Authentic Account of the Twelfth of August, 1819' (*BM* 5.597–*613) prepared the way for 'The Tent', which occupied the whole of the September number, introducing the usual variety of articles and songs as part of an imaginary shooting holiday on Deeside. It was an easy step from this to the first of the noctes eighteen months later. Since Lockhart was well versed in the classics, one may add to internal evolution the models provided by such conversations as Plato's and Xenophon's *Symposia*, Lucian's *Dialogues*, and Varro's *Satirae Menippeae*.

In the present selection, the early noctes are represented by two complete numbers: the first, by Lockhart, and the fourth (with its unique setting in Byron's temporary home Pisa), by Maginn, who may have contributed one or more of the songs to Lockhart's piece. Both of these rely for much of their detailed London literary gossip on sets of memoranda contributed by the periodical and newspaper editor Alaric Watts.[8] This gossip gives a vivid picture of metropolitan letters (and in particular the periodical world) in the age of Byron and Scott, but there is much more in these two noctes to suggest the attractiveness of the early group's exuberance and ingenuity: the imaginary verse original of Byron's widely-published letter on *Cain* (pages 8–10) is a high point, as is Odoherty's Latin version of the venerable 'Backe and side go bare' (35–6); and even when the ingenuity is employed in relentless pursuit of the Cockney School (who included not only Leigh Hunt but also John Keats) most modern readers are likely to find the doggerel Italian hilarious (15). There is self-criticism as well as self-promotion on Maga's part: Odoherty's characterisation of the magazine's coverage of German literature as 'humbug articles' (5) fails, perhaps deliberately, to recognise the importance of this aspect of its work in this area. There is much thumbnail literary criticism to stimulate the reader. And throughout there is the combination, typical of Maga, of teasing inconsistency

and high Tory principle: Kit North undermines Francis Jeffrey's
Edinburgh Review 'by doing all that ever these folks could do in one
Number, and then undoing it in the next', but 'as to two or three
principles—I mean religion, loyalty, and the like, he is always stiff as a
poker' (32).

The later noctes, Wilson's major achievement, are longer, more
homogeneous, less riotous, heavier, more substantial. Maginn found
them rather dull. On 2 August 1826 he wrote to Blackwood: 'I shall
send you a bundle of literary Chat for your noctes. Wilson's are badly
defective in that article—and they are rather too much of Hogg.' Later
in the year he made the same point in a more sweeping manner: 'I am
afraid you have given up the old vein of the magazine—and yet I cannot
help thinking it was a good—at all events an original—one.'[9] But
although there are longueurs in Wilson's later extended noctes, the
vitality of language, thought, and incident of the early days is not lost.
The variety of which Wilson was capable is illustrated in this selection
by two complete noctes, separated by a single scene with an unusual
setting, and followed by a series of short extracts mostly from his pen.

The noctes were often placed at the end of the main matter in
individual numbers of Maga, suggesting that they were seen as the
climax of the issue. Wilson's Noctes 5[10] is clearly intended to set the
seal on a Royal Number, devoted entirely to celebrating George IV's
visit to Edinburgh in August 1822. The number begins with a Wilsonian
panegyric, 'The King', and there follow in turn: an English response to
the Visit, by George Croly; imaginary responses from 'Omai, the
Traveller', perhaps by Galt, and from visitors from the west of Scotland,
certainly by him; a dismissal by Wilson of the *Scotsman*'s liberal doubts
about the occasion; a Wilsonian review of Hogg's *pièce d'occasion*, *The
Royal Jubilee*; an anonymous 'Letter from a Goth'; and an account by
John Cay of the controversy between Glengarry and the Celtic
Society.[11] After all this, Noctes 5 crowns the celebration by providing a
masque to set alongside Hogg's *Jubilee*.[12]

Noctes 5 will not be wholly to many readers' tastes nowadays, but it
is at the very least an important historical document and a remarkable
curiosity, which should ideally be read alongside John Prebble's overtly
disapproving (but curiously celebratory) study of *The King's Jaunt*. It
gives wholehearted expression to a high Tory way of imagining: Whigs
are physical as well as moral weaklings, unable to hold their drink or
tolerate tobacco smoke; the aristocracy play their part, and the poor
know their place, being loyal and religious as well as full of physical
vitality; the Highlanders are willing and honoured participants as well
as traditional figures of fun. The Kingdom is United in friendly rivalry.
The comprehensive semiotics of the piece embrace substantial food,[13]

nautical patriotics, the world of pugilism (prize-fighting), and the defeat of political rationalism. In the background is the figure of the stage-manager of the Visit, Sir Walter Scott, whose *Rob Roy* formed the basis of the entertainment at the Theatre Royal, and whose use of the rhythm of the national anthem for the Boat Song 'Hail to the Chief who in triumph advances' in *The Lady of the Lake* is alluded to in the verses allegedly contributed from Cape Clear (53–4). Also in the background, in the final scene, is Burns's 'The Cotter's Saturday Night', for Wilson and his colleagues a classic picture of an idealised rural way of life now seen as threatened by scepticism and radicalism. This crowning noctes is itself crowned by a sonnet printed on a separate page in what was presumably originally bright red, though it has now faded to an inappropriate pale pink:

L'Envoy,
TO THE KING.
Christopher North.

HERE CLOSE WE FOR THE PRESENT! THIS, O KING!
  THIS NUMBER DO WE DEDICATE TO THEE,
  LOWLY AND REVERENTLY ON BENDED KNEE,
OUR LOYAL TRIBUTE HUMBLY OFFERING.
WHILE WE HAVE HAND TO WRITE, OR VOICE TO SING,
  WHILE WE HAVE MASTERY OF VERSE AND PROSE,
  IN SHORT, WHILE THROUGH OUR HEART THE LIFE-BLOOD FLOWS,—
SIMILAR TRIBUTE SHALL WE JOY TO BRING.
AND THOUGH OLD AGE HATH LAID UPON OUR HEAD
  THE SNOW OF THREESCORE WINTERS, YET IF E'ER
NEED SHOULD ARISE—IF DAYS OF DOUBT AND DREAD
  SUMMON US IN THY CAUSE, THE FIGHT TO DARE,
  AGE-STRICKEN AS WE ARE, WE FORTH SHOULD FARE,
OUR BLOOD, AS CRIMSON AS OUR TYPE, TO SHED!

After the heady brew of the Royal Number, the first scene from Noctes 34 is likely to come as a moment of relaxation. It is in a sense sheer fun, but it is also an excellent example of Wilson's ability to combine intense physicality (and here a distinct sexuality) with a sort of glory: the various pleasures and pains of swimming, in its classical, legendary, poetic, and mundane aspects, are intimately linked with the picture of Edinburgh as 'a glorious city'. The introduction of Wilson's actual dog Bronte brings to perfection this delightful sketch.

    The massive Noctes 48 is constructed on the ground-bass of a gargantuan repast which makes its presence known as more superficial topics die away and yield to others. The prominent figure of the English Opium-Eater had first been introduced in Noctes 12: this partly fictionalised De Quincey is used to contrast (often to comic as well as serious effect) a mind possessed of intense analytical intelligence with the largely instinctive mind of the fictionalised Hogg. This noctes illustrates well the easy manner in which Wilson moves from one field to another. During the soup course the conversation focusses on the current exhibition of the Scottish Academy in a man-in-the-street fashion. The fish course brings the immortal fantasy of the Shepherd on the Bonassus with the Opium-Eater's hilarious but not wholly risible commentary. Meat at first accompanies, or is accompanied by, appropriately tough discussion of political and economic matters, with Reform the spectre at the feast, and then by an even tougher assault on the young liberal 'Macauley'. (Thomas Macaulay has won this argument almost as decisively as John Keats has the Cockney squabble; in Scott's words, 'Yes, yes, the world finds out these things for itself at last').[14] Conversation during the game course first provides an insight into the state of literature in 1830, that interregnum between Romantic and Victorian which is *terra incognita* for most modern readers, and then focusses on a comparison of Scottish and English cultural achievements.

The series of twenty-four short extracts are Wilson's, apart from 1, 4, and 19 which are by Lockhart. No writing is ideologically innocent, and concerns touched on in the complete noctes can be observed here too. But this final section is presented primarily for pure enjoyment, ranging from the slapstick to the sentimental (11), and from the intensely concrete to the enchanted (22). The twenties and early thirties of the last century come to life more vividly in these pages than in almost any others.

Alan Lang Strout has said that in the *Noctes* 'for the first time, Wilson could write as well as he talked, passing from subject to subject with his extraordinary gusto. Inconsistent and contradictory always, here was no need for consistency:—here, above all, was afforded him an opportunity to pour out, by the bucket, his "flamboyant vitality."'[15] Most of what Strout says may be applied to the whole series. From the outset, for all its classical precedents, it struck its readers as something quite new: 'the idea of the *Noctes* was one so entirely novel as set everyone talking about it when it first appeared.'[16] It may be regarded as an outstanding example of second generation Romantic genius, comparable in many ways with Byron's *Don Juan* in its outrageousness, its variety, its virtuoso improvisatory quality, its exploratory and subversive aspect, its allusiveness, and its vast entertainment value. As Hogg wrote to Blackwood, stressing the importance of preserving the anonymity of his *Confessions of a Justified Sinner*, 'This will give excellent and delightful scope and freedom.'[17] Or, as Lockhart (now editor of the *Quarterly Review*) put it in an undated letter from Abbotsford: '*In vino veritas* and *ridentem dicere verum* were I always understood the real mottoes of the N.A. and when you ask if I wd say such & such things in the Quarterly my only answer is alas! no for there I have no such machinery of round table & flowing bowls & *talkers* who of course wd get dull if they all talked in one Strain.'[18]

The whole series of the *Noctes Ambrosianae* amounts to well over a million words. The present selection may appear substantial, but it contains only some eight per cent of the corpus. Concentrating on this representative sample has made it possible for the first time to fill in the background by means of adequate notes. The notes of the pioneering nineteenth-century editors R. Shelton Mackenzie and J.F. Ferrier, though often invaluable, are decidedly exiguous, and while some of the most memorable and enduring passages in the *Noctes* require little or no explanation, so much is so intricately rooted in its own time that attempting to read it with inadequate help is like tackling Pope's *Dunciad* in an unannotated edition. In due course, the *Noctes* will no doubt attain the complete edition which they deserve. In the meantime readers who are attracted by what they have encountered in this volume can only be referred in the first instance to Ferrier's edition of those noctes which he was sure were Wilson's (in one or two cases he omits sections which he believes are by other hands): Ferrier's text is reasonably accurate, and he has an invaluable index and a series of detailed running heads making possible a quick check of the contents of each noctes. For the noctes which do not appear in Ferrier, readers must go to Shelton Mackenzie's edition (which also has detailed running heads and an index, but which is not widely available in Britain), or to the original volumes of *Blackwood's* which are to be found in many university and major public libraries. They can be assured of much instruction, some indignation, and a great deal of most excellent entertainment.

Acknowledgments

The editor gratefully acknowledges the generous help given by the librarians and staff of Aberdeen University Library, the British Library, Edinburgh Public Library, Edinburgh University Library, Leeds University Library, the Mitchell Library, Glasgow, and the National Library of Scotland. The following individuals have made helpful suggestions and contributions of many different kinds: Professor David Buchan, Geoffrey D. Carnall, Peter Cochrane, Dr Janet Cooksey, Professor Wendy A. Craik, Thomas Crawford, Professor David Daiches,

Alastair Elliot, Dr Peter D. Garside, A.P. Gorringe, Dr David Groves, Dr David S. Hewitt, Martin Hopkinson, Dr Gillian H. Hughes, Professor David Irwin, Caroline Jackson-Houlston, Claire Lamont, Dr Douglas S. Mack, Dr Robin MacLachlan, Dr Fiona Pearson, Roy M. Pinkerton, Dr Michael J. Robson, Robert N. Smart, Joanna Soden, Dr Timothy Stevens, Dr Peter Thomas, Professor Derick S. Thomson, Dr Donald Sultana, Donald J. Withrington, Margaret Tait, and Hilda Weir. Mairi Robinson has given expert help with certain linguistic queries. The editor owes a special debt to the Association's General Editor, Dr Christopher MacLachlan, and to its expert reader who in accordance with convention must remain anonymous. The previous editions of the *Noctes Ambrosianae* by J.F. Ferrier (1855, selected), and R. Shelton Mackenzie (1866 and later editions) have been useful, as has Claire Cartmell's edition of the first noctes in her Leeds University dissertation (1974): details are given in the Abbreviated References.

NOTES

1. For Maga's use of Buchanan, see note to 67.9.

2. Gurney's surname is a playful allusion to William Brodie Gurney (1777–1855), official shorthand writer to the Houses of Parliament, immortalised by Byron in *Don Juan*, Canto 1 (1819), stanza 189.

3. The Blackwood papers in the National Library of Scotland contain allusions to Blackwood's own involvement. See for example MS Acc. 5643 B6, p. 135 and MS Acc. 5643 B7, p. 88 (both undated), where Lockhart asks Hogg to send songs for the *Noctes*. Lockhart has an undated letter to Blackwood (MS 4721, f. 236v) saying: 'Your idea of the Noctes is most capital—but the thing must be done at leisure & I rather think when Wilson & I are together. Meantime hint it to the Dr [Maginn] & let me have his hints.'

4. Notably nos 57, 58, 62, and 63.

5. The term 'boozing buffoon' was coined by Lockhart to describe the problems that the Hogg/Shepherd figure presented when James Hogg was hoping for a grant from the Royal Society of Literature: *Quarterly Review*, 44 (January 1831), 82.

6. This case is more fully argued in J.H. Alexander, '*Blackwood's*: Magazine as Romantic Form', *Wordsworth Circle*, 15 (1984), 57–68.

7. The Chaldee Manuscript was replaced in printing the complete volumes of Maga generally available nowadays: it is most easily found in the final volume of Ferrier's edition of the Wilson *Noctes*.

8. The memoranda on which the first noctes draws are to be found in MS 4009, ff. 228–31, 249–56, and 257–60; the corresponding memoranda for most of the fourth noctes have not survived: their existence is indicated by Maginn's remark to Blackwood in a letter to be dated 23 July 1823 that he wrote Noctes 4 'out of Alaric's notes' (MS 4011, ff. 33v–34r), and by Blackwood's statement to Watts on 24 July 1824: 'You will see we have made as much use as we could in the Dialogue betwixt Byron and ODoherty of your Memoranda' (MS Acc. 5643 B3, p. 25): only one of two points from Watts's surviving memoranda appear in this noctes. Some of the most important debts to Watts in the first Noctes are indicated in the editorial notes.

9. MS 4018, f. 9r; f. 11r [4 November 1826].

10. This noctes was originally misnumbered 'VI' instead of 'V'.

11. This subject is discussed in the note to 49.2: Cay also contributed the song 'Deil tak' the Kelts' in the Noctes.

12. The archaising tendency of the fifth Noctes and of Hogg's *Jubilee* is significantly paralleled by Turner's projected series of pictures of the Royal Progress: see Gerald Finley, *Turner and George the Fourth in Edinburgh, 1822* (London and Edinburgh, 1981).

13. Some idea of the regal associations of gargantuan meals may be gained from the almost incredible table plans for the Grand Banquet of 24 August, reproduced as a large pull-out at the end of [Robert Mudie], *A Historical Account of His Majesty's Visit to Scotland*, 2nd edn (Edinburgh, 1822).

14. On meeting John Severn, Keats's friend, in Rome in 1832: Marion Lockhart, *John Gibson Lockhart* (London, 1954), 41.

15. 'Concernng the *Noctes Ambrosianae*', *Modern Language Notes*, 51 (1936), 497.

16. Alaric Watts to Blackwood, 8 August 1822: MS 4009, f. 227r.

17. Hogg to Blackwood, 28 June 1824: MS 4012, f. 184r.

18. MS 4033, f. 238r. The Latin quotations mean 'Truth comes out in wine' (proverbial) and 'And yet why may one not be telling truth while one laughs?' ('Quamquam ridentem dicere verum/ Quid vetat?': Horace, *Odes* 4.12.24–5).

ABBREVIATED REFERENCES

BM or Maga   *Blackwood's Edinburgh Magazine*

Cartmell   Claire Cartmell, 'The Age of Politics, Personalities
                    and Periodicals: The Early Nineteenth Century World
                    of the "Noctes Ambrosianae" of *Blackwood's
                    Edinburgh Magazine*' (unpublished Leeds University
                    Ph.D. dissertation, 1974)

Ferrier   *Noctes Ambrosianæ by Professor Wilson*, ed. J.F.
                    F[errier], 4 vols (Edinburgh and London, [1855])

Mackenzie   *Noctes Ambrosianæ*, ed. R. Shelton Mackenzie, 5 vols
                    (New York, 1866)

ODEP   *The Oxford Dictionary of English Proverbs*, 2nd edn,
                    ed. F.P. Wilson (Oxford, 1970)

Strout   Alan Lang Strout, *A Bibliography of Articles in
                    'Blackwood's Magazine'* ... *1817–1825* (Lubbock,
                    Texas, 1959)

Noctes Ambrosianae.

No. I.

CHRISTOPHER NORTH, Esquire, *Solus.*

Enter Ensign MORGAN ODOHERTY.

EDITOR. I am glad to see you, Odoherty. I am heartily glad of the interruption. I won't write any more to-night—I'll be shot if I write a word more. Ebony may jaw as he pleases. The Number will do well enough as it is. If there is not enough, let him send his devil into the Balaam-box.

ODOHERTY. I have just arrived from London.

EDITOR. From *London?*—The Fleet, I suppose.—How long have you lain there?

ODOHERTY. I have been out these three weeks. I suppose, for any thing you would have advanced, I might have lain there till Kingdom-come.

EDITOR. I can't advance money for ever, Adjutant. You have not sent me one article these four months.

ODOHERTY. What sort of an article do you want?—A poem?

EDITOR. Poems! There's poetry enough without paying you for it. Have you seen Milman's new tragedy?

ODOHERTY. No; but I saw the proofs of a puff upon it for the next Quarterly. He's a clever fellow, but they cry him too high. The report goes, that he is to step into Gifford's shoes one of these days.

EDITOR. That accounts for the puffing; but it will do a really clever fellow, like Milman, no good.

ODOHERTY. It will, Mr North. I know nobody that puffs more lustily than yourself now and then. What made you puff Procter so much at first?

EDITOR. It was you that puffed him. It was an article of your own, Ensign.

ODOHERTY. By Mahomet's mustard-pot, I've written so much, I don't remember half the things I've done in your own lubberly Magazine, and elsewhere. At one time I wrote all Day and Martin's poetry. They were grateful. They kept the whole mess of the 44th in blacking.

EDITOR. Then you wrote the *World*, did not you?

ODOHERTY. I never heard of such a thing. They've been quizzing you, old boy. Impostors are abroad.

EDITOR. Then somebody has been sporting false colours about town.

ODOHERTY. Like enough. Set a thief to catch a thief.

EDITOR. You've been writing in Colbourn, they say, Master Morgan?

ODOHERTY. Not one line. The pretty boys have applied to me a dozen times, but I never sent them any answer except once, and then it was an epigram on themselves.

EDITOR. Let's hear it!

ODOHERTY. Now! By Jupiter, I have forgotten the beginning of it. I think it was something like this:—

> Colbourn, Campbell, and Co. write rather so so,
>   But atone for't by puff and profession—
> Every month gives us scope for the *Pleasures of Hope,*
>   But all ends in the *Pains of Possession.*

EDITOR. How do they get on? Heavily, Ensign?

ODOHERTY. D— heavily! They lay out a cool hundred on advertisements every month; but Campbell does very little—at least so it is to be hoped—and the Subs are no great shakes. They have a miserable set of bullaboos about them—broken-winded *dominies*, from the manufacturing districts, and so forth. Even Hazlitt does the drama better.

EDITOR. O, Hazlitt's a real fellow in his small way. He has more sense in his little finger, than many who laugh at him have in their heads, but he is bothering too long at that *table-talk.*

ODOHERTY. Proper humbug!

EDITOR. Did you see any of the Cockneys? What's the gossip about Murray's, Ridgeway's, and so forth? Did you make a tour of the shops?

ODOHERTY. Of course—I went round them all with a bundle of discarded articles you gave me to line my trunk with, when I went to the moors last year. I passed myself off for a country clergyman, wanting to publish a series of essays. I said I had a wife and seven small children.

EDITOR. You have some tolerable big ones, I believe.

ODOHERTY. Which you never will have, old boy. The booksellers are a very civil set of fellows: Murray took me into a room by myself, and told me about the row between him and the Divan.

EDITOR. What row? and with whom?

ODOHERTY. Why, they call Murray Emperor of the West, and Longman and Company the Divan. They've fallen out about Mother Rundell's book upon cookery. I told Kitchener the next day, that I thought his own book as good a one.

EDITOR. Shameless fellow! Don't you remember how you cut it up? I wonder you could look the doctor in the face.

ODOHERTY. By jing! he thought I was a doctor myself. I had a black rose in my hat, and talked very wisely about the famous mistake touching *a Mr Winton of Chelsea.* I'll tell you about that, too, some other time.

EDITOR. The Bishop's first two volumes are not quite *the potato.* I hope the others are better.

ODOHERTY. Who cares? I shall never read them. Have you seen Horace Walpole's Memoirs?

EDITOR. I have. A most charming book. A most malicious, prying, lying old fox. What a prime contributor he would have made!—but, to be sure, he was a Whig.

ODOHERTY. So am I.—For that matter, half your best contributors are Whigs, I take it.

EDITOR. Mum, for that, Ensign.—But, at least, I have nothing to do with the Scotch Kangaroo Canaille.

ODOHERTY. They have nothing to do with you, you mean to say.

EDITOR. They're a dirty, dull, detestable set.—I hate them all—I despise them all—except little Jeffrey.

ODOHERTY. He's a clever chap, certainly,—I have not given him a dressing these two years;—I shall give you a song upon him one of these days.

EDITOR. Do.—What's a-foot among the Tumbledowns?

ODOHERTY. The Holland-house gentry are chuckling very much over a little tid-bit of blasphemy, sent over by a certain learned Lord from Italy,—'tis call'd the "Irish Advent,"—'tis a base parody on the Advent of our Saviour,—'tis circulated widely among the same Thebans who blarney'd about Hogg's Chaldee.

EDITOR. *Hogg's* Chaldee!—good.

ODOHERTY. You would notice the puffs about another thing, called "the Royal Progress;"—they say 'tis writ by Mrs Morgan's ex-chevalier; and I can believe it, for it is equally dull and disloyal.

EDITOR. Are these all the news you have picked up? How do the minor periodicals sell?

ODOHERTY. Worse and worse. Taylor and Hessey are going down like the devil.—Colburn pays like a hero, for what you would fling into the fire. The copyright of the European was disposed of t'other day for about £1600, back numbers, plates, and all included. 'Twas about the best of them.

EDITOR. I hope old Sir Richard is thriving.

ODOHERTY. Capitally. He circulates between three and four thousand; and his advertisements are very profitable.—Why don't you sport a little extra matter of cover?

EDITOR. At present mine are mostly *preserves.* I'll enlarge them, if you won't poach.

ODOHERTY. Depend on't, 'twill pay.

EDITOR. I hope Nicholls gets on.

ODOHERTY. Very fair. 'Tis the only Gentleman's Magazine, besides your own.

EDITOR. What is that thing called the Gazette of Fashion?

ODOHERTY. 'Tis a poor imitation of the Literary Gazette. Mr — —, they say, patronizes it; but this can't be true, for it attacks, very shamefully, *the man who did* HIM *more good than any body else ever will be able to do him, here or hereafter.*

EDITOR. Hercles' vein with a vengeance! You've been studying the Eclectic, one would think.

ODOHERTY. The Eclectic is not so poor an affair as you insinuate, Mr Christopher. The principal writers tip us a little of the *Snuffle* and *Whine,*—but you are up to that yourself, when it serves your turn. Montgomery's articles are such as you would like very well to lay your own fist upon, I fancy.

EDITOR. If Foster still writes in it, they have one of the first thinkers in England beneath their banner. I wish you would read him, before you begin to the auto-biography you've been talking about these three years.

ODOHERTY. Coleridge's did not pay.

EDITOR. But yours may,—nay, will,—must pay. I'll insure you of £3000 if you go to "the proper man." I intend to give him the first offer of my own great work,—my Armenian Grammar, which is now nearly ready for press.

ODOHERTY. Your name will sell any thing. Is there much personality in the notes?

EDITOR. I have cut up the commentators here and there. I have fixed an indelible stigma on old Scioppius.

ODOHERTY. I'll defy you to write a sermon without being personal.

EDITOR. I'll defy Dr Chalmers to do that. He is deuced severe on the Glasgow Bailies and Professors! I am told.

ODOHERTY. Do many clergymen contribute?

EDITOR. Droves.

ODOHERTY. What do the lads chiefly affect?

EDITOR. Jocular topics. 'Twas an arch-deacon sent me the Irish Melodies, which I know you have been owning every where for your own.

ODOHERTY. I follow one great rule,—never to own any thing that is my own, nor deny any thing that is not my own.

EDITOR. 'Tis the age of owning and disowning. It was a long while or I believed Hope to be Anastasius.

ODOHERTY. It will be a long while ere I believe that Anastasius wrote those quartos about mahogany. I believe he might furnish the wood, but, by Jericho, did he carve it at all?

EDITOR. You are an incorrigible Irishman. Have you any news from your own country? It seems to be in a fine state.

ODOHERTY. Why, for that matter, I think we are very common-place in our national diversions. Sir William Chambers complained of nature being monotonous, for furnishing *only* earth, air, and water. Blood and whisky may sum up all the amusements of the Irish Whigs.—Burning, throat-cutting, shooting an old proctor or policeman—that's all. They fight in a cowardly fashion. There's my cousin, Tom Magrath, writes me he saw 500 of them run away from about forty gentlemen. One of the chief stimulants the poor devils have, is a prophecy of the papist Bishop Walmesley, (the same that goes under the name of Pastorini,) that the Protestant church is to be destroyed in 1825.

EDITOR. Why, some few years ago, a godly Squire in Ayrshire here, published a thumping book, to prove that Buonaparte would die *in* 1825, *at the siege of Jerusalem.* The year 1825 will be a rare one when it comes.

ODOHERTY. These events will furnish fine materials for a new hour's *Tete-a-tete with the public.*

EDITOR. What a world of things will have happened ere 1825!

ODOHERTY. You will be knocked up ere then. You talk about your stomach—only see how little remains in the bottle!

EDITOR. I had finished two ere you came in. I can never write without a bottle beside me. Judge Blackstone followed the same plan, he had always a bottle of port by him while he was at his commentaries. When Addison was composing his Essay on the Evidences, he used to walk up and down the long room in Holland-house—there was a table with the black strap at each end, and he always turned up his little finger twice ere he had polished a sentence to his mind.—I believe he took brandy while he was doing the last act of Cato. There is no good writing without one glass.

"Nemo bene potest scribere jejunus."

ODOHERTY. I prefer smoking, on the whole. But I have no objection to a glass of punch along with it. It clears our mouth.

EDITOR. "Experto crede Roberto."

ODOHERTY. I am glad to see you have dropt your cursed humbug articles on German Plays. I hate all that trash. Is Kempferhausen defunct?

EDITOR. I had a present of two *aums* of Johannisberg from him not a week ago.

ODOHERTY. The piperly fellow once promised me a few dozens; but he took it amiss that I peppered him so at the *Tent.*

EDITOR. I am sure you would have sold it to Ambrose if you had got it,—Will you have some supper?

ODOHERTY. Excuse me, I never eat supper.

EDITOR. (*Rings.*) Waiter, welsh rabbits for five, scolloped oysters for ten, six quarts of porter, and covers for two.

WAITER. It is all ready, sir; Mr Ambrose knew what you would want the moment the Captain came in.

ODOHERTY. I am thinking seriously of writing some book. What shape do you recommend? I was thinking of a quarto.

EDITOR. A duodecimo you mean; will a quarto go into a sabretache, or a work-basket, or a ridicule? Are you the bishop of Winchester?

ODOHERTY. What bookseller do you recommend? [These are prime powldoodies!]

EDITOR. Ebony to be sure, if he will give the best price. But be sure you don't abuse his good temper. There was a worthy young man done up only a few months ago by the Cockney poets. He gave £100 to one for a bundle of verses, (I forget the title,) of which just 30 copies were sold. They were all at him like leeches, and he was soon sucked to the bone. You must not tip Ebony any shabby trash—you must be upon honour, Mr Odoherty. You have a great name, and you must support it. If you mind your hits, you may rise as high as anybody I know in any of the slang lines.

ODOHERTY. You flatter me! Butter!

EDITOR. Not one lick! Egan is not worthy of holding the candle to your Boxiana; and yet Egan is a prime swell. You should get little Cruikshanks to draw the vignettes; your life would sell as well as Hogg's, or Haggart's, or any body else, that I remember.

ODOHERTY. You'll cut a great figure in it yourself.

EDITOR. A good one you mean?

ODOHERTY. No, d—, I scorn to flatter you, or any man. I shall tell the truth, all the truth, and nothing but the truth. Do you expect me to say that you are a handsome man? Or that you have slim ancles? Or that you don't squint? Or that you understand the whole doctrine of quadrille? Or that you are the author of Waverley? Or the author of Anastasius? Are these the bams you expect?

EDITOR. Say that I am the author of the Chaldee, and I am satisfied.

ODOHERTY. No, I'll stick to my own rule. I'll claim it myself. I'll challenge Hogg if he disputes the point.

EDITOR. I hope you'll shoot potatoes; for I could not afford to lose either of you! you are both of you rum ones to look at, but devils to go.

ODOHERTY. I intend to be modest as to my amours.

EDITOR. You had better not. The ladies won't buy if you do so. Your amour with Mrs Macwhirter raised my sale considerably.

ODOHERTY. This is a very delicate age. I fear nothing at all high would go down with it.

EDITOR. Why, there's a vast deal of cant afloat as to this matter; people don't know what they are speaking about. Shew me any production of genius, written in our time, which does not contain what they pretend to abhor.

ODOHERTY. Why, there's the Edinburgh Review—you must at least allow 'tis a decent work.

EDITOR. Have you forgotten Sidney Smith's article about missionaries?—I won't repeat the *names* of some of them.

ODOHERTY. The Quarterly?

EDITOR. Why, Gifford and I are old boys, and past our dancing days; but I believe you will find some very sly touches here and there.

ODOHERTY. Byron?

EDITOR. Poh! you're wild now. We may despise the cant about him, but you must confess that there's always a little of *what's wrong* in the best of his works. Even the Corsair seems to have flirted a bit now and then. And Juan, you know, is a perfect Richelieu.

ODOHERTY. Have you any thing to say against the Waverley novels?

EDITOR. Not much. Yet even old Dame Norna in the Pirate seems to have danced in her youth. I strongly suspect her son was a mere *filius carnalis*.

ODOHERTY. What of Kenilworth, then?

EDITOR. 'Tis all full of going about the bush. One always sees what Elizabeth is thinking about. She has never some handsome fellow or other out of her mind. And then the scene where Leicester and Amy get up is certainly rather richly coloured. There is nothing a whit worse in the Sorrows of Werter, or Julia de Roubigné, or any of that sentimental set.

ODOHERTY. Milman is a very well-behaved boy—You can say nothing of that sort against him.

EDITOR. He is a very respectable man, and a clergyman to boot; but the bridal songs in his Fall of Jerusalem are not much behind what a layman might have done. There are some very luxurious hits in *that* part of the performance. Did you attend old P—'s sale when you were in town?

ODOHERTY. No, I can't say I did; but I hear there was a fine collection of the Facetiæ, and other forbidden fruits. A friend of mine got the editio princeps of Poggio, but he sweated for it. The Whigs bid high. They worked to keep all those tid-bits for themselves.

EDITOR. Does this affair of Lord Byron's Mystery create any sensation in London?

ODOHERTY. Very little. The Parsons about Murray's shop are not the most untractable people in the world, otherwise they would never have abstained so long from attacking Juan, Beppo, and the rest of Byron's improprieties—they that are so foul-mouthed against Shelly, and such insignificant blasphemers as that Cockney crew.

EDITOR. I have often wondered at the *face* they shew in that omission.

ODOHERTY. Really?

EDITOR. No doubt a Bookseller must have something to say as to his own Review. But the thing should not be pushed too far, else a noodle can see through it.

ODOHERTY. Meaning me?

EDITOR. Not at all. But as to Cain, I entirely differ from the Chancellor. I think, if Cain be prosecuted, it will be a great shame. The humbug of the age will then have achieved its most visible triumph.

ODOHERTY. I never saw it, but I thought it had been blasphemous.

EDITOR. No, sir, I can't see that. The Society might have had some pretence had they fallen on Don Juan; but I suppose those well-fed Archdeacons, and so forth, have their own ways of observing certain matters.

ODOHERTY. Have you seen Lord Byron's letter on the subject to Mr Murray?

EDITOR. Yes; 'tis in the papers.

ODOHERTY. A bite! that's the prose edition. It was written originally in verse, but Murray's friends thought it would have more effect if translated into prose; and a young clergyman, who writes in the Quarterly, turned the thing very neatly, considering. I believe I have a copy of Lord Byron's own letter in my pocket.

EDITOR. Let's see it.

ODOHERTY. You shall have it.

BYRON TO MURRAY.*

Attacks on me were what I look'd for, Murray,
    But why the devil do they badger you?
These godly newspapers seem hot as curry,
    But don't, dear Publisher, be in a stew.
They'll be so glad to see you in a flurry—
    I mean those canting Quacks of your Review—
They fain would have you all to their own Set;—
But never mind them—we're not parted yet.

---

* Letter from Lord Byron to Mr Murray.

DEAR SIR,   *Pisa, Feb. 8, 1822.*

Attacks upon me were to be expected; but I perceive one upon *you* in the papers, which, I confess, that I did not expect. How, or in what manner *you* can be considered responsible for what *I* publish, I am at a loss to conceive. If "Cain" be "blasphemous," Paradise Lost is blasphemous; and the very words of the Oxford Gentleman, "Evil be thou my good," are from that very poem, from the mouth of

They surely don't suspect you, Mr John,
  Of being more than *accoucheur* to Cain;
What mortal ever said you wrote the Don?
  I dig the mine—you only fire the train!
But here—why, really, no great lengths I've gone—
  Big wigs and buzz were always my disdain—
But my poor shoulders why throw *all* the guilt on?
There's as much blasphemy, or more, in Milton.—

The thing's a drama, not a sermon-book;
  Here stands the murderer—that's *the old one* there—
In gown and cassock how would Satan look?
  Should Fratricides discourse like Doctor Blair?
The puritanic Milton freedom took,
  Which now-a-days would make a Bishop stare;
But not to shock the feelings of the age,
I only bring your angels on the stage.

Satan: and is there any thing more in that of Lucifer in the Mystery? Cain is nothing more than a drama, not a piece of argument. If Lucifer and Cain speak as the first murderer and the first rebel may be supposed to speak, surely all the rest of the personages talk also according to their characters; and the stronger passions have ever been permitted to the drama. I have even avoided introducing the Deity, as in Scripture, (though Milton does, and not very wisely either;) but have adopted his angel, as sent to Cain, instead, on purpose to avoid shocking any feelings on the subject, by falling short of, what all uninspired men must fall short in, viz. giving an adequate notion of the effect of the presence of Jehovah. The old mysteries introduced him liberally enough, and all this is avoided in the new one.

The attempt to *bully you*, because they think it will not succeed with me, seems to me as atrocious an attempt as ever disgraced the times. What! when Gibbon's, Hume's, Priestley's, and Drummond's publishers have been allowed to rest in peace for seventy years, are *you* to be singled out for a work of *fiction*, not of history or argument? There must be something at the bottom of this— some private enemy of your own—it is otherwise incredible.

I can only say, "*Me—me adsum qui feci,*" that any proceedings directed against you, I beg may be transferred to me, who am willing and *ought* to endure them all; that if you have lost money by the publication, I will refund any, or all of the copyright; that I desire you will say, that both *you* and Mr Gifford remonstrated against the publication, as also Mr Hobhouse; that I alone occasioned it, and I alone am the person who either legally or otherwise should bear the burthen. If they prosecute, I will come to England; that is, if by meeting it in my own person, I can save yours. Let me know—you shan't suffer for me, if I can help it. Make any use of this letter which you please.—Yours ever,

BYRON.

To bully You—yet shrink from battling Me,
   Is baseness. Nothing baser stains "The Times."
While Jeffrey in each catalogue I see,
   While no one talks of priestly Playfair's crimes,
While Drummond, at Marseilles, blasphemes with glee,
   Why all this row about my harmless rhymes?
Depend on't, Piso, 'tis some private pique
'Mong those that cram your Quarterly with Greek.

If this goes on, I wish you'd plainly tell 'em,
   'Twere quite a treat *to me* to be indicted;
Is it less sin to write such books than sell 'em?
   There's muscle!—I'm resolved I'll see you righted.
In me, great Sharpe, *in me converte telum*!
   Come, Doctor Sewell, shew you *have* been knighted!
— On my account you never shall be dunn'd,
The copyright, in part, I will refund.

You may tell all who come into your shop,
   You and your Bull-dog both remonstrated;
My Jackall did the same, you hints may drop,
   (All which, perhaps, you have already said.)
Just speak the word, I'll fly to be your prop,
   They shall not touch a hair, man, in your head.
You're free to print this letter; you're a fool
If you don't sent it first to the JOHN BULL.

EDITOR. Come, this is a good letter. If I had been Murray I would not have thought of the prose. I'll be hanged if I would.

ODOHERTY. Is there any thing new in the literary world here?

EDITOR. Not much that I hear of. There's Colonel Stewart's History of the Highland Regiments, one of the most entertaining books that have been published this long time. You're a soldier, you must review it for me in my next Number.

ODOHERTY. I think I'll tip you a series of articles on the history of the Irish regiments. I'm sure I know as many queer stories about them as any Colonel of them all. Is the book well written?

EDITOR. Plainly, but sensibly, and elegantly too, I think. Not much of the flash that's in vogue, but a great deal of feeling and truth. Some of the anecdotes are quite beautiful, and the Colonel's view of the Highland character is admirably drawn.

ODOHERTY. I'm glad to hear it. Few officers write well except Julius Cæsar, the Heavy Horseman, and myself.

EDITOR. You forget General Burgoyne.

ODOHERTY. Aye, true enough. The General was a sweet fellow.

EDITOR. So are you all. Have you done nothing to your Campaigns? I'm sure they would sell better than Southey's.

ODOHERTY. That's no great matter perhaps. I don't think the Laureate has much of a military eye.

EDITOR. How does the John Bull get on?

ODOHERTY. Famously they say. I'm told they divided L.6000 at the end of the first year. I intend contributing myself if you do not pay me better.

EDITOR. Why, how much would you have? Are you not always sure of your twenty guineas a-sheet? I'm sure that's enough for such articles as yours. You never take any pains.

ODOHERTY. If I did, they would not be worth five.—Have you seen John Home's Life?

EDITOR. To be sure.—'Tis very amusing. The old gentleman writes as well as ever. I wish he would try his hand at a novel once more.

ODOHERTY. Why, no novels sell now except the Author of Waverley's.

EDITOR. Write a good one, and I warrant you 'twill sell.—There's Adam Blair has taken like a shot; and Sir Andrew Wylie is almost out of print already.

ODOHERTY. I don't think Sir Andrew near so good as the Annals of the Parish.—What say you?

EDITOR. I agree with you.—The story is d— improbable; the hero a borish fellow, an abominable bore! but there is so much cleverness in the writing, and many of the scenes are so capitally managed, that one can never lay down the book after beginning it. On the whole, 'tis a very strange performance.—I hear the Provost is likely to be better, however.

ODOHERTY. The Author has a vast deal of humour, but he should stick to what he has seen. The first part of Wylie is far the best.

EDITOR. The scene with old George is as good as possible.

ODOHERTY. It is. Why did he not produce the present King too?

EDITOR. He will probably have him some other time. If he could but write stories as well as the King tells them, he would be the first author of his time.

ODOHERTY. Were you ever in company with the King, North?

EDITOR. Three or four times,—long ago now, when he used to come a-hunting in the New Forest.

ODOHERTY. Will he come to Scotland this summer?

EDITOR. One can never be sure of a King's movements; but 'tis said he is quite resolved upon the trip.

ODOHERTY. What will the Whigs do?

EDITOR. Poh! the Whigs here are nobody. Even Lord Moira could not endure them. He lived altogether among the Tories when he was in

Scotland. The Whigs would be queer pigs at a drawing-room.

ODOHERTY. Sir Ronald Ferguson seems to be a great spoon.

EDITOR. He is what he seems. At the Fox dinner, t'other day, he came prepared with two speeches; one to preface the memory of old Charlie; the other returning thanks for his own health being drunk. He forgot himself, and transposed them. He introduced Fox with twenty minutes harangue about his own merits, and then, discovering his mistake, sat down in such a quandary!

ODOHERTY. Good! they're a petty set. What sort of a thing is the Thane of Fife—Tennant's poem?

EDITOR. Mere humbug—quite defunct.

ODOHERTY. What are they saying about Hogg's new romance, "The Three Perils of Man; or, War, Women, and Witchcraft"—Is not that the name?

EDITOR. I think so. I dare say 'twill be like all his things,—a mixture of the admirable, the execrable, and the tolerable. It is to be published by some London house.

ODOHERTY. Does he never come to Edinburgh now?

EDITOR. Oh yes, now and then he is to be seen, about five in the morning, selling sheep in the Grassmarket. I am told he is a capital manager about his farm, and getting rich apace.

ODOHERTY. I am glad to hear it. I'm sorry I wrote that article on his life. It was too severe, perhaps.

EDITOR. Never mind; 'tis quite forgotten. He is now giving out that he wrote it himself.

ODOHERTY. It was a devilish good article. He could not have written three lines of it.

EDITOR. No, no, but neither could you have written three lines of Kilmeny, no, nor one line of his dedication to Lady Anne Scott. Hogg's a true genius in his own style. Just compare him with any of the others of the same sort; compare him with Clare for a moment. Upon my word, Hogg appears to me to be one of the most wonderful creatures in the world, taking all things together. I wish he would send me more articles than he does, and take more pains with them.

ODOHERTY. Is Dr Scott in town?

EDITOR. No—he's busy writing the Odontist. They say it will be the oddest jumble. All his life—every thing he has seen, or might have seen, from a boy—and some strange anecdotes of the French Revolution.

ODOHERTY. Was he ever in the Bastile?

EDITOR. Oh yes, and in the Temple too. He has been every where but at Timbuctoo.

ODOHERTY. Where is Timbuctoo?

EDITOR. Somewhere in Egypt, I am told. I never was there.

ODOHERTY. What is your serious opinion about the present state of literature?

EDITOR. Why, we live in an age that will be much discussed when 'tis over—a very stirring, productive, active age—a generation of comment-ators will probably succeed—and I, for one, look to furnish them with some tough work. There is a great deal of genius astir, but, after all, not many first-rate works produced. If I were asked to say how many will survive, I could answer in a few syllables. Wordsworth's Ballads will be much talked of a hundred years hence; so will the Waverley Novels; so will Don Juan, I think, and Manfred; so will Thalaba, and Childe Harold's Pilgrimage, and the Pilgrimage to the Kirk of Shotts, and Christabel—

ODOHERTY. And the Essay on the Scope and Tendency of Bacon.

EDITOR. You wag, I suppose you expect to float yourself.

ODOHERTY. Do you?

EDITOR. None of your quizzing here, Mr Odoherty. I'll get Hogg to review your next book, sir, if you don't mend your manners.

ODOHERTY. Do—I would fain have a row, as I say in *my* song,—

"O, no matter with whom—no, nor what it was for."

EDITOR. Aye, you are always in that mood.

ODOHERTY. Sometimes only. Do you disapprove of personality?

EDITOR. No, no. I am not quite fool enough to sport that; least of all to you. In reviewing, in particular, what can be done without personality? Nothing, nothing. What are books that don't express the personal characters of their authors; and who can review books, without reviewing those that wrote them?

ODOHERTY. You get warm, Christopher; out with it.

EDITOR. Can a man read La Fontaine, Mr Odoherty, without perceiv-ing his personal good nature? Swift's personal ill nature is quite as visible. Can a man read Burns without having the idea of a great and a bold man—or Barry Cornwall, without the very uncomfortable feeling of a little man and a timid one? The whole of the talk about personality is, as Fogarty says, cant.

ODOHERTY. Get on.

EDITOR. I have done. Did you pick me up any good new hands when you were in town?

ODOHERTY. Several—two or three, that is. But I think the less you have to do with the Cockney underscrubs the better.

EDITOR. You're right there.

ODOHERTY. Oh yes, I have no love of the "Young Geniuses about town." The glorious army of Parliamentary reporters has no magnific-ence in my eyes. I detest news-writers—paragraphers—spouting-club speechifiers—all equally. You have them writing on different *lays*, but they are at *bottom*, with very few exceptions, the same dirty radicals,—meanly born,—meanly bred,—uneducated adventurers, who have been thrown upon literature only by having failed as attorneys, apothecaries, painters, schoolmasters, preachers, grocers—

EDITOR. Or Adjutants.—ha! ha! This Barry Cornwall, do they still puff him as much as ever?

ODOHERTY. Yes, they do; but the best joke is, that in one of his own prefaces he takes the trouble to tell us that Mirandola, (a character in one of his play-things,) is not the same man with Othello.

EDITOR. One might as well say that Tom Thumb is not the same man as Richard the Third.

ODOHERTY. Or that Joseph Hume is not Edmund Burke.

EDITOR. Or that the friend of Gerrald is not Sir Philip Sidney.

ODOHERTY. Or that a painted broomstick is not an oak.

EDITOR. Or that Baby Cornwall is not Giant Shakespeare. To be serious, do you think Campbell is gaining reputation by his Editorship?

ODOHERTY. No; nor do I think Byron will by his.

EDITOR. How are you sure of that, Ensign?

ODOHERTY. The Duke of Wellington would not raise himself by the best of all possible corn-bills. Hannibal did not raise himself by his excellent conduct at the head of the Carthaginian Police. Even if Tom Campbell had turned out the prince of Editors, I should still have preferred him thinking of

> On Linden when the sun was low,
> All bloodless lay the untrodden snow,
> And dark as winter was the flow
>   Of Iser rolling rapidly.

EDITOR. You are getting sentimental now, I think. Will you have another tumbler?

ODOHERTY. Hand me the lemons. This holy alliance of Pisa will be a queer affair. The Examiner has let down its price from a tenpenny to a sevenpenny. They say the Editor here is to be one of that faction, for they must publish in London of course.

EDITOR. Of course; but I doubt if they will be able to sell many. Byron is a prince; but these dabbling dogglerers destroy every dish they dip in.

ODOHERTY. Apt alliteration's artful aid.

EDITOR. Imagine Shelly, with his spavin, and Hunt, with his staingalt, going in the same harness with such a caperer as Byron, three a-breast! He'll knock the wind out of them both the first canter.

ODOHERTY. 'Tis pity Keats is dead.—I suppose you could not venture to publish a sonnet in which he is mentioned now? The Quarterly (who killed him, as Shelly says) would blame you.

EDITOR. Let's hear it. Is it your own?

ODOHERTY. No, 'twas written many months ago by a certain great Italian genius, who cuts a figure about the London routs—one Fudgiolo.

EDITOR. Try to recollect it.

ODOHERTY. It began

> Signor Le Hunto, gloria di Cocagna
>   Chi scrive il poema della Rimini
> Che tutta apparenza ha, per Gemini,
>   D'esser cantato sopra la montagna
> Di bel Ludgato, o nella compagna
>   D'Amsted, o sulle marge Serpentimini
> Com' esta Don Giovanni d'Endyimini
>   Il gran poeta d'Ipecacuanha?
> Tu sei il Re del Cocknio Parnasso
>   Ed egli il herede apparente,
> Tu sei un gran Giacasso ciertamente,
>   Ed egli ciertamente gran Giacasso!
> Tu sei il Signor del Examinero
> Ed egli soave Signor del Glystero.

EDITOR. I don't see why *Examinero* and *Glystero* should be so coupled together.

ODOHERTY. Both vehicles of dirt, you know.

EDITOR. You have me there. Who is Regent at present during his Majesty's absence?

ODOHERTY. Of course Prince John. I don't think Hazlitt is in the Council of Regency. From the moment King George went to Hanover, King Leigh was in the fidgets to be off.

EDITOR. What a cursed number of sonnets he'll write about the Venus de Medicis and the Hermaphrodite! The pictures and statues will drive him clean out of his wits. He'll fall in love with some of them.

ODOHERTY. If he sees Niobe and her Nine Daughters, he's a lost man.

EDITOR. Quite done for.

ODOHERTY. Will the ladies admire his sonnets when they come over?

EDITOR. According to Dr Colquhoun, there is one parish in London, Mary-le-bone, which contains 50,000 *ladies* capable of appreciating his poetry.

ODOHERTY. Is the new novel nearly ready—The Fortunes of Nigel— is not that it?

EDITOR. I hear it will soon be out, and that it is better than the Pirate.

ODOHERTY. I can believe that.

EDITOR. The subject is better. The time a very picturesque one. I am informed, that we may expect to have the most high and mighty Prince, King Jamie, and old Geordie Heriot, introduced in high style.

ODOHERTY. In London, I hope.

EDITOR. I hope so, too. I think he shews most in a bustle.

ODOHERTY. I don't know. I like the glen in the Monastery.

EDITOR. Your affectation is consummate. You that never breathed at ease out of a tavern, to be sporting romance.

ODOHERTY. I have written as many sentimental verses as any *Sempstress* alive. I once tried an epic in dead earnest.

EDITOR. How did you get on?

ODOHERTY. My heroine was with child at the end of the first canto, but I never had patience to deliver her.

EDITOR. Have you still got the MS.?

ODOHERTY. Yes; I think of sending it to Tom Campbell, or Taylor and Hessey, or the Aberdeen Review, if there be such a book still.

EDITOR. I never heard of it; but Steam-boats and Magazines are all the go at present. They've got a Magazine in Brighton—another at Newcastle, for the colliers—another at Dundee—and, I believe, five or six about Paisley and Glasgow. You may choose which you like best— they're all works of genius—Hogg writes in them all.

ODOHERTY. I'll sing you a song. (*Sings.*)

Thus speaks out Christopher
To his gallant crew—
Up with the Olive flag,
Down with the Blue;

Fire upon Jeffrey,
Fire on Sir James,
Fire on the Benthams,
Fire on the Grahams.

Fire upon Bennet,
Fire on Joe Hume,
Fire upon Lambton,
Fire upon Brougham.

Fire upon Hallam,
Fire upon Moore,
Spit upon Hazlitt,
* * * * * *.

I've forgot the last line. 'Tis my call. Your stave, Christopher!

EDITOR. (*Rings.*) Waiter! If Willison Glass be in the house, desire him to come up stairs, and he shall have a bottle of porter.

Enter WILLISON GLASS. What's your will?

EDITOR. Sing the dialogue between yourself and Jeremy Bentham.

WILLISON GLASS. I have it in my pocket, sir—I will sing it directly, sir—there's a running commentary, sir—would you be pleased to hear it too, sir?

EDITOR. Tip us the affair as it stands, Willison.

DIALOGUE BETWEEN WILLISON GLASS, ESQ. OF EDINBURGH,
AND JEREMY BENTHAM, ESQ. OF LONDON.

1.

Willison inviteth Jeremy to the sign of the Jolly Bacchus, whereof he speaketh in commendation.

Jeremy throw your pen aside,
   And come get drunk with me;
We'll go where Bacchus sits astride,
   Perch'd high upon barrels three;
'Tis there the ale is frothing up,
And genuine is the gin;
So we shall take a liberal sup,
   To comfort our souls within.

2.

Jeremy refuseth the invitation, blandly alleging that he had much rather destroy the young man of the west, and other persons.

O cheerier than the nappy ale,
   Or the Hollands smacking fine,
Is sitting by the taper pale,
   And piling line on line;
Smashing with many a heavy word
   Anti-usurers* in a row,
Or pointing arguments absurd†
   To level the Boroughs low.

* See Essay on the Usury Laws.
† Reform Catechism.

B

3.

Whereupon Wil-
lison remindeth
him of the Quar-
terly, and extol-
leth the good li-
quor.

Jeremy, trust me, 'tis but stuff
    To scribble the live long night,
While the Quarterly bloodhounds howl so rough,
    And so grusome is their bite.
But down at the sign of the triple ton,
    There's nothing like them to fear,
But sweet is its brandy's genial run,
    And barmy is its beer.

4.

Jeremy disvalu-
eth beer, brandy,
and the Quarter-
ly, declares that
he chooseth rather
to eat lawyers
than drink bran-
dy.

Brandy, I know, is liquor good,
    And barmy the beer may be;
But common law is my favourite food,*
    And it must be crunch'd by me:
And I'm writing a word three pages long,
    The Quarterly dogs to rout,
A word which never will human tongue
    Be able to wind about.

5.

Willison prefer-
reth long draughts
to long words.

Jeremy, never shall tongue of mine
    Be put to such silly use;
I'll keep it to smack the brandy-wine,
    Or barleycorn's gallant juice.
Then mount your mitre on your skull,
    And waddle with me, my lad,
To take a long and a hearty pull,
    At the brimmer bumpering glad.

6.

Jeremy bringeth
up his nine
pounders, and de-
clareth that he is
a Berkeleian phi-
losopher.

Though ale be comforting to the maw,
    Yet here I still shall dwell,
Until I prove that judge-made law
    Is uncognoscible,—
That the schools at Canterbury's beck†
    Exist but in the mind,—
And that T.T. Walmsey, Esquire, *Sec.*
    Is no more than a spirit of wind.

---

* Theorie de Legislation.
† Church of Englandism.

7.

Willison compa-
reth Jeremy's Pan-
opticon to a porter
pot in a pretty
simile.

Jeremy, never mind such trash,
  And of better spirits think,
And out of your throat the cobwebs wash
  With a foaming flagon of drink;
For 'tis sweet the pewter pots to spy,
Imprisoning the liquor stout,
As jail-bird rogues are ring'd in by
  Your Panopticon roundabout.

8.

Jeremy calleth on
three great men,
Sir Pythagoras,
George Ensor,
and Master Fran-
cis Jeffrey.

Sweeter it is to see the sheet
  With paradox scribbled fair,
Where jawbreaking words every line you meet,
  To make poor people stare.
And Sir Richard of Bridge-street my books shall
    puff,
  And Ensor will swear them fine,
And Jeffrey will say, though my style is tough,
  Yet my arguments are divine.

9.

Willison dispara-
ging the three
recommendeth to
blow a cloud.

Jeremy, trust me, the puff of the three,
  (I tell you the truth indeed),
Is not worth the puff you'd get from me,
  Of the pure Virginian weed.
And beneath its fume, while we gaily quaff
  The beer or the ruin blue,
You at the world may merrily laugh,
  Instead of its laughing at you.

10.

Jeremy proposeth
pleasant reading
to his friend Mr
Glass,

The world may lay what it likes to my charge,
  May laugh, or may say I'm crack'd.
If it do, I shall swear that the world at large
  Is no more than a jury pack'd;
Such a jury as those on which I penn'd*
  A Treatise genteel and clear;
And I'll read it now to you, my friend,
  For 'twill give you joy to hear.

* Elements of Packing.

11.

who thereupon
recoileth, horror-
struck, and de-
parteth to the sign
of the Jolly Bac-
chus, there to sing
about Prince
Charlie, and other
goodly ballads.
And Jeremy abi-
deth in his place.

Jeremy, not for a gallon of ale
    Would I stay that book to hear;
Why, even at its sight my cheek turns pale,
    And my heart leaps up like a deer.
So I must off without more delay,
    My courage to raise with a glass;
And as you prefer o'er such stuff to stay,
    I'll toast you, my lad, for an ass.

(*Exit Willison Glass.*)

EDITOR. Well, but say candidly, what have you been doing for us? Your active mind must have been after something. I heard lately, (perhaps it was said in allusion to your late detention in London,) that you were engaged with a novel, to be entitled "Fleeting Impressions."

ODOHERTY. You are quite mistaken. I have not patience for a novel. I must go off like a cracker, or an ode of Horace.

EDITOR. Then why don't you give us an essay for our periodical?

ODOHERTY. To prove what? or nothing. When I last saw Coleridge, he said he considered an essay, in a periodical publication, as merely "a say" for the time—an ingenious string of sentences, driving, apparently, with great vehemence, towards some object, but never meant to lead to any thing, or to arrive at any conclusion, (for in what conclusion are the public interested but the abuse of individuals). Fortunately, there is one subject for a critical disquisition, which can never be exhausted.

EDITOR. What is this treasure?

ODOHERTY. The question, whether is Pope a poet?

EDITOR. True! But confess, Odoherty, what have you been after?

ODOHERTY. The truth is, I have some thoughts of finishing my tragedy of the Black Revenge.

EDITOR. Ye gods! what a scheme!

ODOHERTY. The truth is, I must either do this, or go on with my great quarto disquisition, on "The Decline and Fall of Genius."

EDITOR. I would advise to let alone the drama. I do not think it is at present a good field for the exertion of genius.

ODOHERTY. For what reason, Honey?

EDITOR. I think the good novels, which are published, come in place of new dramas. Besides, they are better fitted for the present state of public taste. The public are merely capable of strong sensations, but of nothing which requires knowledge, taste, or judgment. A certain ideal dignity of style, and regularity of arrangement, must be required for a drama, before it can deserve the name of a composition. But what sense have the common herd of barbarians of composition, or order, or any thing else of that kind?

ODOHERTY. But there is also the more loose and popular drama, which is only a novel without the narrative parts.

EDITOR. Yes, the acting is the chief difference. But I think the novel has the advantage in being without the acting, for its power over the feelings is more undisturbed and entire, and the imagination of the reader blends the whole into a harmony which is not found on the stage. I think those who read novels need not go to the theatre, for they are in general beforehand with the whole progress of the story.

ODOHERTY. This is true to a certain extent. But novels can never carry away from the theatre those things which are peculiarly its own; that is to say, the powers of expression in the acting, the eloquence of declamation, music, buffoonery, the splendour of painted decorations, &c.

EDITOR. You are perfectly right. Novels may carry away sympathy, plot, invention, distress, catastrophe, and every thing—(Vide Blair.)

ODOHERTY. Do you mean Dr Blair, or Adam Blair?

EDITOR. The latter. I say the novels may carry away all these things, but the theatre must still be strong in its power of affecting the senses. This is its peculiar dominion. Yet our populace do not much seek after what strikes and pleases the senses; for the elegances of sight and hearing require a sort of abstract taste which they do not seem to have. Any thing which is not an appeal through sympathy to some of their vulgar personal feelings, appears to them uninteresting and unmeaning.

ODOHERTY. They think it has no reference to *meum* and *tuum*.

EDITOR. It probably would not be easy to find a people more lamentably deficient in all those liberal and general feelings which partake of the quality of taste.

ODOHERTY. You sink me into despair. I think I must betake myself to my old and favourite study of theological controversy, and furnish a reply to Coplestone. I perceive that Lord Byron, in his Mystery of Cain, tends very much to go off into the same disputes.

EDITOR. A sceptically disputatious turn of mind, appears a good deal here and there in his poetry.

ODOHERTY. I suppose you think Sardanapalus the best Tragedy he has written.

EDITOR. Yes. The Foscari is interesting to read, but rather painful and disagreeable in the subject. Besides, the dialogue is too much in the short and pointed manner of Alfieri. When a play is not meant to be acted, there is no necessity for its having that hurry in the action and speeches, which excludes wandering strains of poetical beauty, or reflexion and thought, nor should it want the advantages of rhyme. The Faustus of Goethe seems to be the best specimen of the kind of plan fit for a poem of this kind not meant to be acted.

ODOHERTY. Pindarum quisquis.

EDITOR. Byron's Manfred is certainly but an Icarian flutter in comparison; his Sardanapalus is better composed, and more original.

ODOHERTY. How do you like Nimrod and Semiramis?

EDITOR. That dream is a very frightful one, and I admire the conception of Nimrod.

ODOHERTY. You know that I am not subject to nocturnal terrors, even after the heaviest supper; but I acknowledge that the ancestors of Sardanapalus almost made my hair stand on end; and I have some intention of introducing the ghost of Fingal in my "Black Revenge."

EDITOR. The superstitious vein has not lately been waked with much success. I slight the conception of Norna in relation to fear. The scorpion lash, which Mr David Lindsay applied to the tyrant Firaoun, is not at all formidable to the reader; but there is solemnity and sentiment in the conception of the people being called away one by one from the festival, till he is left alone. That same piece of the Deluge would be very good, if it were not sometimes like music, which aims rather at loudness than harmony or expression. The most elegant and well composed piece in Lindsay's book is the Destiny of Cain.

ODOHERTY. How do you like the Nereid's love?

EDITOR. It is vastly pretty, but too profuse in images drawn from mythology. However, there are many fables of the ancients on which poems might be successfully made even in modern times, and according to modern feeling, if the meaning of the fables were deeply enough studied. It does not necessarily follow that all mythological poems should be written in imitation of the manner of the ancients, much less in the pretty style of Ovid, and those moderns who have adopted the same taste.

ODOHERTY. You do not think Mr Lindsay's Nereid French?

EDITOR. By no means. It is free from any fault of that kind. In some of Wordsworth's later poems, there appears something like a reviving imagination for those fine old conceptions, which have been, and always will be.

> An age hath been when earth was proud
>   Of lustre too intense
> To be sustain'd; and mortals bow'd
>   The front in self defence.
> Who, then, if Dian's crescent gleam'd,
> Or Cupid's sparkling arrow stream'd,
> While on the wing the urchin play'd,
> Could fearlessly approach the shade?

Enough for one soft vernal day,
If I, a bard of ebbing time,
And nurtured in a fickle clime,
May haunt this horned bay;
Whose amorous water multiplies
The flitting halcyon's vivid dyes,
And smooths its liquid breast to show
These swan-like specks of mountain snow,
White, as the pair that slid along the plains
Of heaven, while Venus held the reins.

ODOHERTY. Beautifully recited, and now touch the bell again, for we're getting prosy.

EDITOR. Positively, Ensign, we must rise.

ODOHERTY. Having now relinquished the army, I rise by sitting still, and applying either to study, or—Will you ring?

EDITOR. 'Tis time to be going, I believe. I see the day-light peeping down the chimney. But sing one good song more, Odoherty, and so wind up the evening.

ODOHERTY. (*Sings*).

ARIA.

With boisterous expression.

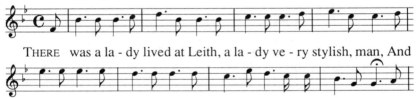

THERE   was a la - dy lived at Leith, a la - dy ve - ry stylish, man, And

yet, in spite of all her teeth, she fell in love with an I - rish- man, A

CHORUS—CHRISTOPHER!

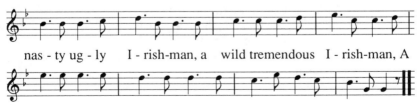

nas - ty ug - ly   I - rish-man, a   wild tremendous   I - rish-man, A

tearing, swearing, thumping, bumping, ramping, roaring I-rishman.

2.

His face was no ways beautiful,
   For with small-pox 'twas scarr'd across;
And the shoulders of the ugly dog
   Were almost double a yard across.
      O, the lump of an Irishman,
      The whisky-devouring Irishman—
The great he-rogue, with his wonderful brogue, the fighting,
   rioting, Irishman.

3.

One of his eyes was bottle-green,
   And the other eye was out, my dear;
And the calves of his wicked-looking legs
   Were more than two feet about, my dear.
      O, the great big Irishman,
      The rattling, battling Irishman—
The stamping, ramping, swaggering, staggering, leathering
   swash of an Irishman.

4.

He took so much of Lundy-Foot,
   That he used to snort and snuffle—O;
And in shape and size, the fellow's neck,
   Was as bad as the neck of a buffalo.
      O, the horrible Irishman,
      The thundering, blundering Irishman—
The slashing, dashing, smashing, lashing, thrashing, hashing,
   Irishman.

5.

His name was a terrible name, indeed,
   Being Timothy Thady Mulligan;
And whenever he emptied his tumbler of punch,
   He'd not rest till he fill'd it full again.
      The boozing, bruising Irishman,
      The 'toxicated Irishman—
The whisky, frisky, rummy, gummy, brandy, no dandy Irish-
   man.

6.
This was the lad the lady loved,
  Like all the girls of quality;
And he broke the skulls of the men of Leith,
  Just by the way of jollity.
      O, the leathering Irishman,
      The barbarous, savage, Irishman—
The hearts of the maids, and the gentlemen's heads, were both-
  er'd, I'm sure, by this Irishman.

I think I hear the rattles, Christopher. By Saint Patrick, there's a row
in the street! Come along, old one! Up with your crutch!
Exeunt AMBO.

Noctes Ambrosianae.

No. IV.

SCENE. — *Transferred (by poetic licence) to Pisa.*

ODOHERTY, (*Solus.*) Jupiter strike me! but that cabbage soup and roasted raisins is an infernal mixture—Blow all Italian cookery, say I. Everything is over-done here—how inferior to the Carlingford! The dishes done to rags.

Enter WAITER. Milordo, here is questo grand Lord is come, for to have the onore of kissing the manos for sua eccellenza.

ODOHERTY. Kissing my what? Shew in the shaver—hand him in upon a clean plate.   [*Exit Waiter.*

Enter LORD BYRON. Mr Doherty,—I trust I——

ODOHERTY. Odoherty, if you please, sir.

BYRON. Mr Odoherty, I have to beg pardon for this intrusion—but really, hearing you were to remain but this evening in Pisa, I could not deny myself the pleasure of at least seeing a gentleman, of whom I have heard and read so much—I need scarcely add, that I believe myself to be in the presence of THE Odoherty.

ODOHERTY. You may say that; but, may I take the liberty of asking, who you are yourself?

BYRON. My name's Byron.

ODOHERTY. Byron! Lord Byron! God bless you, my dear fellow. Sure I was a blockhead not to know you at first-sight.—Waiter! waiter! waiter, I say.—They don't understand even plain English in this house!

Enter WAITER. Milordo!

ODOHERTY. Instantaneously a clean glass—if you have any thing clean in this filthy country—And, my Lord, what will you drink? I drink every thing bating water.

BYRON. Why, Mr Odoherty, to be plain with you—you will find but poor accommodation in these Italian inns—and I should, therefore, recommend you to come with me to my villa. You will meet fellows there—asses of the first water—native, and stranger, whom you can cut-up, quiz, and humbug without end.

ODOHERTY. With deference, my Lord, I shall stay where I am—I never knew any place where a man was so much at home as in a tavern, no matter how shy. Ho! waiter.

WAITER. Milordo!

ODOHERTY. What-a have-a you-a to drink-a, in this damned house-a of yours?—[*Aside.*] I suppose to make the fellow understand, I must speak broken English.

Lord Byron whispers waiter, who exit; and after a moment returns with two flasks of Montifiascone.

BYRON. Fill, Mr Odoherty. Your health, sir; and welcome to Italy.

ODOHERTY. Your health, my lord; and I wish we both were out of it. But this stuff is by no means so bad as I expected. What do you call it?

BYRON. Lacryma Christi.

ODOHERTY. Lacryma Christi! A pretty name to go to church with! Very passable stingo—though Inishowen is, after all, rather stiffer drinking.

BYRON. Inishowen! What's that?

ODOHERTY. Whisky, made in the hills about Inishowen, in the north. General Hart patronizes it much. Indeed the Lord Chancellor, old Manners, is a great hand at it.

BYRON. I cannot exactly say I recognize whom you speak of; nor did I ever hear of the liquor.

ODOHERTY. Why, then, I wrote rather a neat song about it once on a time, which I shall just twist off for the edification of your Lordship.

ODOHERTY *sings.*

1.

I care not a fig for a flagon of flip,
    Or a whistling can of rumbo;
But my tongue through whisky punch will slip
    As nimble as Hurlothrumbo.
So put the spirits on the board,
    And give the lemons a squeezer,
And we'll mix a jorum, by the Lord!
    That will make your worship sneeze, sir.

2.

The French, no doubt, are famous souls,
    I love them for their brandy;
In rum and sweet tobacco rolls,
    Jamaica men are handy.
The big-breech'd Dutch in juniper gin,
    I own, are very knowing;
But are rum, gin, brandy, worth a pin,
    Compared with Inishowen?

Extempore verse additional.
Though here with a Lord, 'tis jolly and fine,
    To tumble down Lacryma Christi,
And over a skin of Italy's wine
    To get a little misty;
Yet not the blood of the Bourdeaux grape,
    The finest grape-juice going,
Nor clammy Constantia, the pride of the Cape,
    Prefer I to Inishowen.

BYRON. Thank ye, Mr Odoherty. Oh! by Jupiter, you have not been flattered; you are a prince of good-fellows; ay, and of good-looking fellows.

ODOHERTY. The same compliment I may pay you, my Lord. I never saw you before. By the bye, you look much older than the print which Murray gave me when I was up at the Coronation.

BYRON. Ah! then you know Murray? Murray is an excellent fellow. Not such a bookseller between the Appenine and the Grampian.

ODOHERTY. Always excepting Ebony, my Lord?

BYRON. How is Ebony? I'm told he's been getting fat since I saw him.

ODOHERTY. A porpoise. No wonder, my lord; let them fatten who win. As for laughing, that you know, we may all screw a mouth to.

BYRON. On the same principle, my old friend Jeffrey must be thinning apace.

ODOHERTY. A perfect whipping-post. But I have not seen the little man this some time. I don't think he goes much into public—his book I know does not.

BYRON. Have you been in London lately, Mr Odoherty?

ODOHERTY. O yes, past through about a fortnight ago. But let me request your Lordship to sink the *mister* entirely, and call me by my name quite plain—Odoherty, as it is.

BYRON. Certainly, Odoherty, as you wish it—but you in return must sink the Lord, and let me be plain Byron.

ODOHERTY. To be sure, Byron. Hunt you know called you "Dear Byron" some years ago in a dedication; and if you would allow the familiarity of a poor devil of a Cockney editor of a sneaking Sunday paper, you would be squeamish indeed if you wanted to be Lorded by me. And yet, after all, Le Hunto is a cleverer fellow than most of the Cockneys.

BYRON. He's worth fifty Hoggs. These *plebs* occasionally write good verses.

ODOHERTY. I sha'nt give up Hogg. Have you seen his last work?

BYRON. His *last* work! I am glad to hear it has come at length.

ODOHERTY. It is quite a Chaldee.

BRYON. Oh! that's his *first* work. Seriously, however, I have heard nothing of him since your good-humoured notice of his Life in Blackwood.

ODOHERTY. Thank you, Baron! I take you. By the bye, what a right good poem that was of yours, on old Bam Rogers. You and I may leave off quizzing one another. We at least are too much up to trap. But the old Banker was as mad as blazes about it.

BYRON. Non mi ricordo.—I was in a state of civilation when I wrote it—if indeed I did ever write such a thing.

ODOHERTY. 'Twas Wordsworth told me of it, and I doubt he's given to humbugging much.

BYRON. Oh! the old Ponder! The great god Pan! is he extant still?

ODOHERTY. Alive and sulky. He has been delivered of two octavos this spring.

BYRON. So have I for that matter. Are his as heavy as mine?

ODOHERTY. The Giants' Causeway to a two-year old paving-stone—thundering fellows, about Roman Catholic Emancipation, which he has dished into little sonnets. Yours, however, were lumpish enough, in the name of Nicholas.

BYRON. The sale, at least, was *heavy*.

ODOHERTY. Your tributary, his Majesty the Emperor of the West, grumbled like a pig in the fits, I suppose.

BYRON. Come, come, no personalities on this side of the Alps.

ODOHERTY. Satan reproving sin. That's pretty from you—the bottle's out—after what Jeffrey has said of you—call for another—in the last number of the Edinburgh—fill your glass—of the Edinburgh Review. No bad bottle this.

BYRON. Why, Odoherty, you and I may joke, but such fellows as these to be preaching about Cain, and canting about Don Juan, is too bad. I once thought Jeffrey had a little brains, but now I see he is quite an old woman.

ODOHERTY. Nay, by the eternal frost, and that's as great an oath as if I swore by the holy bottle, I agree with Jeff. on this point. I don't care a cracked Jews-harp about him in general; but here, faith, I must say I think him quite right. Consider, my Lord—consider, I say, what a very immoral work Don Juan is—how you therein sport with the holiest ties —the most sacred feelings—the purest sentiments. In a word, with every thing—the bottle is with you—with every thing which raises man above a mere sensual being. I say, consider this, and you will not wonder so much that all England is in an out-cry against it, as that Murray, surrounded with the rums and buzzes of parsons as he is, should have the audacity to publish it—or Sir Mungo Malagrowther——

BYRON. Who?

ODOHERTY. His Editor—Now-a-days commonly called Sir Mungo Malagrowther. I say it is really astonishing that Murray should print, or Sir Mungo have the face not to cut up, a book so destructive of every feeling which we have been taught to cherish.

BYRON. Are you serious, Ensign?

ODOHERTY. *Serious* as the rock of Cashel.

BYRON. I did not expect it. I thought this silly out-cry about Don Juan and Cain was confined to the underlings of literature; so much so, that I was astonished to find even Jeffrey joining in it—but that you, one of the first and most enlightened men of the age, should adopt it—that Ensign and Adjutant Morgan Odoherty should be found swelling the war-hoop of my antagonist Dr Southey, is indeed more than I expected.

ODOHERTY. I am not an old quiz, like Malagrowther and the Laureate: Yet, my Lord Byron, I am a man and an Englishman, (I mean an Irishman,) and disapprove of Don Juan.

BYRON. The devil ye do! Why, most illustrious rival of Dr Magnus Oglethorpe, why?

ODOHERTY. I have already sufficiently explained myself.

BYRON. You have uttered nothing, sir, pardon me, but the common old humbug. In Don Juan I meant to give a flowing free satire on things as they are. I meant to call people's attention to the realities of things. I could make nothing of England or France. There every thing is convention—surface—cant. I had recourse to the regions where Nature acts more vividly, more in the open light of day. I meant no harm, upon my honour. I meant but to do what any other man might have done with a more serious face, and had all the Hannah Mores in Europe to answer his Plaudite.

ODOHERTY. I don't follow your Lordship.

BYRON. Not follow me, sir? Why, what can be more plain than my intention? I drew a lively lad, neglected in his education, strong in his passions, active in his body, and lively in his brains; would you have had me make him look as wise as a Quarterly Reviewer? Every boy must sow his wild oats; wait till Don Juan be turned of fifty, and if I don't represent him as one of the gravest and most devout Tories in the world, may I be hanged. As yet he has only been what Dr Southey once was, "a clever boy, thinking upon politics (and other subjects) as those who are boys in mind, whatever their age may be, do think." Have patience. The Don may be Lord Chancellor ere he dies.

ODOHERTY. The serious charge is your warmth of colouring.

BYRON. Look at Homer, remember the cloud-scene. Look at Virgil, remember the cave-scene. Look at Milton, remember the bower-scene, the scene of "nothing loth." Why, sir, poets are like their heroes, and poets represent such matters (which all poets do and must represent) more or less warmly, just as they are more or less men.

ODOHERTY. Well, but what do you say for Cain? 'Tis blasphemous.

BYRON. Not intentionally, at least—but I cannot see that it is so at all. You know—for I suppose you know theology as well as you know every thing else.

ODOHERTY. Like Doctor Magee—an old friend of mine, who has lately been made an Archbishop.

BYRON. You know then that there is no question so puzzling in all divinity—no matter under what light you view it—as the origin of evil. There is no theory whatever—I say not one—and you may take your countryman, Archbishop King's, among them, which is not liable to great objection, if the objectors be determined to cavil. Now I assert, and that fearlessly, that it is quite possible to reconcile my scheme, bating a few poetical flights of no moment, with views and feelings perfectly religious. I engage to write a commentary on Cain, proving it beyond question a religious poem.

ODOHERTY. Warburton did the same for the Essay on Man—but convinced nobody.

BYRON. And yet Warburton was a bishop—yea, more than a bishop—one of your brightest, deepest, profoundest, most brilliant theologians. I only ask you to extend to me the same indulgence you extend to Milton—ay, even to Cumberland—if his Calvary be still extant.

ODOHERTY. Nay, my Lord, there is this difference. The *intention* of Milton and Cumberland makes a vast distinction. They wrote poems to promote religion—your Lordship wrote——

BYRON. Mr Odoherty, I presume—Nay, I know—I am talking to a gentleman. I have disclaimed irreligious intention, and I *demand*, as a gentleman, to be believed. Cain is like all poems in which spiritual matters are introduced. The antagonist of Heaven—of whom the Prometheus of Æschylus is the prototype—cannot be made to speak in such terms, as may not be perverted by those who wish to pervert. I defy any man—I repeat it—I defy any man to shew me a speech—a line in Cain, which is not defensible on the same principle as the haughty speech of Satan, in the fifth book of Milton—or the proud defiance of Moloch in the second. In both poets—I beg pardon—in the poet, and in Cain, speeches torn from the context, and misinterpreted by the malevolent or the weak-minded, may be made to prove what was directly contrary to the intention of the writer.

ODOHERTY. To be sure, as Chief Baron O'Grady says, in his Letter to Mr Gregory, remove the words "the fool has said in his heart," and you can prove by Scripture that "there is no God."

BYRON. I know nothing of your Chief Baron, but what he says is true

—and it is *so,* that I have been criticized. I don't complain of Lord
Eldon. Perhaps it became his high station to deliver the judgment he did
—perhaps it was right he should bend to public opinion—which
opinion, however, I shall for ever assert, was stimulated by a party of
more noise than number. But I do confess—for I was born an aristocrat
—that I was a good deal pained when I saw my books, in consequence
of his decree, degraded to be published in sixpenny numbers by
Benbow, with Lawrence's Lectures—Southey's Wat Tyler—Paine's Age
of Reason—and the Chevalier de Faublas.

ODOHERTY. I am sorry I introduced the subject. If I thought I should
have in the slightest degree annoyed your lordship——

BYRON. I am not annoyed, bless your soul; there is nothing I like better
than free discussion. *That,* you know, can never be, except between men
of sense. As for all your humbug of Reviews, Magazines, &c. why, you
are, at least, as much as any man alive, up to their nothingness.

ODOHERTY. 'Tis the proudest of my reflections, that I have somewhat
contributed to make people see what complete stuff all that affair is.

BYRON. I admire your genius, Mr Odoherty: but why do you claim
this particular merit?

ODOHERTY. Merely as a great contributor to Blackwood. That work
has done the business.

BYRON. As how, friend Morgan?

ODOHERTY. Call another flask, and I'll tell you——Ay, now fill a
bumper to old Christopher.

BYRON. With three times three, with all my heart. The immortal Kit
North!!! !!! !!!   [*Bibunt ambo.*

ODOHERTY. Why, you see, what with utterly squabashing Jeffrey, and
what with giving Malagrowther an odd squeeze or so,—but most of all,
by doing all that ever these folks could do in one Number, and then
undoing it in the next,—puffing, deriding, sneering, jeering, prosing,
piping, and so forth, he has really taken the thing into his own hands, and
convinced the Brutum Pecus that 'tis all quackery and humbug.

BYRON. Himself included?

ODOHERTY. No—not quite that neither. As to two or three principles
—I mean religion, loyalty, and the like, he is always stiff as a poker; and
although he now and then puts in puffs of mediocre fellows, every body
sees they're put in merely to fill the pages; and the moment he or any of
his true men set pen to paper, the effect is instantaneous. His book is just
like the best book in the world—it contains a certain portion of *Balaam.*

BYRON. And this sort of course, you think, has enlightened the public?

ODOHERTY. Certain and sure it has. People have learnt the great
lesson, that Reviews, and indeed all periodicals, merely *quâ* such, are
nothing. They take in his book not as a Review, to pick up opinions of

new books from it, nor as a periodical, to read themselves asleep upon, but as a classical work, which happens to be continued from month to month;—a real Magazine of mirth, misanthropy, wit, wisdom, folly, fiction, fun, festivity, theology, bruising, and thingumbob. He unites all the best materials of the Edinburgh, the Quarterly, and the Sporting Magazine—the literature and good writing of the first—the information and orthodoxy of the second, and the flash and trap of the third.

BYRON. You speak *con amore,* sir: Why the devil am I cut up and parodied in Ebony?

ODOHERTY. Come, come, pop such questions to the marines! Have you ever been half so much cut up there as I have been? Fill your glass! Here's to *Humbug.* Three times three, my lord! No two men alive should fill higher to that toast than we that are here present, thank God; and I'm very glad to be here, with my legs under the same board with the author of Cain and Don Juan.

BYRON. What, after abusing them both so savagely just this moment.

ODOHERTY. So I do still;—but I had rather have written a page of Juan than a ton of Childe Harold—that was too great a bore entirely.

BYRON. Well,—waive my works in toto. How is Sir Walter Scott?

ODOHERTY. I have not seen him for nearly six months; but he is quite well, and writing Peveril of the Peak; that is, if he be the Author of Waverley.

BYRON. Which he is.

ODOHERTY. I won't swear to that, knowing what I do about Anastasius. Did you see how Hope bristled up in the back in Blackwood, when somebody, I forget who, perhaps myself, said that you were guilty of that most admirable book?

BYRON. Yes,—but no matter.—Could you give me any more information *de re periodicali,* as the Baron of Bradwardine would have said?

ODOHERTY. I shall sing a stave touchant that point—

1.

O! gone are the days, when the censure or praise
Of the Monthly was heard with devotion;
When the sight of the blue of old Griffith's Review,
Set each heart in a pit-a-pat motion;
We care not a curse, now, for better or worse,
For the prate of the maundering old mumper;
And, since it is dead,—why, no more can be said,—
Than "Destruction to Cant" in a bumper.

2.

When the sense of the town had the Monthly put down,
    Mr Jeffrey a new caper started;
Every fourth of a year he swore to appear,
    To terrify all the faint-hearted.
Then with vigour and pith, Brougham, Jeffrey, and Smith,
    Began to belabour the natives;
Who, bother'd at first by their bravo and burst,
    Sunk under the scribblers like caitiffs.

3.

Quite vex'd at their blows, Johnny Murray arose,
    Assisted by mild Billy Gifford—
The Edinburgh work he squabash'd like a Turk,
    So that folks do not now care a whiff for't.
But soon such a gang, there grew up slap-bang,
    Of scribblers and nibblers reviewing.
That people got sick of the horrible trick,
    And it almost had set them a-sp——g.

4.

But a figure of light soon burst on their sight,
    In Bill Ebony's beautiful pages—
The immortal Kit North in his glory came forth,
    With his cycle of satellite sages.
He can cant, it is true—he can sport a review,
    Now and then, when it suits his devices;
But who trusts to his prog is a bothersome dog,
    If he says he is stingy of spices.

BYRON. Not a bad song! Cazzo. I have quite lost the knack of song-writing. Tom Moore is the best at it now alive.

ODOHERTY. The present company excepted, you mean; but truly, my Lord, I don't care a tester for that piperly poet of green Erin. I don't think he ever wrote one real good song in his days. He wants pith, by Jericho! and simplicity, and straight-forward meaning. He's always twining and whining. Give me your old stave.

BYRON. You prefer Burns, perhaps, now you've been so long a Scotchman, and heard all their eternal puffing of one another.

ODOHERTY. Poh! Poh! I was too old a cat for that straw. Burns wrote five or six good things,—Tam o' Shanter, M'Pherson's Lament, Farewell thou fair Earth, Mary's Dream, the Holy Fair, the Stanzas to a Louse on a Lady's Bonnet, and perhaps a few more; but the most of his verses are mere manufacture—the most perfect common-place about love and bowers, and poverty, and so forth. And as for his prose, why, Gad-a-mercy! 'tis execrable. 'Tis worse than Hogg's worst, or Allan Cunningham's best. His letters are enough to make a dog sick.

BYRON. Come, you are too severe; Burns was a noble fellow, although Jeffery abused him: But indeed that was nothing. After praising the Cockneys, who cares what he reviles?

ODOHERTY. Not I.

BYRON. No, no; I don't suspect you of any such folly. Pray, have you seen any of our Italian Improvisatores as yet? What do think of their art?

ODOHERTY. That I can beat it.

BYRON. In English or Irish?

ODOHERTY. In any language I know—Latin or Greek, if you like them.

BYRON. Try Latin then.

ODOHERTY. Here's Ritson. Turn him over; I'll translate any song you like off-hand.

BRYON. Here, take this one—"Back and side go bare." 'Tis not the worse for having a bishop for its father.

ODOHERTY. Old Still must have been a hearty cock,—here goes. Read you the English, and I'll chant it in Latin.

BYRON READS.	CANTAT DOHERTIADES.
1.	1.
Backe and side go bare, go bare,	Sint nuda dorsum, latera—
Both foot and hande go colde:	Pes, manus, algens sit;
But bellye, God sende thee good ale ynoughe,	Dum Ventri veteris copia
Whether it be newe or olde.	Zythi novive fit.
I cannot eat but lytle meate,	Non possum multum edere,
My stomacke is not good;	Quia stomachus est nullus;
But sure I thinke that I can drynke	Sed volo vel monacho bibere
With him that weares a hood.	Quanquam sit huic cucullus.
Though I go bare, take ye no care,	Et quamvis nudus ambulo,
I am nothing a colde;	De frigore non est metus;
I stuff my skyn so full within,	Quia semper Zytho vetulo
Of joly good ale and olde.	Ventriculus est impletus.
Backe and side go bare, go bare,	Sint nuda dorsum, latera—
Both foote and hande go colde:	Pes, manus, algens sit;
But, belly, God send thee good ale enoughe,	Dum Ventri veteris copia
Whether it be newe or olde.	Zythi novive fit.

2.

I love no rost, but a nut-browne toste,
　And a crab laid in the fyre;
A little breade shall do me stead,
　Much breade I not desyre.
No frost nor snow, nor winde, I trowe,
　Can hurt me if I wolde:
I am so wrapt, and throwly lapt,
　Of jolly good ale and olde.
　　　Backe and side go bare, &c.

2.

Assatum nolo—tostum volo—
　Vel pomum igni situm;
Nil pane careo—parvum habeo
　Pro pane appetitum.
Me gelu, nix, vel ventus vix
　Afficerent injuria;
Hæc sperno, ni adesset mî
　Zythi veteris penuria.
　　　Sint nuda, &c.

3.

And Tyb, my wyfe, that, as her lyfe,
　Loveth well good ale to seeke;
Full oft drynkes shee, tyll ye may see
　The teares run down her cheeke:
Then doth she trowle to mee the boule,
　Even as a mault-worme shuld;
And sayth, "Sweete hart, I took my parte
　Of this jolly good ale and olde."
　　　Back and side go bare, &c.

3.

Et uxor Tybie, qui semper sibi
　Vult quærere Zythum bene,
Ebibit hæc persæpe, nec
　Sistit, dum madeant genæ.
Et mihi tum dat cantharum,
　Sic mores sunt bibosi;
Et dicit "Cor, en! impleor
　Zythi dulcis et annosi."
　　　Sint nuda, &c.

4.

Now let them drynke, tyll they nod and
　　winke,
　Even as good felowes should doe:
They shall not mysse to have the blysse
　Good ale doth bringe men to.
And all poore soules that have scowr'd
　　boules,
　Or have them lustely trolde,
God save the lyves of them and their
　　wyves,
　Whether they be yonge or old.
　　　Back and syde go bare, &c.

4.

Nunc ebibant, donec nictant
　Ut decet virum bonum;
Felicitatis habebunt satis,
　Nam Zythi hoc est donum.
Et omnes hi, qui canthari
　Sunt haustibus lætati,
Atque uxores vel juniores
　Vel senes, Diis sint grati.
　　　Sint nuda, &c.

BYRON. Bravo—bravissimo!—why, you would beat old Camillo Querno if you would only learn Italian.

ODOHERTY. I intend to learn it between this and the end of the week. There is no language on the face of the earth I could not learn in three days,—except Sanscrit, which took me a week. It took Marsham of Serampore seven years. Would your lordship wish to hear a Sanscrit ode I wrote to A.W. Schlegel?

BYRON. No, thank you, not just now. You are not doing the Lacryma justice.

ODOHERTY. Curse it,—it is getting cold on my stomach. Is there no more stout potation in the house?

BYRON. Brandy, I presume,—but the sugar is execrable.

ODOHERTY. No matter, it makes superb grog,—almost as good as rum —far better than whisky. Have you any objection, Byron?

BYRON. Not the least; whatever is agreeable to you. Hola!——

Enter waiter—exits—and returns with a skin of brandy.

ODOHERTY. Ay, this skin is a pretty thing. It puts a man instinctively in mind of a skinful. Gargle it most delicately. Flow thou regal amber stream. Talk of the Falls of the Rhone in comparison with such a cascade as this! Here—water—aqua pura. Ay, that will do.—You are putting too much water, my Lord—it will rise on your stomach, as old Doctor Rumsnout often told me.

BYRON. Nay, mix as you please, and let me settle my own tipple.

ODOHERTY. Oh! of course, freedom of will. But this is far superior to the rascally quaff we have been drinking. By all accounts your lordship leads a gay life here.

BYRON. Not more gay than you have led elsewhere. But if you allude to what you see in the papers, and the travels of impertinent and underbred tourists;—underbred they must be, else they would not publish anecdotes of the private life of any gentleman, to satisfy the multitude, even if they were true—nothing can be more false or ridiculous. I sedulously cut the English here, on purpose to avoid being made food for journals, and Balaam to swell the pages of gabbling tourists. Indeed, I have not been in general treated well by these people. Then there are my Memoirs, published by Colburn——

ODOHERTY. A most audacious imposture! He had heard the report of your having given your Life to Moore, and, accordingly, thinking he might make a good thing of it, he hires at once Dictionary Watkins, to set about Memoirs, which, to give old Gropius credit for industry, he touched up in a fortnight; and advertised it was, as *the* Memoirs of Lord B., particularly in the country papers.

BYRON. Industry! it was only the industry of the scissars, for half the book is merely cut out of the Peerage, giving an account of my old grim ancestors—and newspapers, magazines, and other authentic vehicles of intelligence supply the rest.

ODOHERTY. I can assure you, my Lord, it imposed on many simple, chuckleheaded, open-mouthed people, as your autobiography.

BYRON. Impossible. An idiot must have known that I had not any thing to do with it, even from its style.

ODOHERTY. Style—as to style, that is all fudge. I myself have written in all kind of styles, from Burke to Jeremy Bentham. But I assure your Lordship the mob charge you with these Memoirs.

BYRON. Why, really some people believe me capable of any kind of stuff. You remember I was accused of writing puffs for Day and Martin.

ODOHERTY. A calumny, I *know*, my dear Byron, for *I* am myself author of them. By the way, have you heard the epigram on your disclaimer?

BYRON. No—tell it me—I hope it is good.

ODOHERTY. You shall judge.

ON READING THE APPENDIX TO LORD BYRON'S TRAGEDY
OF THE TWO FOSCARI.
Is Byron surprised that his enemies say
He makes puffing verses for Martin and Day?
Why, what other task could his Lordship take part in
More fit than the service of Day, and of Martin?
So shining, so dark—all his writing displays
A type of this liquid of Martin and Day's—
Gouvernantes—Kings—laurel-crown'd Poets attacking—
Oh! he's master complete of the science of Blacking!

BYRON. No great affair. But there are "many more too long" to trouble you with, which the public give me credit for.

ODOHERTY. As, for instance, the attack on Ebony. Give me a specimen of that—or give me the thing itself, and I shall make him print it.

BYRON. It is too stale now; besides, I have quite forgotten it. Murray has the only copy I know of—and I shall write to him to give it you on your return.

ODOHERTY. Thank you—and a copy of the Irish Advent too?

BYRON. Hush! Hush!

ODOHERTY. You need not be afraid of me, my Lord, I *have* seen it; there are a dozen copies in existence.

BYRON. Let's change the subject. Giving my Memoirs was not the first trick Colburn served me. You remember the Vampire affair.

ODOHERTY. Ah! poor Jack Polidori! Lord rest him. Polidori was bribed on the occasion.

BYRON. I am sorry for it. I once thought him a fair fellow. But you see in this catchpenny Life how Colburn's hack pretends to censure the forgery, though his employer was the *sole* planner and manager of the affair—and it was he who got some people in the Row to father the published pamphlet—the separate one, you know.

ODOHERTY. Ay—and I heard, on authority which I believe, that Colburn cancelled a disavowal of your being the author, which some person had written and prefixed to the notice of the Vampire in the New Monthly.

BYRON. Hand me the brandy, that I may wash my mouth after mentioning such things. How is the New Monthly?

ODOHERTY. Dying hard. Nobody of talent about it except Campbell himself, who is too lazy. As for * * * * * * * __ * * * * * __ * * * * * and other mere asses—

BYRON. I have never heard of the worthies you mention.

ODOHERTY. By jingo, I am sure of that. * * * * is a great officer. He sits in the theatre taking notes, as magisterially as a judge does on a trial, and with as much dignity.

BYRON. Transeat. Murray sends me shoals of periodicals. There appears to be a swarm of them lately, and I find I am a popular subject for all. Not a fellow takes pen in hand without criticizing me.

ODOHERTY. Oxoniensis gave you, or rather Murray, a good ribroasting. I trouble you for the bottle.

BYRON. I think too harshly—but the Oxonians are great big-wigs.

ODOHERTY. Oh! thundering tearers, in their own opinion. I remember * * * * , who, n'importe—going into Covent-Garden a few years ago, simultaneously with the Prince Regent. The audience, of course, rose out of respect to his Royal Highness, and remained for some time standing; on which the delighted Tyro—hot from Rhedycina, exclaimed—God bless my soul—these good people, who mean well I dare say, have been informed that I am in the first class, and about to stand for Oriel.

BYRON. Ha! ha! ha! I shall, however, look back always with pleasure to the days,

> When smitten first with sacred love of song,
> I roamed old Oxford's hoary piles among;

and forgive Oxoniensis, whom I know. But let us return. I do not want information about the great magnates of your English literature—or those reputed such—but I should wish to hear something of the minors —the insect tribes. Who are your magazine, &c. scribblers?

ODOHERTY. Innumerable as the snipes in the bog of Allen. There is Clare poetizing for the London.

BYRON. An over-puffed youth that ploughboy appears to be.

ODOHERTY. He may have written some pretty things, but he is taken now to slum, scissorsing, namby pamby, and is quite spoiled. But it is a good thing to have a good conceit of one's self, and that's the boy who has it. He has pitted himself against Hogg, whom he considers as his inferior.

BYRON. Quelle gloire! they should have an amabean contention, like the clowns in Virgil. Suggest this to North, with my compliments.

ODOHERTY. Surely—it is a good hint. But Clare never will write any thing like the "Dedication to Mr Grieve," or "The flying tailor of Ettrick," until he is boiled again.

BYRON. I am told he is a delicate retiring young man. And that's more than can be said of you, Ensign and Adjutant. You have been always too much a lady's man.

ODOHERTY. Ay,—and so has somebody else who shall be nameless. I have had, I take it, somewhere about 144 pretty little bantlings—God bless them—of all colours, in various quarters of the globe.

BYRON. You would be a useful man in a new colony. Why don't you take the Quarterly hint, and settle in Shoulder of Mutton Bay, Van Diemen's Land?

ODOHERTY. Thank you for the hint—as much as to say, I ought to be sent across the water to Botany. But to the insects. Taylor, also, its publisher, is a writer for the London. He continues Johnson's Lives of the Poets!

BYRON. Surely you joke. It is as good a jest as if Hazlitt were to take it into his head to continue Chesterfield.

ODOHERTY. Yet such is the fact. But don't mention it; for Taylor, who really is a decent fellow, wishes it to be kept secret, being heartily sick of the concern. There are fifty other "Gentlemen of the Press," but really they are too obscure to bother your Lordship with. Some new periodical —name unknown—is supported by Proctor, the great tragedian.

BYRON. Nay, I am jealous of Cornwall, as of a superior poet. His Mirandola floated proudly through the theatre. My Faliero was damned.

ODOHERTY. I know it was d—d ungenteel in Elliston to put it in the way of being so. But there is no making a silk purse out of a sow's ear.

BYRON. How is my old friend, "My Grandmamma's Review, the British?"

ODOHERTY. Just as merry and jocular as ever—but the British Critic is dying. Rivington has started the Monthly Literary Censor, it is said, to supersede it.

BYRON. And my old foe, the Literary Gazette?

ODOHERTY. Doing well. But what need you be so thin-skinned as to mind such little flea-bites?

BYRON. *Flebit* et insignis tota cantabitur urbe. Faith, I don't like to be pestered with impunity. Has it any rivals?

ODOHERTY. Lots. Valpy set up the Museum, a weekly paper, the other day, against it. When I tell you that black-letter Tom Fogrum Dibdin is the chief hand, I need not add that it is dull and harmless.

BYRON. No—that's pretty evident. But truce with periodical chit-chat.

ODOHERTY. Shall I give you news from Parnassus?

BYRON. No—no—no—I am sick of that. Did you see my Werner and my New Mystery?

ODOHERTY. Yes—Murray shewed them to me in sheets.

BYRON. Well, what did you think of them?

ODOHERTY. Like every thing that comes from your lordship's pen, they are tinged with the ethereal hues of genius,—and perfumed with fragrance of the flowers that grow upon the brink of Helicon.

BYRON. Ho! I see, my friend, you have joined the Irish school of oratory. But as that goes for nothing, what do you, without trope or figure, think of them?

ODOHERTY. Seriously, my Lord, I admire them when they are good, and dislike them when they are bad.—[*Aside*] That is, I like five pages, and dislike fifty.—[*To Lord B.*] But, my Lord, why do you not try your hand at your own old style—the tale—the occasional poetry;—you know what I mean?

BYRON. Because I am sick of being imitated. I revolt at the idea of the lower orders making desperate attempts to climb the arduous mount. I have been publicly accused of seducing, by my example, youths

> Doom'd their father's hopes to cross,
> To pen a stanza when they should engross.

And I shall not,—at least just now I think I shall not—lead the way for sentimental and poetical hard-handed and hard-headed good people to follow. There is no danger of their following me into the lofty region of tragedy.

ODOHERTY. Whew! Why, you are playing the aristocrat with a vengeance. There is, however, one lowly poet whom I would recommend to your attention.

BYRON. Whom?

ODOHERTY. He is so modest, that he does not wish his name to be mentioned, and writes his "lays" under the title of Ismail Fitz-Adam.

BYRON. I never heard of him.

ODOHERTY. I did not imagine you did; and yet he has written some things which would not have disgraced the pen of a Byron. I could not say more of any man. (*Lord B. bows and smiles.*) Nay, my Lord, I am quite in earnest; and though very poor, and only a common sailor, he has that spirit of independence which I hope will always animate our navy, and refuses all direct pecuniary assistance.

BYRON. What, in heroics again! But he is quite right. Do his books sell?

ODOHERTY. Not as they ought—Very slowly.

BYRON. I am sorry for it. On your return, bid Murray put my name down for fifty copies.

ODOHERTY. You were always a gentleman, my Lord: But the bottle is out, and I am some hundred yards distant from civilation yet.

BYRON. Pardon me—do as you like; but I shall not drink any more.

ODOHERTY. Not till the next time, you mean. Could I get a song out of your lordship?

BYRON. On what subject?

ODOHERTY. On any. Parody one of your own serious humbugs.—Suppose—"There's not a joy that life can give."—

BYRON. Very well—here goes—accompany me on the pipes, which I see you have brought with you to alarm the Italians.

SONG.

THERE'S NOT A JOY THAT LIFE CAN GIVE, &C.

Tune.—GRAND MARCH *in Scipio.*

1.

There's not a joy that WINE *can give like that it takes away,*
When slight intoxication yields to drunkenness the sway,
'Tis not that *youth's smooth cheek* its *blush* surrenders to the nose;
But the stomach turns, the forehead burns, and all our pleasure goes.

2.

Then the few, who still can keep their chairs amid the smash'd decanters,
Who wanton still in witless jokes, and laugh at pointless banters—
The magnet of their course is gone—for, let them try to walk,
Their legs, they speedily will find as jointless as their talk.

3.

Then the mortal hotness of the brain, like hell itself, is burning,
It cannot feel, nor dream, nor think—'tis whizzing, blazing, turning—
The heavy wet, or port, or rum, has mingled with *our tears,*
And if by chance we're weeping drunk, each drop our cheek-bone sears.

4.

Though fun still flow from fluent lips, and jokes confuse our noddles
Through midnight hours, while punch our powers insidiously enfuddles,
'Tis but as ivy leaves were worn by Bacchanals of yore,
To make them still look fresh and gay while rolling on the floor.

5.

Oh! could I walk *as I have* walk'd, *or* see *as I have* seen;
Or even roll as I have done on many a carpet green—
As port at Highland inn seems sound, all corkish though it be,
So would I the Borachio kiss, and get blind drunk with thee.

ODOHERTY. Excellent—most excellent!

BYRON. Nay, I don't shine in parody—Apropos, de bottes—Do you know anything of Bowles?

ODOHERTY. Your antagonist?

BYRON. Yes.

ODOHERTY. I know he's a most excellent and elegant gentleman, who gave your Lordship some rubbers.

BYRON. I flatter myself he had not the game altogether in his own hands. He, indeed, is a gentleman-like man, and so was Ali Pacha—but a heretic with respect to Pope. By the bye, is not Murray going to give a new edition of the great Ethic, the Bard of Twickenham?

ODOHERTY. No, not now. He was, but in the mean time Roscoe, the gillyflower of Liverpool, announced his intention of coming forth—and Murray's editor declined. His Western Majesty, however, took the merit of declining it himself, and made a great matter of his condescension to Roscoe, who swallowed it. In the meantime, one of Murray's huff-caps cut Roscoe to pieces, in the review of Washington Irving's Sketch-Book, in the Quarterly.

BYRON. Ha! ha! Well done, Joannes de Moravia. But is Bowles as thin-skinned as ever with respect to criticism?

ODOHERTY. No—I should think not. Tickler, at Ambrose's, drew rather a droll description of him the other night, painting him in a shovel-hat, &c., which some how or other got into print, and Bowles was quite tickled by it.

BYRON. The devil he was!

ODOHERTY. Ay, and accepted the office of bottle-holder to North, in the expected turn-up between Christopher and Tom Moore, in the most handsome manner possible, chaunting, *à la Pistol,*

> Thou hast produced me in a gown and band,
> And shovel, oh! sublimest Christopher!
> And I shall now thy bottle-holder be,
> Betting my shovel to a 'prentice cap,
> That neither Tom nor Byron [*meaning you, my Lord.*] will stand up
> A single moment 'gainst your powerful facers,
> When you set to in fistic combat fairly.

But now that I have told you so much about British literature, give me something of the literature of this, I am sorry to say it, your adopted country.

BYRON. I might perhaps shock your political principles.

ODOHERTY. I have not any. So push on.

BYRON. This poor country is so misgoverned——

ODOHERTY. Ay, so your man Hobhouse says—

BYRON. What, Hobbio—mobbio—Psha! But really the Austrian domination is so abom——

Left speaking.

𝔑octes 𝔄mbrosianae.

No. V.

ACT I.

Scene, Back Parlour—Cold Supper just set.
Manet MR AMBROSE *solus.*

MR AMBROSE. I think it will do. That plate of lobsters is a little too near the edge. Softly, softly, the round of beef casts too deep a shadow over these pickles. There—that is right. Old Kit will be unable to criticise—

Enter MR NORTH. Old Kit! will be unable to criticise!!—Why, upon my honour, Mr Ambrose, you are rather irreverent in your lingo.

MR AMBROSE. (*much confused.*) I really, sir, had not the least idea you were at hand. You know, sir, with what profound respect——

MR NORTH. Come, Ambrose, put down the pots of porter. The King has left the Theatre, and we shall be all here in a few seconds. I made my escape from the Manager's box, just before the row and the rush began. Hark! that is the clank of the Adjutant.

Enter ODOHERTY, TICKLER, SEWARD, BULLER, HIGHLAND CHIEFTAIN,
and MR BLACKWOOD.

ODOHERTY. Allow me, my dear North, to introduce to you my friend, the Chief of the Clan—

MR NORTH. No need of a name. I know him by his Father's face.— Sir, I will love you for the sake of as noble a Gael as ever slaughtered a Sassenach. Sit down, sir, if you please.—(*Highland Chieftain sits down at Mr North's right hand.*)

MR SEWARD. Well, did not he look every inch a King, this evening? A King of Great Britain, France, and Ireland, ought, if possible, to be a man worth looking at. His subjects expect it, and it is but reasonable they should.

MR NORTH. Fame does no more than justice to his bow. It is most princely—so—or rather so. Is that like him?

ODOHERTY. No more than a hop-pole is like a palm-tree, or the Editor of the Edinburgh Review like him of Blackwood's Magazine. The King's bow shews him to be a man of genius; for, mark me, he has no model to go by. He must not bow like the Duke of Argyll, or Lord Fife, well as they bow, but like a King. And he does so. The King is a man of genius.

MR BLACKWOOD. Do you think, sirs, that the King would become a contributor to the Magazine? I have sent his Majesty a set splendidly bound, by—

MR NORTH. Hush, Ebony, leave that to me. You must not interfere with the Editorial department.

MR BULLER. What do you Scotch mean by calling yourselves a grave people; and by saying that you are not, like the Irish, absurd in the expression of your loyalty? I never heard such thunder in a Theatre before.

ODOHERTY. I would have given twenty ten-pennies that some of the young ladies in the pit had remembered that a pocket handkerchief should not be used longer than a couple of days. Some of the literary gentlemen too, shewed snuffy signals. But the *coup d'œil* was imposing.

BULLER. I hate all invidious national distinctions. Let every people hail their King in their own way.

ODOHERTY. To be sure they should. But then the Scotch are "a nation of Gentlemen;" and the Irish "a nation of ragamuffins;" and the English a "nation of shop-keepers." How then?

MR NORTH. His Majesty knows better than to satirize us. We are not a nation of gentlemen—thank God;—but the greater part of our population is vulgar, intelligent, high-cheeked, raw-boned, and religious.

MR SEWARD. I could not help smiling, when I looked across the pit and along the boxes this evening, at the compliment towards yourselves as a nation, which some self-sufficient soul put into his Majesty's mouth. I never saw a more vulgar pit in my life. The women looked as if——

ODOHERTY. One and all of them could have kissed the King. But, Seward, my boy, you are mistaken in calling the pit vulgar. Your taste has been vitiated, Seward, by Oxford milliners, and————

MR NORTH. The conversation is wandering. (*Turning to the Chieftain.*) I saw you talking to the Thane in the Theatre. Would to Heaven you had brought him here!

CHIEFTAIN. He is gone to Dalkeith, or he would have come.

MR NORTH. How popular the Thane is all over Scotland. Depend upon it, Gentlemen, that the best man is, in general, the most popular. Nothing but generosity and goodness will make peasants love peers.

MR BLACKWOOD. His Lordship never comes to town without calling at the shop.

Enter Mr AMBROSE *and Waiters, with rizzard haddocks,*
cut of warm salmon, muirfowl, and haggis.

MR TICKLER. Adjutant, I will drink a pot of porter with you—THE KING,—(three times three—*surgunt omnes*)—Hurra, hurra, hurra—Hurra, hurra, hurra—Hurra, hurra, hurra! (*Conticuere omnes.*)

MR NORTH. Odoherty, be pleased to act as croupier.

ODOHERTY. More porter.

MR TICKLER. Did you see how the whole pit fixed its face on the King's—till the play began? It was grand, North. His eye met that loyal "glower" with mild and dignified composure. The King, North, was happy. I'll swear he was. He saw that he had our hearts. Every note of "God save the King" went dirling through my very soul-strings. I'm as hoarse as a howlet.

MR NORTH. I think the people feel proud of their King. As he past the platform where I stood, on his entrance into Edinburgh, I heard a countryman say to his neighbour,— "Look, Jock; look, Jock,—isna he an honest-looking chiel? Gude faith, Jock, he's just like my ain father."

MR SEWARD. Curse the Radicals! A King must abhor even a single hiss from the vilest of his subjects. The King, Mr North, is with us as popular a King as ever reigned in England. He has only to shew himself oftener, and——

MR BULLER. I have seen the King in public often; but I never saw him insulted except in the Newspapers. The "Scotsman in London" is a common character.

ODOHERTY. Mr Seward, a little haggies. See "its hurdies like twa distant hills."

MR SEWARD. What are hurdies?

MR TICKLER. See Dr Jamieson.

CHIEFTAIN. Mr North, I am delighted. I hope I may say so without flattery. I never drank better Glenlivit.—Why, gentlemen, not come and pay me a visit this autumn? No occasion for a tent. I am a bachelor, and have few children.

ODOHERTY. Settled.—Name your day.

CHIEFTAIN. 14th of September. I cannot be home sooner. Is it a promise?

OMNES. 14th of September. WE SWEAR!!

ODOHERTY. Well done, old Mole, in the cellarage.—Hamlet—See Shakespeare.

Enter MR AMBROSE. Mr North, a communication.

MR TICKLER. Read—read.

MR NORTH. I cannot say I am quite able to do so. My eyes are a little hazy or so. But there is the letter, Tickler.—Up with it.

MR TICKLER (*reads.*)

De'il tak the kilts! For fifty year, nae honest son of Reikie's
Wad ever think to walk the streets, denuded o' his breekies.
And ony kilted drover lad, wi' kyloes or a letter,
Was pitied, or was glower'd at, "Puir chiel he kens nae better;"
And apple-wives look'd sidelins, and thocht he came to steal or beg,
Whene'er they saw a callant wi' his hurdies in a philabeg.

And even chiefs o' clans themselves, whene'er they ran to towns, man,
Were fain to clothe their hairy knees in breeks, or pantaloons, man.
But now! Lord bless your soul! there's no a Lawland writer laddie
Can wheedle a pund note or twa frae his auld canker'd daddie,
But aff he sets, (though born betwixt St Leonard's and Drumsheugh) an
He fits himsel' wi' bannet, plaid, and hose, and kilt, and spleuchan.
Ye'se ken the cause o' a' the steer;—the Heeland Dhuine Wassals
Began to tire o' wearin' breeks whene'er they left their castles;
So they coax'd the honest citizens to join in a convention
To tak' the corduroy from off the pairt I daurna mention;
That, like the tod that tint his tail, they mightna cause derision,
And find their faces in a flame, while elsewhere they were freezin.—
The town's-lads snappit at the plan, and thus began the Celtic,
A medley strange frae every land, frae off the shores o' Baltic;
Frae England, Ireland, Scotland; Border lairds and ancient British,
There were Dutchmen, Danes, and Portuguese, and French and Otaheitish;
And a' professions, frae the lad that's only just apprenticed,
To the great hero of the west—e'en Doctor Scott the Dentist—
And they wad dine, and drink, and strut, as big's Maccallum More, sir,
And skraigh attempts at Gaelic words, until their throats were sore, sir.
An' a' was canty for a while, for these were still their gay days,
An' a' could lend a hand to pay for balls gi'en to the ladies;
And there they danc'd the Highland fling, and kick'd their kilts and toes up,
Tho' whiles their ruler-shapit legs refused to keep their hose up.
But when the pawky Highland lairds had fairly set the fashion,
Up gets an angry Chief o' Chiefs in a prodigious passion:
"Fat Teil hae you to do wi' kilts, gae wa' and get your claes on,
Get out, ye nasty Lowland poys, and put your preeks and stays on;
Ye shanna wear your claes like me, I look on you as fermin,
Ye hae nae mair o' Highland pluid than if ye were a Cherman."*
This sets them up, "Chairman indeed! Ye never sall be ours, sir!
Except it be to carry us when we go out of doors, sir!
Like ithers o' your kintra men." And thus they flyte thegither,
And haud the hail town in a steer, expelling' ane anither.
And how the bus'ness is to end, is mair than I can tell, sir,
Indeed it seems to fickle and perplex the Sherriff's sell, sir;
But this I ken, that folk that's wise think they maun be nae witches,
Wha ever let a Highland kerne entice them out o' breeches.

---

* German.

HIGHLAND CHIEF. Come, gentlemen, if you please, I will propose a toast,—"Glengarry!" His Majesty would not have sent the message he did to the Chiefs, if he had not been pleased with them and their Highlanders.

OMNES. Glengarry. Hurra, hurra, hurra!

ODOHERTY. What does Glengarry mean, by saying that few members of the Celtic Society could shoot an eagle? It is easier, a damned deal easier, to shoot an eagle than a peacock. But the easiest way of any is to knock an eagle down with a shillala.

MR SEWARD. Do you shy the shillala at his head from a distance?

ODOHERTY. No. I refer to the Chieftain. You must walk slowly up to him at the rate of about four miles an hour, (Townsend, the pedestrian, would do it half backwards and half forwards,) and hit him over the periwig with your sapling.

CHIEFTAIN. Perfectly true. When an eagle has eat a sheep or a roe, he sits as heavy as a Dutchman—cannot take wing—and you may bag him alive if you chuse. The shepherds often fling their plaids over him. But let him take wing, and he darkens the sun-disk like an eclipse.

MR BLACKWOOD. I beg your pardon, sir, but I should wish much to have a sound, sensible Article on the State of the Highlands of Scotland. I suspect there is much misrepresentation as to the alleged cruelty and impolicy of large farms. Dog on it, will any man tell me, sir, that——

CHIEFTAIN. Mr Blackwood, I wish I could write an article of the kind you mention. You are a gentleman of liberal sentiments. In twenty years the Highlands will be happier than they ever have been since the days of Ossian. Lowland Lairds have no right to abuse us for departing from the savage state.

MR BLACKWOOD. Could you let us have it for next Number, sir? We stand in need of such articles prodigiously—sound, sensible, statistical articles, full of useful information. We have wit, fun, fancy, feeling, and all that sort of thing in abundance, but we are short of useful information. We want facts—a Number now and then, with less fun and more facts, would take, and promote the sale with dull people. Yes, it is a fact, that we want facts.

ODOHERTY. Damn your Magazine, Ebony! You gave Napoleon no rest at St Helena till he became a contributor. You are beginning to send sly hints to the King. And here we have you smelling as strong of the shop as a bale of brown paper, dunning the Chieftain the very first time he has come among us.

MR SEWARD. Chieftain, you mentioned Ossian—may I ask if his Poems are authentic?

CHIEFTAIN. As authentic as the heather and the hail on our misty mountains.

C

MR SEWARD. Wordsworth the poet says, that in Ossian's Poems, every thing is looked at as if it were one, but that nothing in nature is so looked at by a great poet. Therefore, Ossian's poetry is bad, and written by Macpherson.

CHIEFTAIN. I have not the pleasure of being familiar with Mr Wordsworth's name or writings. Neither do I understand one syllable of what you have now said. Ossian's poetry is not bad. Did the gentleman you speak of ever see a lake or a mountain?

MR BULLER. He lives on the banks of a tarn about a mile round about.

CHIEFTAIN. I am sorry for him.

MR NORTH. He also says, if I recollect rightly, that Ossian speaks of car-borne chiefs in Morven—but that Morven is inaccessible to cars.

ODOHERTY. So it is to jaunting cars. Wordsworth was in a sort of mongrel shandrydan, a cross between a gig and a tax-cart; and no wonder he was shy of Morven. But unless he had been a most ignorant person indeed, (all poets are ignorant,) he would have known that there are cars in Morven to this day.

CHIEFTAIN. There are—and scientifically constructed, though of old date. I have seen the Highlanders coming down the steep and rocky hills with them, full of peats, with a rapidity that would have pleased Fingal himself. Besides, there are many straths and level places in Morven.

MR NORTH. Pray, were not all the Highlands once called "Morven?"

CHIEFTAIN. They were, not unfrequently, nor by a few.

ODOHERTY. So goes the flummery of the water-drinking laker about Ossian,—the bard who brewed his own whisky, and drank like a whale.

MR TICKLER. Tell Wordsworth to let other people's poetry alone, from Ossian to Pope, and make his own a little better. Who prefers Alice Fell to Malvina? or Peter Bell to Abelard? Oh! that the English lakes were all connected by canals! A few steam-boats from Glasgow would soon blow up their poetry. Wishy-washy stuff indeed!

MR NORTH. Our conversation, gentlemen, is degenerating into literature. I will fine the first of you that tattles in a bumper.

ODOHERTY. The Paradise Lost of Milton has ever ap——

MR TICKLER. He blabs for a bumper. But in with the salt.

MR BLACKWOOD. One of the great merits of *The Magazine* is, that it has less literature——

ODOHERTY. Than libels.

MR BLACKWOOD, (*rising.*) Mr Odoherty, I have lately seen you walking on all occasions with the enemy. Did you review O'Meara in the Edinburgh?

ODOHERTY. No, no, my good fellow; they throw out their bait, but I wont nibble.

MR BLACKWOOD. All I know is, that it is at once more honourable and more lucrative to write in our Maga, than in any other existing work.

MR TICKLER, (*ringing the bell.*) What cackling, as of geese, is that we hear through the partition?—Mr Ambrose, remove that side-board, and throw open these folding-doors.

MR AMBROSE. There is a small party in the next room, Mr Tickler.

MR TICKLER. I want to count them. (*Side-board is removed, and doors flung open.*)

SCENE II.

ODOHERTY. Whigs—Whigs—a nest of Whigs. A conspiracy against our Lord the King. How do you, Mr Bunting?

MR BUNTING. I scarcely understand this, Mr Odoherty. But, during the King's Visit, all party distinctions should be forgotten. I hope you did not cry, Whigs, Whigs, Whigs, offensively.

MR NORTH. Young gentlemen, we have been all Whigs in our day. It is a disease of the constitution. Will you and your friends join our table? Help Mr Bunting to some haggis.

MR BULLER. This is a formidable coalition. It is as bad as Mr Fox joining Lord North.

MR BLACKWOOD. Mr Bunting, I seldom see you or any of your friends about the shop now-a-days. I hope, now that the King comes to see us, you will step up the front-steps.—(*Aside, to Mr Bunting in a whisper.*) Are not these three of the seven young men?

MR BUNTING. I was glad to see the King, and I trust he will not be misinformed of our sentiments towards him. I respect him as the chief magistrate.

MR TICKLER. That is infernal nonsense, Master Bunting, begging your pardon. Have you no feeling, no fancy, no imagination, Master Bunting? Your heart ought to leap at the word King, as at the sound of a trumpet. Chief magistrate!—humbug. Do you love your own father, because he was once Provost of Crail? No, no, Master Bunting—that won't pass at Ambrose's.

YOUNG MAN. I hope that the King's Visit will be productive of some substantial and lasting benefit to this portion of the united empire.

MR NORTH. What do you mean? Mention what ought to be done, and I will give a hint to Mr Peel.

YOUNG MAN. In my opinion the question of borough reform——

ODOHERTY. Sheep's head or trotters, sir?

MR BUNTING. Unless his Majesty's ministers assist the Greeks, and ransom the young women ravished from their native Scio into Turkish harems, the inhabitants of modern Athens will——

ODOHERTY. What will they do?—But I agree with you, Mr Bunting, in thinking the Greek girls deucedly handsome. Were you ever in Scio?

MR BUNTING. No. But I attended a meeting t'other day, at which the affairs in general of Greece were admirably discussed. And are we to countenance rape, robbery, and murder?

ODOHERTY. Why, I don't know. As an Irishman, I am scarcely entitled to answer in the negative. But what has all this blarney to do with King George the Fourth's Visit to Scotland?

MR BLACKWOOD. I will be very happy to give Mr Bunting, or any of his Whig friends, five guineas for an article of moderate size, containing a few facts about the Greeks. Pray, Mr Bunting, what may be the population of the isle of Scio?

MR BUNTING (*after a pause.*) Well—well—I shall not push the conversation any farther in that direction. The haggis is most excellent. Mr North, may I have the honour to pledge you in a pot of porter?

ODOHERTY (*ringing the bell.*) Pipes. (*They are brought in.*)

MR TICKLER. No spitting-boxes. They are filthy.

MR NORTH. Where art thou, Odoherty? I discern thee not through this dense cloud of smoke.

ODOHERTY. We may all come and go without being missed. I have an appointment at one o'clock.

Voice, as of one of the Young Men. I have just been perusing the fresh number of the Edinburgh Review. I scarcely think that the Duke of Wellington will go to the Congress—after it.

MR TICKLER. Has Frank Jeffrey stultified the Duke of Wellington?

Voice, as of one of the Young Men. Bonaparte, Benjamin Constant, Madame de Stael, John Allan, Esq., Sir James Macintosh, and Jeffrey himself, all think him *un homme bornè.*

MR SEWARD. Pray, sir,—I beg your pardon, but I do not see you very distinctly; what do they mean by *un homme bornè?* How do you translate the words?

Voice, as of one of the Young Men. I am no French scholar; but it sounds like French. It is an epithet of opprobrium. The precise meaning is of no consequence to our argument.

ODOHERTY. Oh! the Duke of Wellington is an ass! What a pity!—Who is that sick in that corner?—Waiter, waiter. Throw open the window—down pipes, till it clears off a little. Soho! it is my eloquent young Man of the Mist?—Carry him out, Ambrose—there he is *un homme bornè.*

MR BUNTING. We, all of us, hate smoking. But, Mr North—gentlemen—goodnight.

Exeunt Mr BUNTING *and the Young Men.*

MR BULLER. Are these a fair specimen of your young Edinburgh Whigs?

MR NORTH. I fear they are. Their feebleness quite distresses us. Jeffrey himself, I am told, is unhappy about it.—What am I doing? lighting my pipe with an article that I have not read. There, (*flinging it*

over to Buller) read it aloud for the general edification and delight.
   BULLER *reads.*

TO CHRISTOPHER NORTH, ESQ.
From an occasional Contributor, living at Cape Clear,
who was applied to for an article about the King in Edinburgh.

1.
Chief of scribblers! Wondrous Editor!
   Why d'ye seek assistance here?
Little you'd gain of praise, or credit, or
   Any thing else by me, my dear.
         Those who, like Boreas,
         Greeted uproarious,
Visit so glorious, loudly should sing,
         How Miss Edina,
         Looking so fine-a,
Smart and divine-a, welcomed the King.

2.
One would think it only rational,
   That you had poets there on the spot:
Stir up your own Bard truly national,
   First of all Minstrels, Sir Walter Scott:
         High o'er Fahrenheit,
         Our hearts *are* in heat,
When that Baronet thrums the string.
         Can he refuse us
         Aid from his Muses?
No, no, he chuses to welcome the King.

3.
Have you not there, too, Crabbe the veteran?
   Ask that old poet to do the job.
For describing, shew me a better one,
   Bailies or beggarmen, flunkies or mob:
         Hubbub, bobbery,
         Crowd and mobbery,
For all such jobbery he's the thing.
         So then for a bard,
         List the Borough Bard,
Being a thorough bard to welcome the King.

4.

Mr Croly, my brother Irishman,
    Was there with you, as I am told;
He, I think, could give you a flourish, man,
    In verses bright of gems and gold.
            Soho, Cataline!
            Prime hand at a line!
Haste, and rattle in your verse to bring;
            Singing so gorgeous,
            How knight and burgess,
Throng'd round Great Georgius, welcomed the King.

5.

Then, there's another to do it cleverly,
    He, the great poet, who writes in prose;
Sure I mean the Author of Waverley,
    Whoe'er he be, if any one knows.
            Truce to Peveril!
            There are several
People who never will miss the thing,
            If he will vapour
            On hot-press'd paper,
And cut a caper to welcome the King.

6.

Or ask Wilson, the grave and serious
    Poet, who sung of the Palmy Isle;
Or the sweet fellow who wrote Valerius
    (Pray, what's his name?) would do it in style.
            Could you get once
            Some of these great ones,
Tender or sweet ones, for you to sing,
            We'd think the lasses
            Had left Parnassus,
To sing trebles and basses, to welcome the King.

MR SEWARD. I have had enough of "tobacco reek." O for a gulp of fresh air!

CHIEFTAIN. The barge of the Duke of Athol is now lying near the Chain Pier. It is under my orders. Might I propose a water-party? I can have her manned with ten oars in ten minutes.

MR NORTH. With all my heart. I am fond of aquatics.

OMNES (*crowding round the Editor.*) Take my box-coat—No, no, my cloak—here is my wrap rascal. Tie my Barcelona round your neat neck. Ring for a coach and six.

> *Exeunt Mr* NORTH, *leaning on the arm of the Highland Chief—and Mr* AMBROSE *with a flaming branch of wax-lights in each hand.*
> END OF ACT FIRST.

ACT II.—SCENE I.

Duke of Athole's Barge off the Chain Pier, Newhaven.

CHIEFTAIN. She pulls ten oars. Mr North, will you take the helm? I ask no better Palinurus.

MR NORTH. I am but a fresh-water sailor; yet in my day I have sailed a few thousand leagues. Byron says he has swam more leagues than all the living poets of Britain have sailed, with one or two exceptions. Had he said the living critics, he had grossly erred.

ODOHERTY. Coxswain, give North the tiller. Now, lads, down with your oars—splash—splash. Are we all on board?

OMNES. All—all—all—pull away.

MR NORTH. For the King's yacht. Beautifully feathered! Remember whom you have on board.

MR BULLER. Seward! this beats Brazen-nose. Yet I wish one of old Davis' wherries were here, to shew how an arrow whizzes from a bow.

MR NORTH. Seward—Buller, behold the Queen of the North! What think you of the Castle, with the crescent moon hung over her for a banner? The city lights are not afraid to confront the stars. I hope Arthur's Ghost is on his mountain-throne to-night. Yonder goes a fire-balloon. See how the stationary stars mock that transient flight of rockets. Yonder crown of gas-light burns brightly to-night,—now it is half veiled in cloud-drapery,—now it is gone. Hurra! Again it blazes forth, and tinges Nelson's Pillar with its ruddy splendour.

ODOHERTY. By the powers, North, you are poetical!

MR TICKLER. Nelson's Pillar—ay—may it stand there for ever! Did they not talk of pulling it down for the Parthenon? *We* held it up. Pull down a Monument to the greatest of all British admirals! Fie—fie.

MR BULLER. We Englishmen thought the proposal an odd one. But the Pillar, it was said, was in bad taste, and disfigured the modern Athens.

MR NORTH. It is in bad taste. What then? Are monuments to the illustrious dead to lie at the mercy of Dilettanti? But, as Mr Tickler said, *we* preserved that Monument.

MR SEWARD. I admire the Parthenon. Most of you will recollect my prize poem on that subject. I am glad the foundation-stone has been laid.

MR NORTH. So am I. Let Scotland shew now that she has liberality as well as taste, and not suffer the walls to be dilapidated by time before they have been raised to their perfect height.

ODOHERTY. The Parthenon will be an elegant testimonial. Is it not, too, a national testimonial? Why then should not the Scottish nation pay the masons? Why sue for Parliamentary grants? Are you not "a nation of Gentlemen?" Put your hands then into your breeches-pockets, (I beg your pardon, Chieftain,) and pay for what you build.

MR TICKLER. The Standard-Bearer speaks nobly. We admire the Parthenon. We resolve to build it. We call ourselves Athenians, and then implore Parliament to pay the piper. Poor devils! we ought to be ashamed of ourselves.

MR BULLER. Mr Odoherty, I agree with you. A rich nation does well to be magnificent. Up with towers, temples, baths, porticos, and what not; but for one nation to build splendid structures, and then call on another for their praises and their purses, is, in my opinion, not exactly after the fashion of the Athenians.

MR BLACKWOOD. I have no objection to publish an additional Number any month in behoof of the Parthenon. I think Mr Linning deserves the highest praise for his zeal and perseverance.

ODOHERTY. And I hope you will also publish an additional Number the month following for behoof of the Foundling Hospital, Dublin, which is generally over-stocked. There is not milk for half the brats.

MR NORTH. Shall I steer under her stern, or across her bows?

COXSWAIN. Under her great clumsy stern, and be damned to her—Jung-frau! Dung-cart! She can't keep her backside out of the water.

MR SEWARD. Whom are you speaking of? Not a female, I hope.

ODOHERTY. Sir William Curtis's yacht—a female, to be sure. Look, you may read her name on her bottom by moonlight.

MR BLACKWOOD. How many guns does she carry?

COXSWAIN. Twenty stew-pans.

CHIEFTAIN. Lord bless the worthy Baronet, however; he wins the hearts of us Highlanders by mounting a kilt. I hope he will wear it occasionally in Guildhall. I believe he is an honorary member of the Celtic Society.

MR SEWARD. Are turtles ever caught on the coast of Scotland?

CHIEFTAIN. Occasionally—but they are found in greatest numbers in the inland lochs. They were originally fresh-water fish.

MR SEWARD. You surprise me. Have these inland lochs no communication with the sea?

CHIEFTAIN. Many of them only by means of torrents precipitous, several miles high, and inaccessible, I suspect, to turtles.

COXSWAIN. Old gentleman, helm-a-lee, or we run foul of that hawser. Helm-a-lee, old gentleman, helm-a-lee, or we all take our grog in Davy's locker.

MR BLACKWOOD. Dog on it, Mr North, you would steer, and you would steer, and a pretty kettle of fish you are making of it—I wish I were safe at Newington! These boating expeditions never answer. My brother Thomas told me not to——

COXSWAIN. All's well.—Unship oars.

SCENE II.
State-cabin Royal Yacht.

MR NORTH. Admirable simplicity! nothing gorgeous and gawdy,— one feels at sea in such a cabin as this. The King, who designed it, knows the spirit of the British navy.

MR TICKLER. No broad glittering gilding; there is no smell of ginger-bread; one can think of grog and sea-biscuit. A man might be sick in squally weather here, without fear of the furniture.

ODOHERTY. Would it not be a pretty pastime to spend a honey-moon now and then in such a floating heaven as this? Calm weather and a clear conscience, soft sofa, liberty and love.

MR BULLER. Nay, confound it, the prettiest girl looks forbidding when she is squeamish. The dim orange hue of sea-sickness is an antidote to all foolish fondness.—Terra firma for me.

MR TICKLER. Unquestionably. I gave Mrs Tickler, a few days after our union, a voyage on the New Canal. The track-boat of this Cut was appropriately called The Lady of the Lake. We were hauled along, at the rate of three miles an hour, by a couple of horses, "lean, and lank, and brown, as is the ribbed sea-sand." Yet, even then, Mrs Tickler felt queer, and we had to disembarge before changing cattle.

THE ADJUTANT. One may travel now for twenty pounds all over Great Britain. Go it toe and heel in cool weather—take a lift occasionally in cart, buggy, or shandrydan, by the side of a fat farmer—tip the guard of Heavies a sly wink, and get up behind in the basket, thirty miles for a couple of shillings; now for a cheap circuitous cut by a canal, when you live cheap with the chaw-bacons, and see a fine flat country—into a steam-boat before the mast, and smoke it away fifty leagues for six and eight pence—*da capo*—and in about six weeks you return to your wife and family, with a perfect geographical and hydrographical knowledge of this Island, and with a five pound note, out of the twenty, for a nest-egg.

MR BLACKWOOD. That looks all very well upon paper.

ODOHERTY. On paper, Mr Blackwood!

MR BLACKWOOD. I say it is a mere theory, and cannot be reduced to practice. I cannot go to London, stay a fortnight, see my friends, and return, under fifty guineas.

ODOHERTY. But then you indulge in luxuries, extraneous expenses— works of supererogation.

MR BLACKWOOD. Not at all, Adjutant. To be sure hunting costs a good deal.

MR BULLER. Hunting!——Are you a sportsman? Do you join the Surrey? and conspire with your friend, Leigh Hunt, to worry hares in the dog-days?

MR BLACKWOOD. No, no. It is hunting contributors. For example, I hear of a clever young man having been at a tea-and-turn-out in the city. I lay on a few idle dogs to scent him out—I trace him to Temple Bar— there he is lost, and the chase may be repeated for several days before we secure him. Then I have to dinner him divers times, and, before leaving town, to advance money on his articles. Perhaps I never hear more of him, till I read the identical article, promised and paid for, in the London or New Monthly.

ODOHERTY. There is a melancholy want of principle indeed among literary men. Nobody will accuse me of being straight-laced; but while the love-fit lasts, I am true as steel to one mistress and to one Magazine. I look upon an attachment to either, quite as an affair of the heart. When mutually tired of each other, then part with a kiss, a squeeze of the hand, a curtsey, and a bow. But no infidelity during the attachment. What sort of a heart can that man have, who, while he is openly living with the New Monthly, insidiously pays his addresses to the modest and too unsuspecting Maga? It is a shocking system of promiscuous Cockney concubinage, that must at no distant period vitiate the taste, harden the sensibility, vulgarize the manners, and deprave the morals of the people of Great Britain. It ought to be put down.

MR BULLER. Do you seriously opine, Mr North, that much money is made by periodical literature in London?

MR NORTH. Assuredly not. There is little available talent there. The really good men are all over head and ears in wigs and work. There do not seem to be above a dozen idlers in all London who can get up a decent article; these are all known, and their intellects are measured as exactly as their bodies by a tailor;—each man has his measure lying at Colburn's, &c. and is paid accordingly. When a spare young man quarrels with one employer, he attempts another; but his wares are known in the market, and "he drags at each remove a heavier chain."

ODOHERTY. The contributors are all as well known as the pugilists— height, weight, length, bottom, and science. Mr F. can hit hard, but is a cur, like Jack the butcher. Mr R. can spar prettily, like Williams the swell, with the gloves, but can neither give nor take with the naked mauleys. Mr T. is like the Birmingham Youth, and "falls off unaccountably." And Mr —— is a palpable cross—fights booty, and it ends in a wrangle or a draw.

MR BLACKWOOD. Dog on it, Adjutant, why don't you give us some more Boxiana articles?

ODOHERTY. I do not wish to interfere with old —— in the "Fancy Gazette." He is a rum one to go——a most pawky and prophetic pugilist. He knows the whole business of the ring better than any man alive, and writes scholastically and like a gemman; but he was rather out there about Barlow and Josh. Hudson. Ebony, you should exchange Magazines. The prime object of the "Fancy Gazette" is to kick curs and crosses out of the ring. It is full of the true English spirit. Why, I gave a few Numbers of it to my friend the Rev. Dr Wodrow, who was once, as you know, Moderator of the General Assembly of the Kirk of Scotland, and nothing would satisfy the old divine but a couple of pairs of gloves. I sent them out from Christie's; and on my next visit, there were he and Saunders Howie, one of his elders, ruffianing it away like old Tom Owen and Mendoza. "That's a chatterer," quoth the elder, as I entered the study, he having hit Wodrow on his box of ivories. "There's a floorer," responded the ex-Moderator, and straightway the Covenanter was on the carpet.

CHIEFTAIN. Is not this a somewhat singular conversation for the state-cabin of our most gracious Sovereign's yacht?

ODOHERTY. Not at all. I saw Randal welt Macarthy in a room about this size, and Jack Scroggins serve out Holt—

MR SEWARD. Where is North? I hope he has not leapt out of the cabin window.

OMNES, (*rising from the King's sopha.*) North—North—Editor—Christopher—Kit,—where the devil are you?

MR NORTH, (*from within his Majesty's bed-room.*) Come hither, my dear boys, and behold your father reposing on the bed of royalty!
They all rush in.

MR BULLER. Behold him lying alive in state! Let us kneel down by the bed-side.
They all kneel down.

OMNES. Hail, King of Editors! Long mayest thou reign over us, thy faithful subjects. *Salve, Pater!*

MR NORTH. Oh! my children, little do you know what a weary weight is in a crown! Alas, for us Monarchs! Oh! that I could fall asleep, and never more awake! Posterity will do me justice.

MR BLACKWOOD (*in tears.*) Oh! my good sir—my good sir—it is quite a mistake, I assure you—every living soul loves and admires you. You must not talk of dying, sire—(*handing over the gem to Mr North*)—The world can ill spare you at this crisis.—Here is Canning, Secretary of State for Foreign Affairs. With yourself, in the Home Department, things will go on gloriously; and I calculate on 1000 additional subscribers to our next Number.

ODOHERTY. Let me smooth his pillow.

MR NORTH. How many of my poorest subjects are now asleep!

CHIEFTAIN (*aside to Mr Tickler.*) Is he subject to moody fits of this kind? Is he liable to the blue devils?

MR TICKLER. Only to printer's devils, Chieftain; but let him alone for a few minutes.—Strong imagination is working within him, as he lies on the King's couch.—See, he is recovering—what a grey piercing eye the old cock turns up! He is game to the back-bone.

MR NORTH. Would I had a bowl of punch-royal!

YOUNG MIDSHIPMAN. That you shall have, Mr North, in the twinkling of a bed-post. We drink nothing else on board, on a trip of this kind.— Hollo, Jenkins, bring the crater. (*Enter Jenkins with punch-royal.*) We call this the crater.

MR NORTH (*drinks.*) Punch-royal indeed!

ODOHERTY. Fair play is a jewel, North. Leave a cheerer to the Chieftain.

MR NORTH (*rising.*) Gentlemen, let us re-embark. My soul is full.— Adjutant, lend me your arm up the gang-way. Kings lie on down—but, oh, oh, oh! (*Striking his forehead.*)

MR BLACKWOOD. This will end in an article.

SCENE III.
The Deck of Mr Smith's Cutter, the Orion.

CHIEFTAIN. Bargemen, there are five guineas for you to drink the King's health, from Mr North and his friends.

BARGEMEN. KIT and the KING! Huzza—North for ever!

MR SEWARD. Let us beat up the Frith; the breeze is freshening. I only wish the worthy Commander had been on board—He can lay a bowsprit in the wind's eye with any man that ever touched a tiller.

ODOHERTY. Where the devil is the moon? Well tumbled porpus.—A sea-mew—lend me a musket. There, madam, some pepper for your tail —roundabouts like a whirligig—up like an arrow—and then off "right slick away," and down upon the billow, safe and sound, as dapper as a daisy. I always miss, except with single ball. I recollect killing Corney Macguire at the first fire, like winking, and hardly ever an aim at all at all.

MR BULLER. She will lie nearer the wind, Seward,—thereabouts— thereabouts—her mainsail has the true Ramsay-cut.—She looks quite snakish.

ODOHERTY. Put her about. The breeze is snoring from the kingdom of Fife. See now, Seward, that you don't let her miss stays. She goes round within her own length as on a pivot.—Well done, Orion!

MR TICKLER. I vote we set off for the Western Isles.

ODOHERTY. I have too much regard for Mrs Tickler to allow her husband to leave her in her present interesting situation. Besides, it would not be civil to the absent commander of the cutter, to overpower the crew, and carry her off, like pirates.

MR SEWARD. Demme—there's a schooner, about our own tonnage, beating up in ballast to Alloa for table beer—let us race her. I will lay the Orion on her quarter. There, lads—all tight—now she feels it—gunwale in—grand bearings—I could steer her with my little finger.—We are eating him out of the wind.

ODOHERTY, (*through his hands as a speaking trumpet.*) Whither bound?—What cargo?—Timber and fruit, staves and potatoes? Son of a sea-cow, you are drifting to leeward.

MR NORTH. I have been glancing over O'Meara. Buonaparte's tone, when speaking of the intended invasion of this country, did not a little amuse me. He laid his account with conquering Great Britain.

MR BULLER. Great insolence. Did his troops conquer divided and degenerate Spain? The British nation would have trampled him under foot. O'Meara records his ravings, as if he went along with them. I hate the French for snivelling so through their noses. No nasal nation could conquer a great guttural people.

MR NORTH. Good. It is quite laughable to hear him telling the surgeon what he intended to have done with the Bank of England, and what sort of a constitution he had cut and dried for us.

ODOHERTY. Buonaparte says sneeringly, that Wellington *could not* have left the field of battle, if he had been defeated at Waterloo. Does he mean, that his position was a bad one, in case of retreat? I ask, was his own a good one? Was not his army cut to pieces as it fled?

MR TICKLER. Odoherty, did you read t'other day, in the newspapers, of a Liverpool barber shaving eighty chins, in a workmanlike style, within the hour?

ODOHERTY. I did; but a Manchester shaver has since done a hundred.

MR TICKLER. It must have been a serious affair for the last score of shaveès. When the betting became loud, 6 to 4 on time, I am surprised the barber got his patients to sit.

MR NORTH. Was he allowed to draw blood?

ODOHERTY. Only from pimples. I like these sort of bets. They encourage the useful arts. I won a cool hundred last winter, as you may have heard, by eating a thousand eggs in a thousand hours.

MR TICKLER. Hard or soft?

ODOHERTY. Both—raw, roasted, and poached. It was a sickening business. I ate a few rotten ones, for the sake of variety.

CHIEFTAIN. One of my tail drank a thousand glasses of whisky in a thousand hours; and we had great difficulty in keeping him to a single glass an hour. He did it without turning a hair.

MR NORTH. Suppose we take a look at the Dollar Academy?

MR TICKLER. Tennant's in town; he dined with me last week. I have a copy of Anster Fair in my pocket. I took it to Holland with me on my last trip, and read it in the Zuyder Zee. It is a fine thing, North, full of life, and glee, and glamour. So is Don Juan.

MR NORTH. I shall not permit any more poetry to be published before the year 1830, except by fresh ones. The known hands are all stale. Poetry is the language of passion. But no strong deep passion is in the mind of the age. If it be, where? Henceforth I patronize prose.

MR TICKLER. So does Mr Blackwood. Confound him, he is inundating the public. I wish to God Galt was dead!

MR BLACKWOOD. You are so fond of saying strong things. Gracious me! before he has finished the Lairds of Grippy?

MR TICKLER. Well, well, let him live till then, and then die. Yet better is a soil, like that of Scotland, that produces a good, strong, rough, coarse crop, than the meagre and mangy barrenness of England.

MR SEWARD. Buller, take the helm.—The meagre and mangy barrenness of England! Do you speak, sir, of the soil or the soul of England? You Scotch do wonders both in agriculture and education; but you cannot contend against climate.

MR NORTH. Come, come—you don't thoroughly understand Tickler yet. But the moon is sunk, the stars are paling their ineffectual fires,— and, what is worse, the tide is ebbing. So let us put about, and back to the Chain Pier. Or shall we make a descent on the coast? See, we are off Hopetoun House.

ODOHERTY. Hark! the sound of the fiddle from that snug farm-house, amidst a grove of trees! Pity they should be Scotch firs,—a damnable tree, and a grove of them is too bad. Let us land.

BOATSWAIN. The water is deep close to the water-edge. Down helm, master. There, her gunwale is on the granite!

Mr NORTH leaps out, followed by the Standard Bearer,
Chieftain, &c.; and the Orion, her sails soon filling, wears,
and goes down the Frith, goose-winged, before the wind.

ACT III.

SCENE I.

Kitchen of the Farm-house of Girnaway. Gudeman in his arm-chair, by
the ingle—Mr NORTH on his right hand—Gudewife, in her arm-chair,
opposite—ODOHERTY on her right—Lads and Lasses all round.
Reel of Tullochgorum.

GUDEMAN. Ma faith, but the Highlander handles his heels weel. You were saying he is a Chieftain—Has he his tail in the town wi' him?

MR NORTH. He has a tail twenty gentlemen long.

GUDEMAN. I'm thinkin' it wad be nae jeest to cast saut on his tail. He's a proud, fierce-lookin' fallow. He's bringing the red into Meg's face yonner, with his kilt flaff flaffing afore her, wi' that great rough pouch. Hear till him, hoo he's snappin' his fingers, and crying out, just wi' perfect wudness. The fiver o' his young Hieland bluid wunna let him rest. Safe us! look at him whirling Meg about like a tee-totum.

GUDEWIFE. Gudeman, this gentleman here, he is an Irisher, is priggin' on me to tak the floor. I fin' as gin I couldna refuse him.

GUDEMAN. Do as thou likes, Tibbie, thou'rt auld eneugh to take care o' thyself.

MR BLACKWOOD (*to a pretty young Girl in a white gown and pink ribbons.*) My dear, it's to be a foursome reel. May I have the pleasure of standing before you. Fiddlers, play "I'll gang nae mair to yon town,"— it's the King's favourite.

CHIEFTAIN (*to his Partner, after a kiss.*) Let me hand you to the dresser.

MEG. I'm a' in a drench o' sweat, see it's just pooran down. My sark's as wat's muck.

CHIEFTAIN. You had better step out to the door for a few minutes, and take the benefit of the fresh air.

MEG. Wi' a' my heart, sir.

Exeunt Chieftain and MEG.

ODOHERTY. Madam, you cannot go wrong, it is just the eight figure— so—8. Jig, or common time?

GUDEWIFE. Oh! Jig—jig.

A Foursome Reel by the Standard-bearer,
the Gudewife, Mr BLACKWOOD, *and Maiden.*

GUDEMAN. Mr North, you hae brocht a band o' rare swankies wi' you. I'm thinking you're no sae auld's you look like.

MR NORTH. I'm quite a young man, just the age of the King, God bless him. I hope we'll both live thirty years yet.

MR TICKLER, (*to Mr North.*) Look how busy Buller is yonder in the corner, at the end o' the kitchen dresser.

MR NORTH. Laird, the gudewife foots it away with admirable agility. I never saw a reel better danced in my life.

GUDEMAN. She's a gay canny body; see hoo the jade pits her twa neives to the sides o' her, and hauds up her chin wi' a prie-my-mou sort o' a cock.—Tibby, ye jade, the ee o' your auld gudeman's on you.— What ca' ye that lang land-louper that's wallopping afore her? said you, the Stawner-bearer? Is he a Flag-Staff-Lieutenant on half pay?

MR TICKLER. Fiddler, my boy, you with that infernal squint, I beg your pardon, with the slight cast of your eye, will you lend me your

fiddle for a few seconds?
Takes the fiddle, and plays with prodigious birr.

GUDEWIFE. Stap him—stap him, that's no the same tune. I canna keep the step. That's Maggy Lauder he's strumming at; they're playing different tunes.

Dance is stopped.

MR BLACKWOOD. I beg your pardon, Mr Tickler; but you have put us all out; I was just beginning to get into the way of it.

MR TICKLER. Come, I volunteer a solo. The Bush aboon Traquair.

Plays.

ODOHERTY. The Hen's March, by jingo.

ONE FIDDLER (*to another.*) He fingers bonny, bonny, but he has a cramp bow-hand. He's shouther-bun'. I like to see the bow gaun like a flail back and forward.

GUDEWIFE. Mr Odoherty, sit down aside me again, and let's hear something about the King.

ODOHERTY. Mrs Girnaway, you are quite a woman to please the King—fat, fair, and forty. And I assure you, that the King is quite a man to please any woman. The expression of the under part of his face is particularly pleasing; his mouth, madam, is not unlike your own, especially when you both smile.

GUDEWIFE. Do you hear that, gudeman? Mr Odocterme says, that I am like the King about the mouth, when I smile.

GUDEMAN. When you smile, gudewife? Whan's that? Your mouth, ony time I see't, is either wide open, wi' a' its buck-teeth in a guffaw, or as fast as a vice, in a dour fit of the sourocks.

MR NORTH. May I ask, sir, who is that maiden with the silken snood, whose conversation is now enjoyed by my young friend, Mr Buller of Brazen-nose?

GUDEMAN. That's our auldest dochter, Girzzy Girnaway; she'll be out o' her teens by Halloween; and she's as gude's she's bonny, sir,—she never gied her parents an ill word, nor a sair heart.

MR NORTH. The dancing is kept up with wonderful spirit, and you and I now have all the conversation to ourselves.—A country-dance, I declare! See, the gudewife, sir, is coming over to join us. We shall just have a three-handed crack.

GUDEWIFE. Ae reel's eneugh for me. My daft days are ower; but I couldna thole his fleeching—that ane you ca' the Adjutant. Look at yon lang deevil how he is gaun down the middle wi' Mysie below his oxter. Ca' ye him Tickler? Hech, sirs, but he's well named. He's kittlin her a' the way down.

MR NORTH. There is much happiness, Laird, now before us. My heart enjoys their homely hilarity. We must take human life as we find it.

GUDEMAN. What for did ye say that Mr Buller had a brazen nose? I think him a very douce, quate, blate callan, an' less o' the brass nose than ony single ane o' your forbears.

MR NORTH. He belongs to an English college called Brazen-nose.

GUDEMAN. Na, na, Mr North, that'll no gang down with Gibby Girnaway. An English college called Brazen-nose! Na, na.

GUDEWIFE. He's gane fain on our Girzzy. But he can mean nae ill. He wadna be a man, to come down frae England and say aught amiss to our bairn. Oh! Gibby, but he's a neat dancer, and has sma' sma' ankles, but gude strong calves. I thocht the English had been a' wee bit fat bodies. Aiblins his mither may hae been frae Scotland.

MR NORTH. Laird Girnaway, I fear the times are extremely bad.

GUDEMAN. They are so. But if the landlords will let down their rents, and indeed they must, and if the crops are as good next year as they are this, and if, and if, and if—then, Mr North, I say the times will not be bad. They will be better for poor people than I ever remember them. And let rich people take care of themselves.

MR NORTH. Can the landlords afford to do so? Will it not ruin them?

GUDEMAN. I cannot tell what they can afford, or who may be ruined. But what I say must happen; and the warld will not be warse off than before. They must draw less, and spend less. That's the hail affair.

GUDEWIFE. I'm a wee dull o hearing, and thae fiddles mak sic a din— and there is sic a hirdum dirdum on the floor, I canna hear either my gudeman or you, sir. But I'm awa' into the spence to mak some plotty, and baste the guse. [*Exit.*

MR NORTH. It does my heart good to see such a scene as this. I hope our dancers are all loyal subjects. Or do they care nothing about their King?

GUDEMAN. I daresay, sir, not ane o' them is thinking o' his Majesty at this minute.—But why should they? a time for a' things. But they've been maist o' them in to Embro', to hae a keek o' him. There's no a chiel on the floor that wadna fecht for the King till his heart's blood flooded the grass aneath his tottering feet.

MR NORTH. Have you any sons, Mr Girnaway?

GUDEMAN. Twa—that's ane o' them, the big chiel wi' the curly pow clapping his hauns, and the ither is a schoolmaster in Ayrshire—a douce laddie, that may ae day be a minister. Davie there is a yeoman, and a fearfu' fallow with the sword. And then he wad ride the Deevil himsel'.

MR NORTH. Have you yourself seen his Majesty, Mr Girnaway?

GUDEMAN. Not yet; but I will see him, God willing, when he takes his leave o' his ain Scotland, frae Hopetoun-house. The auld royal bluid o' Scotland, I ken, is in his veins; and there is something, sir, in the thocht o' far-back times that's grand and fearsome, and suits the head o' a crowned Monarch. The folk in this parish dinna respeck me the less, that I am ane o' the Girnaways, whose family has lived here for generations and generations; and it maun be just the same wi' a King, whose ancestors hae lang ruled the land. If we hae a feeling o' sic a thing, sae maun he; and Davie said, "O, father, but he was a proud man when he looked up to the Calton, and doun on auld Holyrood. I couldna help greeting."

MR NORTH. I trust, Mr Girnaway, that your enlightened sentiments are general.

GUDEMAN. Wha doubts't? Now and then, ye hear a dauner'd body telling ye that the King is just like ither men; and that Kings care naething for puir people; and that the twa Houses o' Parliament should haud him in wi' baith snaffle and curb; but that doctrine doesna gang doun just the now; and the very women-folk, who, in a general way, are rather sillyish, you ken, laugh at it, and praise the King up to the very ee-brees.

MR NORTH. Never beheld I so much mirth, happiness, and innocence. I have often thought, Mr Girnaway, of becoming a farmer in the evening of life.

GUDEMAN. There's mirth eneugh and happiness eneugh, and, as the world goes, innocence eneugh, too, on the floor, Mr North. But you maunna deceive yoursel' wi' fine words. Mirth isna for every day in the year; and we are often a' sulky and dour, and at times raging like tigers. Happiness is a kittle verb to conjugate, as our dominie says; and as to innocence, while lads and lasses are lads and lasses, there'll be baith sin and sorrow. But there's ae thing, sir, keepit sacred amang us, and that is religion, Mr North. We attend the kirk, and we read the Bible.

MR NORTH. I hope, Mr Girnaway, that when you come to Edinburgh, you will take pot-luck with me.

GUDEMAN. Dinna Mr me ony mair, sir; call me just Girnaway. I'll do't. Now, sir, may I ask, cannily, what trade ye may be when you are at hame?

MR NORTH. I am Editor of Blackwood's Magazine, of which you may have heard.

GUDEMAN. Gude safe us! are you a loupin', livin', flesh and bluid man, with real rudiments and a wooden crutch, just as gien out in that ance-a-month peerioddical? Whan will wonders cease? Gies your haun. Come awa' into the spence; the wife maun hae made the plotty by this time. Come into the spence.—Come awa—come awa. This is maist as gude's a visit frae the King himself.

Exeunt NORTH *and* GIRNAWAY *into the Spence.*

SCENE II.

The Spence.

GUDEWIFE (*sola.*) It's no every ane can set down a bit supper like Tibbie Girnaway. Had that guse been langer on the stubble, he might hae been a hantle fatter about the doup. But he'll do as he is, wi' the apple sauce.

Enter GIRNAWAY *and* NORTH.

GIRNAWAY. Gudewife, you ken that buik our son sends us every month, wi' the face of Geordie Buchanan on't.—Would ye believe that we hae under our roof-tree the very lads that write it. Here's the cock o' the company, Mr North himself.

GUDEWIFE. I jaloused something wonderfu', whene'er I saw the face of him, and that Adjutant ane. Siccan a buik I never read afore. It gars ane laugh, they canna tell how; and a' the time ye ken what ye're reading is serious, too—Naething ill in't, but a' gude—supporting the kintra, and the King, and the kirk.

GIRNAWAY. Mr North, I hae not much time to read, but I like fine to put my specs on to a sensible or droll buik, and your Magazine is baith. I'm a friend to general education.

MR NORTH. Girnaway, do you think that there are many profane or seditious books hawked about the country? It seems to be the opinion of the General Assembly.

GIRNAWAY. 'Deed, sir, I can only speak o' my ain experience. Doubtless, there are some, but no great feck; and I hae seen my ain weans and servants, after glowring at them a while on the dresser or the bunker, fling them frae them, like rowans, and neist time I see them it's on the midden. Hawkers come mair speed wi' ribbons, and shears, and knives, and bits o' funny ballads, than profanity and sedition. But the General Assembly should ken best.

GUDEWIFE. Now, ma man, Gibbie, the guse is getting cauld. I maun inveet the lave o' them in. The fiddles and the skirling is baith quate.

Exit the Gudewife, and enters with the STANDARD-BEARER, CHIEFTAIN, BULLER, SEWARD, TICKLER, *and* MR BLACKWOOD.

MR NORTH. Might I take the liberty of requesting the pleasure of your daughter's company, maäm. Mr Buller will go for his partner.

BULLER *darts off.*

GUDEWIFE. I like to see my bairns respecket, sir, and Grace can show her face ony where,—sae can her cousin Mysie.—(TICKLER *darts off.*) And her friend, Miss Susy, the only dochter o' the Antiburgher minister, wha was dancing wi' Mr Blackwood.—(MR BLACKWOOD *darts off.*) And Meg herself, though she hasna ta'en on muckle o' a polish, sin' she came from about Glasgow, is a decent hizzie.—(*Chieftain darts off.*) Yon bit white-faced lassie, wi' the jimp waist, and genteel carriage, is the butcher's only bairn, and a great heiress.—(SEWARD *darts off.*) Preserve us, are they a' coming to soop? Weel, weel, we maun sit close. Where's Mr Odocterme?

ADJUTANT. Here, maäm.

Gudeman says grace, and the Company fall to.

GUDEWIFE. I fear, Mr Adjutant, that you fin' that spawl o' the gusy rather teuch?

ODOHERTY. As tender as a chicken, I assure you, maäm. If it were as tough as timber, I care not. I never made a better supper in my life, than I did one night in Spain, on the tail of an old French artillery horse.—It was short, but sweet.

GUDEWIFE. Let me lay sum mair rumble-te-thumps on your plate, Colonel Odocterme. The tail o' a horse!—What some brave sodgers hae gone through in foreign parts, for our sakes at hame! I could greet to think on't.

MR NORTH. Mrs Girnaway, I propose to drink the health of your absent son, Mr Gilbert Girnaway, student of divinity, and teacher at Torbolton.

GUDEMAN. He couldna leave his scholars, or he would hae been to Embro' to see the King, like the lave. I'se drink the callan's health wi' richt good will.—"Here's our Gilbert."—Hoots, Tibbie, you silly thing, what for are you greeting?

ODOHERTY. "Oh! Beauty's tear is lovelier than her smile." But, gentlemen, Miss Grace Girnaway will give us a song.—Mr Buller, will you prevail upon Miss Girnaway for a song—something plaintive and pathetic, if you please.

MISS GRACE *sings.*

Oh! white is thy bosom, and blue is thine eye,
The light is a tear, and the sound is a sigh!
Thy love is like friendship, thy friendship like love,
And that is the reason I call thee—my Dove.

Oh! sweet to my soul is the balm of thy breath,
As a dew-laden gale from the rich-blossom'd heath;
Can it be that all beauty doth fade in an hour?
Then let that be the reason I call thee—my Flower.

On the wide sea of life shines one unclouded light,
And still it burns softest and clearest by night;
But its lustre, though lovely, alas! is afar,
And that is the reason I call thee—my Star.

But the dove seeks her nest in the forest so green,
And the flower in its fragrance is fading unseen;
The star in its brightness the sea-mist will hide,
So come to my heart, while I call thee—my Bride.

GUDEMAN. She's no a taucht singer, our Grace; but neither is a lint-white nor a laverock. Her father, Mr North, likes to hear her singing by the ingle—and he likes to hear her singing in the kirk.—Mr Buller, you English winna like the hamely lilt o' a Scottish farmer's dochter?

MR BULLER. Liveliness, modesty, cheerfulness, innocence, and beauty, Mr Girnaway, I hope can be felt by an English heart, loved and respected, wherever they smile before his eye, or melt upon his ear. "Your fair and good daughter's health and song—and may she long live to be a blessing and a pride to her parents."

GUDEWIFE. Ay, ay, a blessing, but no a pride. Pride's no for human creatures—but gratitude is; and we thank God, Gilbert and I, for naething mair than for gieing us weel-liked and dutiful bairns.

MR TICKLER. If ever I saw a singing face in my life, it is that of my sweet Mysie's. My dear, will you sing, now that your fair cousin has broken the ice?

GUDEWIFE. Will she sing? We'll gar her sing. We maun a' contribute.

MR BLACKWOOD (*starting.*) We maun a' contribute! Whose voice was that promising an article?

GUDEWIFE. I say, sir, we maun a' contribute. Mysie's gaun to gie you a sang. Aiblins it may get into print.—Come, Mysie, clear your pipes.

MISS MYSIE. Grace, let us sing THE SHEPHERDESS AND THE SAILOR. I shall be the Sailor this time.

SAILOR.
When lightning parts the thunder-cloud
That blackens all the sea,
And tempests sough through sail and shroud,
Even then I think on thee, Mary.

SHEPHERDESS.
I wrap me in that keep-sake plaid,
And lie doun 'mang the snaw;
While frozen are the tears I shed
For him that's far awa', Willy!

SAILOR.
We sail past mony a bonny isle,
Wi' maids the shores are thrang;

Before my ee there's but ae smile,
Within my ear ae sang, Mary.

SHEPHERDESS.
In kirk, on every Sabbath day,
For ane on the great deep
Unto my God I humbly pray—
And as I pray, I weep, Willy.

SAILOR.
The sands are bright wi' golden shells;
The groves wi' blossoms fair;
And I think upon the heather-bells
That deck thy glossy hair, Mary.

SHEPHERDESS.
I read thy letters sent from far,
And aft I kiss thy name,
And ask my maker, frae the war
If ever thou'lt come hame, Willy.

SAILOR.
What though your father's hut be lown
Aneath the green hill-side?
The ship that Willy sails in, blown
Like chaff by wind and tide, Mary?

SHEPHERDESS.
Oh! weel I ken the raging sea,
And a' the stedfast land,
Are held, wi' specks like thee and me,
In the hollow of his hand, Willy.

SAILOR.
He sees thee sitting on the brae,
Me hanging on the mast;
And o'er us baith, in dew or spray,
His saving shield is cast, Mary.

*Song interrupted by loud cries of murder heard from the Kitchen,
and a crash of chairs, and tumbling of tables. Omnes rush out.*

SCENE III.
The Kitchen.

SAUNDERS M'MURDO—*Smith.* I'll no tak a blow frae the haun o' ony leevin' man.—Kate Craigie, I say, ma woman, tak awa your grips. He may be the Miller, but I awe him nae thirlage; and mak room, and I'll gie him the floor, like a sack o' his ain meal.

PATE MUTER. He wud rug Kate aff my knee, so I gied him a clour on his harn-pan. I'm no for fechtin'. I haena fochten since Falkirk Tryst, when I brak the ribs o' that Hieland drover. Peace is best. But stand back, Burniwin', or you may as weel rin into the fanners or the mill-wheel at ance.

DAVIE GIRNAWAY. I'll hae nae fechtin' in my father's house.—Mysie, bring my sword.—Saunders M'Murdo, you're an unhappy man when you get a drap drink.—Lowsen his neckcloth, he's getting black i' the face.

MR NORTH. Saunders M'Murdo, Pate Muter,—I speak to you both as a peace-maker. Why this outrage in the family of the Girnaways? Has party instigated this unbecoming, this shameful brawl? Party! and the King in Scotland? Smith, Miller, you are both honourable men. Your professions are indispensable. Without you, what is this agricultural parish? Will you shake hands, and be friends? I see you will. Advance towards each other like men. There, there. Go where I will, I am a peace-maker.

Smith and Miller shake hands, and quiet is restored.

GUDEWIFE. Weel, weel; little dune's soonest mended. But I never saw a kirn yet without a fecht, sometimes half-a-dozen. After a storm comes a calm; ye may say that. There ye a' sit, every lad beside his lass, as douce as gin the Gudeman were gaun to tak the Book. It's a curious world.

GUDEMAN. Haud your tongue, Tibbie. Bring ben the plotty and a' the spirits into the kitchen; and a' bad bluid shall be at an end, when ilka ane, lad and lass, wife and widow, drinks a glass to the KING.

DAVIE GIRNAWAY. Here's the plotty; put out the tables.—Thank ye, Mr Odoherty.—Tak tent ye dinna lame yourself, Mr North. Hooly and fairly—hooly and fairly.

The tables are set out, and quaichs and coups laid.

GUDEMAN. Now, Mr North, we're a' looking to you. Ye maun gie us twa or three words to the King's health. I canna speechify, but I can roar. And I'se do that wi' a vengeance at the hip, hip.—Fill a' your quaichs till they're sooming ower.

MR NORTH. MR AND MRS GIRNAWAY, LADIES AND GENTLEMEN, We are now assembled round the table of a Scottish yeoman, to drink to the health of his Most Gracious Majesty King George the Fourth. He is within about twelve miles, as the crow flies, of where we now stand. Is it not almost the same thing as if he were actually here, in this very room, standing there beside the Laird himself, and with the light of that very fire shining upon his royal visage? I speak now to you, who have, most of you, seen the King. You saw him surrounded with hundreds of thousands of his shouting subjects, who had then but one great heart, whose looks were lightning, and whose voice was thunder. You had all heard, read, thought of your King. But he was to you but the image of a dream—a shadowy phantom on a far-off throne. Even then you were leal and loyal, as Scotsmen have ever been, who in peace prove their faith by the sweat of their brows, and in war by the blood of their hearts. Now, do not the elder among you feel like the brethren, and the younger like the children, of your King? He has breathed our free northern air—he has felt one of our easterly haars upon his brows—he has heard our dialect— He has trodden our soil—he has eaten our bread, and drunk our water— he has hailed, and been hailed, by countless multitudes, on the ramparts of our unconquered citadel—and he has prayed to the God of his, and our fathers, in our ancient and holy temple. Therefore, by our pride, by our glory, and by our faith, do we now love great George our King. What if he had not known the character of the people over whom he reigned? Their patience—their fortitude—their courage—their unquaking confidence in their own right arms—and their sacred trust in God? What if he had trembled on his throne, and imagined in that terror that its foundations were shaken by that great earthquake that shook to pieces the powers on the Continent? We had then been lost. England, Scotland, would, at this hour, have been peopled by slaves.—Our harvests would not have been reaped, as they now are, by the hands of free men—the stack-yard would not have belonged to him who built it—we should not have been assembled round this ingle—nor would there have been on the earth these faces, fair and bright with beauty, intelligence, and virtue. The British monarchy would have been destroyed—equal liberties and equal laws abrogated, effaced, and obliterated, for ever—our parish schools and our kirks levelled with the dust, religion scorned, and education proscribed—the light of knowledge and of love equally extinguished, and darkness on the hearth, and on the altar. It was he, George the Fourth, who, under God, saved us and our country from such evils, and who has preserved to us, unscathed by the fire through which they have passed, our liberties and our laws. He saw into our hearts, and knew of what stuff they were made. He saw that to us death was nothing —but that disgrace and degradation was more than we could—more than we *would* bear. Toil, taxes, tears, and blood, were demanded of us, not by the voice of our own King, but by the voice of all our Kings and heroes speaking through him—by the voices of our own Wallace and our own Bruce. We fought, and we conquered—and we are free. Therefore, now let each maiden smile upon her friend or lover—fill your cups to the brim—join hands—take a kiss, my lads, if you will—THE KING.

Hip, hip, hip—hurra, hurra, hurra—hip, hip, hip—hurra, hurra, hurra —Hip, hip, hip—hurra, hurra, hurra—hip, hip, hip—hurra, hurra, hurra!

THE SMITH. I was in the wrang, I was in the wrang—I acknowledge't. Gies your haun again, Miller. If ever need be, we'll fecht thegither, baith on ae side, for the King.

THE MILLER. There's flour of speech for you. Gif he were but in Parliament, he would lay his flail about him till the chaff flew into the een o' the Opposition frae the threshing-floor.—Will ye stan' for the borough, Mr North? I'll secure you the brewer's vote o'er bye yonder; or would you prefer the county? Ye'se hae either for the asking.

MR NORTH. My highest ambition, Mr Muter, is to retire into the rural shades, and become a farmer.

THE MILLER. Come out, then, near the Ferry. Tak a lease frae Lord Hopetoun. I'll grin' a' your meal, wheat, aits, and barley, for naething. A' the time you were speaking, I felt as if I could hae made a speech mysel. When you stopt, it was like the stopping of a band o' music on the street, when the sodgers are marching by. It was like the stopping o' the happer o' the mill.

GUDEWIFE. Mysie, Grizzy, Meg, or some o' you, open the wunnock-shutters. [*They do so.*

MR NORTH. A burst of day! The sun has been up for hours. What a bright and beautiful harvest morning! The sea is rolling in gold. See, there is the Orion beating up—close hauled. The best of friends must part.

The whole Party breaks up, and accompany NORTH, *&c.*
to the Beach.
END OF ACT III.

𝔑octes 𝔄mbrosianae.

No. XXXIV.

ΧΡΗ Δ'ΕΝ ΣΥΜΠΟΣΙΩ ΚΥΛΙΚΩΝ ΠΕΡΙΝΙΣΣΟΜΕΝΑΩΝ
ΗΔΕΑ ΚΩΤΙΛΛΟΝΤΑ ΚΑΘΗΜΕΝΟΝ ΟΙΝΟΠΟΤΑΖΕΙΝ.

Σ.

PHOC. *ap. Ath.*

[*This is a distich by wise old Phocylides,*
An ancient who wrote crabbed Greek in no silly days;
Meaning, "'Tis RIGHT FOR GOOD WINEBIBBING PEOPLE,
"NOT TO LET THE JUG PACE ROUND THE BOARD LIKE A CRIPPLE;
"BUT GAILY TO CHAT WHILE DISCUSSING THEIR TIPPLE."
An excellent rule of the hearty old cock 'tis—
And a very fit motto to put to our Noctes.]

C.N. *ap. Ambr.*

SCENE I.—*Two Bathing-machines in the Sea at Portobello.*
SHEPHERD *and* TICKLER.

SHEPHERD. Halloo, Mr Tickler, are you no ready yet, man? I've been a mother-naked man, in my machine here, for mair than ten minutes. Hae your pantaloons got entangled amang your heels, or are you saying your prayers afore you plunge?

TICKLER. Both. These patent long drawers, too, are a confounded nuisance—and this patent short under-shirt. There is no getting out of them, without greater agility than is generally possessed by a man at my time of life.

SHEPHERD. Confound a' pawtents. As for mysell I never wear drawers, but hae my breeks lined wi' flannen a' the year through; and as for thae wee short corded under-shirts that clasp you like ivy, I never hae had ane o' them on syn last July, when I was forced to cut it aff my back and breast wi' a pair o' sheep-shears, after having tried in vain to get out o't every morning for twa months. But are ye no ready, sir? A man on the scaffold wud na be allowed sae lang time for preparation. The minister or the hangman wud be jugging him to fling the handkershief.

TICKLER. Hanging, I hold, is a mere flea-bite—

SHEPHERD. What, tae doukin?—Here goes.

The SHEPHERD *plunges into the sea.*

TICKLER. What the devil has become of James? He is nowhere to be seen. That is but a gull—that only a seal—and that a mere pellock.

James, James, James!

SHEPHERD, (*emerging.*) Wha's that roaring? Stop awee till I get the sawt water out o' my een, and my mouth, and my nose, and wring my hair a bit. Noo, whare are you, Mr Tickler?

TICKLER. I think I shall put on my clothes again, James. The air is chill; and I see from your face that the water is as cold as ice.

SHEPHERD. Oh, man! but you're a desperate cooart. Think shame o' yoursell, staunin' naked there, at the mouth o' the machine, wi' the hail crew o' yon brig sailin' up the Frith, looking at ye, ane after anither, frae cyuck to captain, through the telescope.

TICKLER. James, on the sincerity of a shepherd, and the faith of a Christian, lay your hand on your heart, and tell me was not the shock tremendous? I thought you would never have reappeared.

SHEPHERD. The shock was naething, nae mair than what a body feels when waukenin' suddenly during a sermon, or fa'in' ower a stair-case in a dream.—But I'm aff to Inchkeith.

TICKLER. Whizz.—(*Flings a somerset into the sea.*)

SHEPHERD. Ane—twa—three—four—five—sax—seven—aught—but there's nae need o' coontin—for nae pearl-diver, in the Straits o' Madagascar or aff the coast o' Coromandel, can haud in his breath like Tickler. Weel that's surprisin'. Yon chaise has gaen about half a mile o' gate towards Portybelly syn he gaid fizzin' outower the lugs like a verra rocket. Safe us, what's this gruppin' me by the legs? A sherk—a sherk—a sherk!

TICKLER, (*yellowing to the surface.*) Blabla—blabla—bla—

SHEPHERD. He's keep't soomin' aneath the water till he's sick; but every man for himself, and God for us all—I'm aff.

SHEPHERD *stretches away to sea in the direction*
*of Inchkeith—*TICKLER *in pursuit.*

TICKLER. Every sinew, my dear James, like so much whip-cord. I swim like a salmon.

SHEPHERD. O, sir! that Lord Byron had but been alive the noo, what a sweepstakes!

TICKLER. A Liverpool gentleman has undertaken, James, to swim four-and-twenty miles at a stretch. What are the odds?

SHEPHERD. Three to one on Saturn and Neptune. He'll get numm.

TICKLER. James, I had no idea you were so rough on the back. You are a perfect otter.

SHEPHERD. Nae personality, Mr Tickler, out at sea. I'll compare carcasses wi' you ony day o' the year. Yet, you're a gran' soomer—out o' the water at every stroke, neck, breast, shouthers, and half way doon the back—after the fashion o' the great American serpent. As for me, my style o' soomin's less showy—laigh and lown—less hurry, but mair speed. Come, sir, I'll dive you for a jug o' toddy.

TICKLER *and* SHEPHERD *melt away like foam-bells in the sunshine.*

SHEPHERD. Mr Tickler!

TICKLER. James!

SHEPHERD. It's a drawn bate—sae we'll baith pay.—O sir! Is na' Embro a glorious city? Sae clear the air, yonner you see a man and a woman stannin' on the tap o' Arthur's Seat! I had nae notion there were sae mony steeples, and spires, and columns, and pillars, and obelisks, and doms, in Embro! And at this distance, the ee canna distinguish atween them that belangs to kirks, and them that belangs to naval monuments, and them that belangs to ile-gas companies, and them that's only chimley-heeds in the auld toun, and the taps o' groves, or single trees, sic as poplars; and aboon a' and ahint a', craigs and saft-broo'd hills sprinkled wi' sheep, lichts and shadows, and the blue vapoury glimmer o' a Midsummer day—het, het, het, wi' the barometer at ninety;—but here, to us twa, bob-bobbin amang the wee, fresh, cool, murmurin', and faemy wi' waves, temperate as the air within the mermaid's palace. Anither dive!

TICKLER. James, here goes the Fly-Wheel.

SHEPHERD. That beats a'! He gangs round in the water like a jack roastin' beef. I'm thinkin' he canna stop himsell. Safe us, he's fun' out the perpetual motion.

TICKLER. What fish, James, would you incline to be, if put into scales?

SHEPHERD. A dolphin—for they hae the speed o' lichtnin'. They'll dart past and roun' about a ship in full sail before the wind, just as if she was at anchor. Then the dolphin is a fish o' peace—he saved the life o' a poet of auld, Arion, wi' his harp—and oh! they say, the creatur's beautifu' in death—Byron, ye ken, comparin' his hues to those o' the sun settin' ahint the Grecian Isles. I sud like to be a dolphin.

TICKLER. I should choose to sport shark for a season. In speed he is a match for the dolphin—and then, James, think what luxury to swallow a well-fed chaplain, or a delicate midshipman, or a young negro girl occasionally——

SHEPHERD. And feenally to be grupped wi' a hyuck in a cocked hat and feather, at which the shark rises, as a trout does at a flee, hawled on board, and hacked to pieces wi' cutlasses and pikes by the jolly crew, or left alive on the deck, gutted as clean as a dice-box, and without an inch o' bowels.

TICKLER. Men die at shore, James, of natural deaths as bad as that——

SHEPHERD. Let me see—I sud hae nae great objections to be a whale in the Polar Seas. Gran' fun to fling a boatfu' o' harpooners into the air—or, wi' ae thud o' your tail, to drive in the stern-posts o' a Greenlandman.

TICKLER. Grander fun still, James, to feel the inextricable harpoon in your blubber, and to go snoving away beneath an ice-floe with four mile of line connecting you with your distant enemies.

SHEPHERD. But then whales marry but ae wife, and are passionately attached to their offspring. There, they and I are congenial speerits. Nae fish that swims enjoys so large a share of domestic happiness.

TICKLER. A whale, James, is not a fish.

SHEPHERD. Is na he? Let him alane for that. He's ca'd a fish in the Bible, and that's better authority than Buffon. Oh! that I were a whale!

TICKLER. What think you of a summer of the American Sea-Serpent?

SHEPHERD. What? To be constantly cruized upon by the hale American navy, military and mercantile! No to be able to show your back aboon water without being libelled by the Yankees in a' the newspapers, and pursued even by pleasure-parties, playin' the hurdy-gurdy and smokin' cigars! Besides, although I hae nae objection to a certain degree o' singularity, I sudna just like to be sae very singular as the American Sea-Serpent, who is the only ane of his specie noo extant; and whether he dees in his bed, or is slain by Jonathan, must incur the pain and the opprobrium o' defunckin' an auld bachelor.—What's the matter wi' you, Mr Tickler?—(*Dives.*)

TICKLER. The calf of my right leg is rather harder than is altogether pleasant. A pretty business if it prove the cramp; and the cramp it is, sure enough—hallo—James—James—James—hallo—I'm seized with the cramp—James—the sinews of the calf of my right leg are gathered up into a knot about the bulk and consistency of a sledge-hammer——

SHEPHERD. Nae tricks upon travellers. You've nae cramp. Gin you hae, streek out your richt hind leg, like a horse giein' a funk—and then ower on the back o' ye, and keep floatin' for a space, and your cauf'll be as saft's a cushion. Lord safe us, what's this? Deevil tak me if he's no droonin'. Mr Tickler, are you droonin'? There he's doon ance, and up again—twice, and up again;—but it's time to tak haud o' him by the hair o' the head, or he'll be doon amang the limpets!—(SHEPHERD *seizes* TICKLER *by the locks.*)

TICKLER. Oho—oho—oho—ho—ho—ho—hra—hra—hrach—hrach.

SHEPHERD. What language is that? Finnish? Noo, sir, dinna rug me doon to the bottom alang wi' you in the dead-thraws.

TICKLER. Heaven reward you,—James—the pain is gone—but keep near me.

SHEPHERD. Whammle yoursell ower on your back, sir. That 'ill do. Hoo are you now, sir? Yonner's the James Watt steam-boat, Captain Bain, within half a league. Lean on my airm, sir, till he comes alang-side, and it 'ill be a real happiness to the captain to save your life. But what 'ill a' the leddies do whan they're hoistin' us a-board? They maun just use their fans.

TICKLER. My dear Shepherd, I am again floating like a turtle,—but keep within hail, James. Are you to windward or leeward?

SHEPHERD. Right astarn. Did you ever see, sir, in a' your born days, sic a sky? Ane can scarcely say he sees't, for it's maist invisible in its blue beautifu' tenuity, as the waters o' a well! It's just like the ee o' ae lassie I kent lang ago—the langer you gazed intil't, the deep, deep, deeper it grew—the cawmer and the mair cawm—composed o' a smile, as an amythist is composed o' licht—and seeming something impalpable to the touch, till you ventured, wi' fear, joy, and tremmlin' to kiss it— just ae hesitatin', pantin', reverential kiss—and then to be sure your verra sowl kent it to be a bonny blue ee, covered wi' a lid o' dark fringes, and drappin' aiblins a bit frichten'd tear to the lip o' love.

TICKLER. What is your specific gravity, James? You float like a sedge.

SHEPHERD. Say rather a Nautilus, or a Mew. I'm native to the yelement.

TICKLER. Where learned you the natatory art, my dear Shepherd?

SHEPHERD. Do you mean soomin'? In St Mary's Loch. For a hail simmer I kept plouterin' alang the shore, and pittin' ae fit to the grun, knockin' the skin aff my knees, and makin' nae progress, till ae day, the gravel haein' been loosened by a flood, I plowpped in ower head and ears, and in my confusion, turnin' my face the wrang airt, I swom across the loch at the widest, at ae streatch, and ever after that cou'd hae soomed ony man in the Forest for a wager, excep Mr David Ballantyne, that noo leeves ower by yonner, near the Hermitage Castle.

TICKLER. Now, James, you are, to use the language of Spenser, the Shepherd of the Sea.

SHEPHERD. O that I had been a sailor! To hae circumnavigated the warld! To hae pitched our tents, or built our bowers, on the shores o' bays sae glitterin' wi' league-lang wreaths o' shells, that the billows blushed crimson as they murmured! To hae seen our flags burnin' meteor-like, high up amang the primæval woods, while birds bright as ony buntin' sat trimmin' their plummage amang the cordage, sae tame in that island where ship had haply never touched afore, nor ever might touch again, lying in a latitude by itsell, and far out o' the breath o' the treddwunds! Or to hae landed wi' a' the crew, marines and a', excep a guard on ship-board to keep aff the crowd o' canoes, on some warlike isle, tossin' wi' the plumes on chieftains' heads, and soun'-soun'-soundin' wi' gongs! What's a man-o'-war's barge, Mr Tickler, beautifu' sicht though it be, to the hundred-oared canoe o' some savage Island-king! The King himsell lyin' in state—no dead, but leevin', every inch o' him—on a platform—aboon a' his warriors standin' wi' war-clubs, and stane-hatchets, and fish-bane spears, and twisted mats, and tattooed faces, and ornaments in their noses, and painted een, and feathers on their heads a yard heigh, a' silent, or burstin' out o' a sudden intil shootin' sangs o' welcome or defiance, in a language made up o' a few lang strang words—maistly gutturals—and gran' for the naked priests to yell intil the ears o' their victims, when about to cut their throats on the altar-stane that Idolatry had incrusted with blood, shed by stormy moonlicht to glut the maw of their sanguinary God. Or say rather—O rather say, that the white-winged Wonder that has brought the strangers frae afar, frae lands beyond the setting sun, has been hailed with hymns and dances o' peace—and that a' the daughters of the Isle, wi' the daughter o' the King at their head, come a' gracefully windin' alang in a figur, that, wi' a thousan' changes, is aye but ae single dance, wi' unsandalled feet true to their ain wild singin', wi' wings fancifully fastened to their shouthers, and, beautifu' creaturs! a' naked to the waist —But whare the deevil's Mr Tickler? Has he sunk during my soliloquy? or swum to shore? Mr Tickler—Mr Tickler—I wush I had a pistol to fire into the air, that he might be brought to. Yonner he is, playin' at porpuss. Let me try if I can reach him in twenty strokes—it's no abune a hunder yards. Five yards a-stroke—no bad soomin' in dead water.——There, I've done it in nineteen. Let me on my back for a rest.

TICKLER. I am not sure that this confounded cramp——

SHEPHERD. The cramp's just like the hiccup, sir—never think o't, and it's gane. I've seen a white lace-veil, sic as Queen Mary's drawn in, lyin' afloat, without stirrin' aboon her snawy broo, saftenin' the ee-licht—and it's yon braided clouds that remind me o't, motionless, as if they had lain there a' their lives; yet, wae's me! perhaps in ae single hour to melt away for ever!

TICKLER. James, were a Mermaid to see and hear you moralizing so, afloat on your back, her heart were lost.

SHEPHERD. I'm nae favourite noo, I suspec, amang the Mermaids.

TICKLER. Why not, James? You look more irresistible than you imagine. Never saw I your face and figure to more advantage—when lying on the braes o' Yarrow, with your eyes closed in the sunshine, and the shadows of poetical dreams chasing each other along cheek and brow. You would make a beautiful corpse, James.

SHEPHERD. Think shame o' yoursell, Mr Tickler, fur daurin' to use that word, and the sinnies o' the cawf o' your richt leg yet knotted wi' the cramp. Think shame o' yoursell! That word's no canny.

TICKLER. But what ail the Mermaids with the Shepherd?

SHEPHERD. I was ance lyin' half asleep in a sea-shore cave o' the Isle o' Sky, wearied out by the verra beauty o' the moonlicht that had keepit lyin' for hours in ae lang line o' harmless fire, stretching leagues and leagues to the rim o' the ocean. Nae sound, but a bit faint, dim plash— plash—plash o' the tide—whether ebbin' or flawin' I ken not—no against, but upon the weedy sides o' the cave——

TICKLER.
> As when some shepherd of the Hebride Isles,
> Placed far amid the melancholy main!

SHEPHERD. That soun's like Thamson—in his Castle o' Indolence. A' the hail warld was forgotten—and my ain name—and what I was—and where I had come frae—and why I was lyin' there—nor was I onything but a Leevin' Dream.

TICKLER. Are you to windward or leeward, James?

SHEPHERD. Something—like a caulder breath o' moonlicht—fell on my face and breast, and seemed to touch all my body and my limbs. But it canna be mere moonlicht, thocht I, for, at the same time, there was the whisperin'—or say rather, the waverin' o' the voice—no alang the green cave wa's, but close intil my ear, and then within my verra breast,—sae, at first, for the soun' was saft and sweet, and wi' a touch o' plaintive wildness in't no unlike the strain o' an Eolian harp, I was rather surprised than feared, and maist thocht that it was but the wark o' my ain fancy, afore she yielded to the dwawm o' that solitary sleep.

TICKLER. James, I hear the Steamer.

SHEPHERD. I opened my een, that had only been half steekit—and may we never reach the shore again, if there was not I, sir, in the embrace o' a Mermaid!

TICKLER. James—remember we are well out to Inchkeith. If you please, no——

SHEPHERD. I would scorn to be droon'd with a lee in my mouth, sir. It is quite true that the hair o' the cretur is green—and it's as slimy as it's green—slimy and sliddery as the sea-weed that cheats your unsteady footing on the rocks. Then what een!—oh, what een!—Like the boiled een o' a cod's head and shouthers!—and yet expression in them—an expression o' love and fondness, that would hae garred an Eskimaw scunner.

TICKLER. James, you are surely romancing.

SHEPHERD. Oh, dear, dear me!—hech, sirs! hech sirs!—the fishiness o' that kiss!—I had hung up my claes to dry on a peak o' the cliff—for it was ane o' thae lang midsummer nichts, when the sea-air itself fans ye wi' as warm a sugh as that frae a leddy's fan, when you're sittin' side by side wi' her in an arbour——

TICKLER. Oh, James—you fox——

SHEPHERD. Sae that I was as naked as either you or me, Mr Tickler, at this blessed moment—and whan I felt mysell enveloped in the hauns, paws, fins, scales, tail, and maw o' the Mermaid o' a monster, I grued till the verra roof o' the cave let down drap, drap, drap upon us—me and the Mermaid—and I gied mysell up for lost.

TICKLER. Worse than Venus and Adonis, my dear Shepherd.

SHEPHERD. I began mutterin' the Lord's Prayer, and the Creed, and the hundred and nineteenth Psalm—but a' wudna do. The Mermaid held the grup—and while I was splutterin' out her kisses, and convulsed waur than I ever was under the waarst nicht-mare that ever sat on my stamach, wi' ae desperate wallop we baith gaed tapsalteerie—frae ae sliddery ledge to anither—till, wi' accelerated velocity, like twa stanes, increasin' accordin' to the squares o' the distances, we played plunge like porpusses into the sea, a thousand fadom deep—and hoo I gat rid o' the briny Beastliness nae man kens till this day; for there was I sittin' in the cave, chitterin' like a drookit cock, and nae Mermaid to be seen or heard; although, wad ye believe me, the cave had the smell o' crabs, and labsters, and oysters, and skate, and fish in general, eneuch to turn the stamach o' a whale or a sea-lion.

TICKLER. Ship, ahoy!—Let us change our position, James. Shall we board the Steamer?

SHEPHERD. Only look at the waves, hoo they gang welterin' frae her prow and sides, and widen in her wake for miles aff! Gin we venture ony nearer, we'll never wear breeks mair. Mercy on us, she's bearin' doon upon us. Let us soom fast, and passing across her bows, we shall bear up to windward out o' a' the commotion.—Captain Bain! Captain Bain! it's me and Mr Tickler, takin' a soom for an appeteet—stop the ingine till we get past the bowsprit.

TICKLER. Heavens, James! what a bevy of ladies on deck. Let us dive.

SHEPHERD. You may dive—for you swim improperly high; but as for me, I seem in the water to be a mere Head, like a cherub on a church. A boat, captain—a boat!

TICKLER. James, you aren't mad, sure? Who ever boarded a steamer in our plight? There will be fainting from stem to stern, in cabin and steerage.

SHEPHERD. I ken that leddy in the straw-bannet and green vail, and ruby sarsnet, wi' the glass at her ee. Ye ho—Miss——

TICKLER. James—remember how exceedingly delicate a thing is a young lady's reputation. See, she turns away in confusion.

SHEPHERD. Captain, I say, what news frae London?

CAPTAIN BAIN, (*through a speaking trumpet.*) Lord Wellington's amendment on the bonding clause in the corn bill again carried against Ministers by 133 to 122. Sixty-six shillings!

TICKLER. What says your friend M'Culloch to that, Captain?

SHEPHERD. Wha cares a bodle about corn bills in our situation? What's the Captain routin' about noo out o' his speakin' trumpet? But he may just as well haud his tongue, for I never understand ae word out o' the mouth o' a trumpet.

D

TICKLER. He says, the general opinion in London is, that the Administration will stand—that Canning and Brougham——

SHEPHERD. Canning and Brougham, indeed! Do you think, sir, if Canning and Brougham had been soomin' in the sea, and that Canning had ta'en the cramp in the cawf o' his richt leg, as you either did, or said you did, a short while sin syne, that Brougham wad hae safed him as I safed you? Faith, no he indeed! Hairy wad hae thocht naething o' watchin' till George showed the croon o' his head aboon water, and then hittin' him on the temples.

TICKLER. No, no, James. They would mutually risk lives for each other's sake. But no politics at present, we're getting into the swell, and will have our work to do to beat back into smooth water. James, that was a facer.

SHEPHERD. Dog on it, ane wad need to be a sea-mew, or kittywake, or stormy pettrel, or some ither ane o' Bewick's birds—

TICKLER. Keep your mouth shut, James, till we're out of the swell.

SHEPHERD. Em—hem—umph—humph—whoo—whoo—whurr—whurr—herrachvacherach.

TICKLER. Whsy—whsy—whsy—whugh—whugh—shugh—shugh—prugh—ptsugh—prgugh.

SHEPHERD. It's lang sin' I've drank sae muckle sawt water at ae sittin' —at ae soomin', I mean—as I hae dune, sir, sin' that Steam-boat gaed by. She does indeed kick up a deevil o' a rumpus.

TICKLER. Whoo—whoo—whoof—whroo—whroo—whroof—proof—ptroof—sprtf!

SHEPHERD. Ae thing I maun tell you, sir, and that's, gin you tak the cramp the noo, you maunna expect ony assistance frae me—no gin you were my ain faither. This bates a' the swalls! Confoun' the James Watt, quoth I.

TICKLER. Nay, nay, James. She is worthy of her name—and a better seaman than Captain Bain never boxed the compass. He never comes below, except at meal-times, and a pleasanter person cannot be at the foot of the table. All night long he is on deck, looking out for squalls.

SHEPHERD. I declare to you, sir, that just noo, in the trough o' the sea, I did na see the top o' the Steamer's chimley. See, Mr Tickler—see, Mr Tickler—only look here—only look here—HERE'S BRONTE! MR NORTH'S GREAT NEWFUNLAN' BRONTE!

TICKLER. Capital—capital. He has been paying his father a visit at the gallant Admiral's, and come across our steps on the sands.

SHEPHERD. Puir fallow—gran' fallow—did ye think we was droonin'?

BRONTE. Bow—bow—bow—bow, wow, wow—bow, wow, wow.

TICKLER. His oratory is like that of Bristol Hunt versus Sir Thomas Lethbridge.

SHEPHERD. Sir, you're tired, sir. You had better tak haud o' his tail.

TICKLER. No bad idea, James. But let me just put one arm round his neck. There we go. Bronte, my boy, you swim strong as a rhinoceros!

BRONTE. Bow, wow, wow—bow, wow, wow.

SHEPHERD. He can do onything but speak.

TICKLER. Why, I think, James, he speaks uncommonly well. Few of our Scotch members speak better. He might lead the Opposition.

SHEPHERD. What for will ye aye be introducin' politics, sir? But really, I hae fund his tail very useful in that swall; and let's leave him to himsell noo, for twa men on ae dowg's a sair doondracht.

TICKLER. With what a bold kind eye the noble animal keeps swimming between us, like a Christian!

SHEPHERD. I hae never been able to perswade my heart and my understandin' that dowgs haena immortal sowls. See how he steers himsell, first a wee towarts me, and then a wee towarts you, wi' his tail like a rudder. His sowl *maun* be immortal.

TICKLER. I am sure, James, that if it be, I shall be extremely happy to meet Bronte in any future society.

SHEPHERD. The minister wad ca' that no orthodox. But the mystery o' life canna gang out like the pluff o' a cawnle. Perhaps the verra bit bonny glitterin' insecks that we ca' ephemeral, because they dance out but ae single day, never dee, but keep for ever and aye openin' and shuttin' their wings in mony million atmospheres, and may do sae through a' eternity. The universe is aiblins wide eneuch.

TICKLER. Eyes right! James, a boatful of ladies—with umbrellas and parasols extended to catch the breeze. Let us lie on our oars, and they will never observe us.

BRONTE. Bow—wow—wow—bow—wow—wow.

Female alarms heard from the pleasure-boat. A gentleman in
the stern rises with an oar and stands in a threatening attitude.

TICKLER. Ease off to the east, James—Bronte, hush!

SHEPHERD. I houp they've nae fooling-pieces—for they may tak us for gulls, and pepper us wi' swan-shot or slugs. I'll dive at the flash. Yon's no a gun that chiel has in his haun?

TICKLER. He lets fall his oars into the water, and the "boatie rows— the boatie rows"—Hark, a song!

Song from the retiring boat.

SHEPHERD. A very good sang, and very well sung—jolly companions every one.

TICKLER. The fair authors of the Odd Volume!

SHEPHERD. What's their names?

TICKLER. They choose to be anonymous, James; and that being the case, no gentleman is entitled to withdraw the veil.

SHEPHERD. They're sweet singers, howsomever, and the words o' their sang are capital. Baith Odd Volumes are maist ingenious, well written, and amusing.

TICKLER. The public thinks so—and they sell like wild-fire.

SHEPHERD. I'm beginning to get maist desperat thrusty, and hungry baith. What a denner wull we make! How mony miles do ye think we hae swom?

TICKLER. Three—in or over. Let me sound,—why, James, my toe scrapes the sand. "By the Nail six!"

SHEPHERD. I'm glad o't. It'll be a bonny bizziness, gif ony neer-do-weels hae ran aff wi' our claes out o' the machines. But gif they hae, Bronte 'll sune grup them—Wull na ye, Bronte?

BRONTE. Bow—wow—wow—bow—wow—wow.

SHEPHERD. Now, Tickler, that our feet touch the grun, I'll rin you a race to the machines, for anither jug.

TICKLER. Done—But let us have a fair start.—Once, twice, thrice!

TICKLER *and* SHEPHERD *start, with* BRONTE *in the van, amid loud acclamations from the shore.—Scene closes.*

𝕹octes 𝕬mbrosianae.

No. XLVIII.

ΧΡΗ Δ᾽ΕΝ ΣΥΜΠΟΣΙΩ ΚΥΛΙΚΩΝ ΠΕΡΙΝΙΣΣΟΜΕΝΑΩΝ
ΗΔΕΑ ΚΩΤΙΛΛΟΝΤΑ ΚΑΘΗΜΕΝΟΝ ΟΙΝΟΠΟΤΑΖΕΙΝ.

Σ.

PHOC. *ap. Ath.*

[*This is a distich by wise old Phocylides,*
An ancient who wrote crabbed Greek in no silly days;
Meaning, "'TIS RIGHT FOR GOOD WINEBIBBING PEOPLE,
NOT TO LET THE JUG PACE ROUND THE BOARD LIKE A CRIPPLE;
BUT GAILY TO CHAT WHILE DISCUSSING THEIR TIPPLE."
An excellent rule of the hearty old cock 'tis—
And a very fit motto to put to our Noctes.]

C.N. *ap. Ambr.*

SCENE—*The Saloon, illuminated by the grand Gas Orrery.*
TIME—*First of April—Six o' clock.* PRESENT—NORTH, *the*
ENGLISH OPIUM-EATER, *the* SHEPHERD, TICKLER, *in Court Dresses.—*
The three celebrated young Scottish LEANDERS, *with their horns,*
in the hanging gallery. AIR, *"Brose and Brochan and a'."*

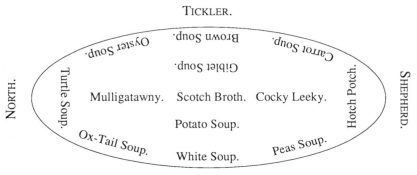

SHEPHERD. An' that's an Orrery! The infinitude o' the starry heavens reduced sae as to suit the ceilin' o' the Saloon!—Whare's Virgo?

TICKLER. Yonder she is, James—smiling in the shade of——

SHEPHERD. I see her—just aboon the cocky-leeky. Weel, sic anither contrivance! Some o' the stars and planets—moons and suns lichter than ithers, I jalouse, by lettin' in upon them a greater power o' coal-gas; and ithers again, just by moderatin' the pipe-conductors, faint and far awa' in the system, sae that ye scarcely ken whether they are lichted wi' the gawzeous vapour ava', or only a sort o' fine, tender, delicate porcelain, radiant in its ain transparent nature, and though thin, yet stronger than the storms.

NORTH. The first astronomers were shepherds——

SHEPHERD. Aye, Chaldean shepherds like mysell—but no a mother's son o' them could hae written the Manuscripp. Ha, ha, ha!

TICKLER. What a misty evening!

SHEPHERD. Nae wonder—wi' thirteen soups a' steamin' up to the skies! O! but the Orrery is sublime the noo, in its shroud! Naethin like hotch-potch for gien a dim grandeur to the stars. See, yonder Venus— peerless planet—shining like the face o' a virgin bride through her white nuptial veil! He's a grim chiel yon Saturn. Nae wonder he devourit his weans—he has the coontenance o' a cannibal. Thank you, Mr Awmrose, for opening the door—for this current o' air has swept awa the mists from heaven, and gien us back the beauty o' the celestial spheres.

NORTH (*aside to the* ENGLISH OPIUM-EATER.) You hear, Mr De Quincey, how he begins to blaze even before broth.

ENGLISH OPIUM-EATER (*aside to* NORTH.) I have always placed Mr Hogg, *in genius*, far above Burns. He is indeed "of imagination all compact." Burns had strong sense—and strong sinews—and brandished a pen pretty much after the same fashion as he brandished a flail. You never lose sight of the thresher——

SHEPHERD. Dinna abuse Burns, Mr De Quinshy. Neither you nor ony ither Englishman can thoroughly understaun three sentences o' his poems——

ENGLISH OPIUM-EATER (*with much animation.*) I have for some years past longed for an opportunity to tear into pieces that gross national delusion, born of prejudice, ignorance, and bigotry, in which, from highest to lowest, all literary classes of Scotchmen are, as it were incar- nated—to wit, a belief strong as superstition, that all their various dialects must be as unintelligible, as I grant that most of them are uncouth and barbarous, to English ears—even to those of the most accomplished and consummate scholars. Whereas, to a Danish, Norwegian, Swedish, Saxon, German, French, Italian, Spanish—and let me add, Latin and Greek scholar, there is not even a monosyllable that——

SHEPHERD. What's *a gowpen o' glaur?*

ENGLISH OPIUM-EATER. Mr Hogg—Sir, I will not be interrupted——

SHEPHERD. You cannot tell. It's just *tua neif-fu's o' clarts.*

NORTH. James—James—James!

SHEPHERD. Kit—Kit—Kit. But beg your pardon, Mr De Quinshy—afore dinner I'm aye unco snappish. I admit you're a great grammarian. But kennin' something o' a language by bringin' to bear upon't a' the united efforts o' knowledge and understaunin'—baith first-rate—is ae thing, and feelin' every breath and every shadow that keeps playin' owre a' its syllables, as if by a natural and born instinct, is anither—the first you may aiblins hae—naebody likelier—but to the second, nae man may pretend that hasna had the happiness and the honour o' havin' been born and bred in bonny Scotland. What can ye ken o' Kilmeny?

ENGLISH OPIUM-EATER (*smiling graciously.*) 'Tis a ballad breathing the sweetest, simplest, wildest spirit of Scottish traditionary song—music, as of some antique instrument long-lost, but found at last in the Forest among the decayed roots of trees, and touched, indeed, as by an instinct, by the only man who could reawaken its sleeping chords—the Ettrick Shepherd.

SHEPHERD. Na—if you say that sincerely—and I never saw a broo smoother wi' truth than your ain—I maun qualify my former apophthegm, and alloo you to be an exception frae the general rule. I wish, sir, you wou'd write a Glossary o' the Scottish Language. I ken naebody fitter.

NORTH. Our distinguished guest is aware that this is "All Fool's Day,"—and must, on that score, pardon these court-dresses. We consider them, my dear sir, appropriate to this Anniversary.

SHEPHERD. Mine wasna originally a coort-dress. It's the uniform o' the Border Club. But nane o' the ither members wou'd wear them, accept me and the late Dyuk o' Buccleuch. So when the King came to Scotland, and expeckit to be introduced to me at Holyrood-House, I got the tiler at Yarrow-Ford to cut it doon after a patron frae Embro'——

ENGLISH OPIUM-EATER. Green and gold—to my eyes the most beautiful of colours—the one characteristic of earth, the other of heaven—and, therefore, the two united, emblematic of genius.

SHEPHERD. Oh! Mr De Quinshy—sir, but you're a pleasant cretur—and were I ask't to gie a notion o' your mainners to them that had never seen you, I shou'd just use twa words, Urbanity and Amenity—meanin', by the first, that saft bricht polish that a man gets by leevin' amang gentlemen scholars in towns and cities, burnished on the solid metal o' a happy natur' hardened by the rural atmosphere o' the pure kintra air, in which I ken you hae ever delighted; and, by the ither, a peculiar sweetness, amaist like that o' a woman's, yet sae far frae bein' feminine, as masculine as that o' Allan Ramsay's ain Gentle Shepherd—and breathin' o' a harmonious union between the heart, the intelleck, and the imagination, a' the three keepin' their ain places, and thus makin' the vice, speech, gesture, and motion o' a man as composed as a figur' on a pictur' by some painter that was a master in his art, and produced his effects easily—and ane kens na hoo—by his lichts and shadows. Mr North, am na I richt in the thocht, if no in the expression?

NORTH. You have always known my sentiments, James——

SHEPHERD. I'm thinkin' we had better lay aside our swurds. They're kittle dealin', when a body's stannin' or walkin'; but the very deevil's in them, when ane claps his doup on a chair; for here's the hilt o' mine interferin' wi' my ladle-hand.

TICKLER. Why, James, you have buckled it on the wrong side.

SHEPHERD. What? Is the richt the wrang?

NORTH. Let us all untackle. Mr Ambrose, hang up each man's sword on his own hat-peg.—There.

SHEPHERD. O, Mr De Quinshy! but you luk weel in a single-breested snuff-olive, wi' cut-steel buttons, figured waistcoat, and——

ENGLISH OPIUM-EATER. There is a beautiful propriety, Mr Hogg, in a court-dress, distinguished as it is, both by material and form, from the apparel suitable to the highest occasions immediately below the presence of royalty, just as *that other* apparel is distinguished from the costume worn on the less ceremonious——

SHEPHERD. Eh?

ENGLISH OPIUM-EATER. Occasions of civilized life,—and *that* again in due degree from *that* sanctioned by custom, in what I may call, to use the language of Shakspeare, and others of our elder dramatists, the "workyday" world,—whether it be in those professions peculiar, or nearly so, to towns and cities, or belonging more appropriately,—though the distinction, perhaps, is popular rather than philosophical—to rural districts on either side of your beautiful river the Tweed.

SHEPHERD. Oh, sir! but I'm unco fond o' the English accent. It's like an instrument wi' a' the strings o' silver,—and though I canna help thinkin' that you speak rather a wee owre slow, yet there's sic music in your vice, that I'm just perfectly enchanted wi' the soun', while a sense o' truth prevents me frae sayin' that I aye a'thegether comprehend the meaning,—for that's aye, written or oral alike, sae desperate metapheesical.—But what soup will you tak, sir? Let me recommend the hotchpotch.

ENGLISH OPIUM-EATER. I prefer vermicelli.

SHEPHERD. What? Worms! They gar me scunner,—the verra luk o' them. Sae, you're a worm-eater, sir, as weel's an Opium-eater?

ENGLISH OPIUM-EATER. Mr Wordsworth, sir, I think it is, who says, speaking of the human being under the thraldom of the senses,—

"He is a slave, the meanest we can meet."

SHEPHERD. I beseech ye, my dear sir, no to be angry sae sune on in the afternoon. There's your worms—and I wuss you muckle gude o' them—only compare them—Thank you, Mr Tickler—wi' this bowl-deep trencher o' hotch-potch—an emblem of the haill vegetable and animal creation.

TICKLER. Why, James, though now invisible to the naked eye, boiled down as they are in baser matter, that tureen on which your face has for some minutes been fixed as gloatingly as that of a Satyr on a sleeping Wood-nymph, or of Pan himself on Matron Cybele, contains, as every naturalist knows, some scores of snails, a gowpen-full of gnats, countless caterpillars, of our smaller British insects numbers without number numberless as the sea-shore sands—

SHEPHERD. No at this time o' the year, you gowk. You're thinking o' simmer colleyfloor——

TICKLER. But their larvæ, James——

SHEPHERD. Confound their larvæ! Awmrose! the pepper. (*Dashes in the pepper along with the silver-top of the cruet.*) Pity me! whare's the cruet? It has sunk doon intill the hotch-potch, like a mailed horse and his rider intill a swamp. I maun tak tent no to swallow the bog-trotter. What the deevil, Awmrose, you've gien me the Cayawne!!

MR AMBROSE (*tremens.*) My dear sir, it was Tappytourie.

SHEPHERD (*to* TAPPY.) You wee sinner, did ye tak me for Moshy Shawbert?

ENGLISH OPIUM-EATER. I have not seen it recorded, Mr Hogg, in any of the Public Journals, at least it was not so in the Standard,—in fact the only newspaper I now read, and an admirable evening paper it is, unceasingly conducted with consummate ability,—that that French charlatan had hitherto essayed Cayenne-pepper; and indeed such an exhibition would be preposterous, seeing that the lesser is contained within the greater, and consequently all the hot varieties of that plant—all the possibilities of the pepper-pod—are included within Phosphorus and Prussic acid. Meanly as I think of the logic——

SHEPHERD. O ma mouth! ma mouth!—Logic indeed! I didna think there had been sic a power o' pepper about a' the premises.

ENGLISH OPIUM-EATER. The only conclusion that can be legitimately drawn——

SHEPHERD. Whisht wi' your College clavers—and, Awmrose, gie me a caulker o' Glenlivet to cool the roof o' my pallet. My tongue's like red-het airn—and blisters my verra lips. Na! it'll melt the siller-spoon——

NORTH. I pledge you, my dear James——

ENGLISH OPIUM-EATER. Vermicelli soup, originally Italian, has been so long naturalized in this island, that it may now almost be said, by those not ambitious of extremest accuracy of thought and expression, to be indigenous in Britain—and as it sips somewhat insipid, may I use the freedom, Mr Tickler,—scarcely pardonable, perhaps, from our short acquaintance,—to request you to join me in a glass of the same truly Scottish liquor?

TICKLER. Most happy indeed to cultivate the friendship of Mr De Quincey.

The Four turn up their little fingers.

SHEPHERD. Mirawcolous! My tongue's a' at aince as cauld 's the rim o' a cart-wheel on a winter's nicht! My pallet cool as the lift o' a spring-mornin! And the inside o' ma mouth just like a wee mountain-well afore sun-rise, when the bit moorland birdies are hoppin' on its margin, about to wat their whustles in the blessed beverage, after their love-dreams amang the dewy heather!

ENGLISH OPIUM-EATER. I would earnestly recommend it to you, Mr Hogg, to abstain——

SHEPHERD. Thank you, sir, for your timeous warnin'—for, without thinkin' what I was about, I was just on the verra eve o' fa'in' to again till the self-same fiery trencher. It's no every body that has your philosophical composure. But it sits weel on you, sir—and I like baith to look and listen to you; for, in spite o' your classical learning, and a' your outlandish logic, you're at a' times—and I'm nae bad judge—shepherd as I am—*intus et in cute*—that is tooth and nail—naething else but a perfeck gentleman. But oh! you're a lazy cretur, man, or you would hae putten out a dizzen vollumms syne the Confessions.

ENGLISH OPIUM-EATER. I am at present, my dear friend,—allow me to call myself so,—in treaty with Mr Blackwood for a novel——

SHEPHERD. In ae vollumm—in ae vollumm, I hope—and that'll tie you doon to whare your strength lies, condensation at aince vigorous and exquisite—like a man succinct for hap-step-and-loup on the green-sward—each spang langer than anither—till he clears a peat hand-barrow at the end like a catastrophe.—Hae I eaten anither dish o' hotch-potch, think ye, sirs, without bein' aware o't?

TICKLER. No, James—North changed the fare upon you, and you have devoured, in a fit of absence, about half-a-bushel of peas.

SHEPHERD. I'm glad it was na carrots—for they aye gie me a sair belly.—But hae ye been at the Exhibition o' Pictures by leevin' artists at the Scottish Academy, Mr North, and what think ye o't?

NORTH. I look in occasionally, James, of a morning, before the bustle begins, for a crowd is not for a crutch.

SHEPHERD. But ma faith, a crutch is for a crood, as is weel kent o' yours, by a' the blockheads in Britain.—Is't gude the year?

NORTH. Good, bad, and indifferent, like all other mortal exhibitions. In landscape, we sorely miss Mr Thomson of Duddingstone.

SHEPHERD. What can be the matter wi' the minister?—He's no deed?

NORTH. God forbid! But Williams is gone—dear delightful Williams—with his aerial distances into which the imagination sailed as on wings, like a dove gliding through sunshine into gentle gloom—with his shady foregrounds, where Love and Leisure reposed—and his middle regions, with towering cities grove-embowered, solemn with the spirit of the olden time—and all, all embalmed in the beauty of those deep Grecian skies!

SHEPHERD. He's deed. What matters it? In his virtues he was happy, and in his genius he is immortal. Hoots, man! If tears are to drap for ilka freen "who is not," our een wud be seldom dry.—Tak some mair turtle.

NORTH. Mr Thomson of Duddingstone is now our greatest landscape painter. In what sullen skies he sometimes shrouds the solitary moors!

SHEPHERD. And wi' what blinks o' beauty he aften brings out frae beneath the clouds the spire o' some pastoral parish kirk, till you feel it is the Sabbath!

NORTH. Time and decay crumbling his castles seem to be warring against the very living rock—and we feel their endurance in their desolation.

SHEPHERD. I never look at his roarin' rivers, wi' a' their precipices, without thinkin' some hoo or ither, o' Sir William Wallace! They seem to belang to an unconquerable country.

NORTH. Yes, James! he is a patriotic painter. Moor, mountain and glen—castle, hall and hut—all breathe sternly or sweetly o' auld Scotland. So do his seas and his friths—roll, roar, blacken and whiten with Caledonia—from the Mull of Galloway to Cape Wrath. Or when summer stillness is upon them, are not all the soft shadowy pastoral hills Scottish, that in their still deep transparency, invert their summits in the transfiguring magic of the far-sleeping main?

TICKLER. William Simpson, now gone to live in London, is in genius no whit inferior to Mr Thomson, and superior in mastery over the execution of the Art.

NORTH. A first-rater. Ewbank's moonlights this season are meritorious; but 'tis difficult to paint Luna, though she is a still sitter in the sky. Be she veiled nun—white-robed vestal—blue-cinctured huntress—full-orbed in Christian meekness—or, bright misbeliever! brow-rayed with the Turkish crescent—still meetest is she, spiritual creature, for the Poet's love!

SHEPHERD. They tell me that a lad o' the name of o' Fleming frae the west kintra has shewn some bonny landscapes.

NORTH. His pictures are rather deficient in depth, James—his scenes are scarcely sufficiently like portions of the solid globe—but he has a sense of beauty—and with that a painter may do almost any thing—

without it, nothing. For of the painter as of the poet, we may employ the exquisite image of Wordsworth, that beauty

> "Pitches her tents before him."

For example, there is Gibb, who can make a small sweet pastoral world, out of a bank and a brae, a pond and a couple of cows, with a simple lassie sitting in her plaid upon the stump of an old tree. Or, if a morning rainbow spans the moor, he shews you brother and sister—it may be—or perhaps childish lovers—facing the showery wind—in the folds of the same plaid—straining merrily, with their colley before them, towards the hut whose smoke is shivered as soon as it reaches the tops of the sheltering grove. Gibb is full of feeling and genius.

SHEPHERD. But is na his colourin' owre blue?

NORTH. No—James. Shew me any thing bluer than the sky—at its bluest—Not even *her* eye——

SHEPHERD. What? Mrs Gentle's? Her een aye seemed to me to be greenish.

NORTH. Hush—blasphemer! Their zones are like the sky-light of the longest night in the year—when all the earth lies half asleep and half awake in the beauty of happy dreams.

SHEPHERD. Hech! hech!

> "O love! love! love!
>   Love's like a dizziness;
> It wunna let a puir bodie
>   Gang about his bizziness!"

ENGLISH OPIUM-EATER. I have often admired the prodigious power of perspective displayed in the large landscapes of Nasmyth. He gives you at one *coup-d'œil* a metropolitan city—with its river, bridges, towers, and temples—engirdled with groves, and far-retiring all around the garden-fields, tree-dropped, or silvan-shaded, of merry England. I allude now to a noble picture of London.

NORTH. And all his family are geniuses like himself. In the minutiæ of nature, Peter is perfect—it would not be easy to say which of his unmarried daughters excels her sisters in truth of touch—though I believe the best judges are disposed to give Mrs Terry the palm—who now—since the death of her lamented husband—teaches painting in London with eminent success.

TICKLER. Colvin Smith has caught Jeffrey's countenance at last—and a fine countenance it is—alive with intellect—armed at all points—acute without a quibble—clothed all over with cloudless perspicacity—and eloquent on the silent canvass, as if all the air within the frame were murmuring with winged words.

NORTH. Not murmuring—his voice tinkles like a silver bell.

SHEPHERD. But wha can tell that frae the canvass?

NORTH. James, on looking at a portrait, you carry along with you all the characteristic individualities of the original—his voice—his gesture—his action—his motion—his manner—and thus the likeness is made up "of what you half-create and half-perceive,"—else dead—thus only spiritualized into perfect similitude.

SHEPHERD. Mr De Quinshy should hae said that!

ENGLISH OPIUM-EATER. Pardon me, Mr Hogg, I could not have said it nearly so well—and in this case, I doubt not, most truly—as Mr North.

NORTH. No one feature, perhaps, of Mr Jeffrey's face is very fine, except, indeed, his mouth, which is the firmest, and, at the same time, the mildest—the most resolute, and yet, at the same time, the sweetest, I ever saw—inferior in such mingled expression only to Canning's, which was perfect; but look on them all together, and they all act together in irresist- ible union; forehead, eyes, cheeks, mouth, and chin, all declaring, as Burns said of Matthew Henderson, that "Francis is a bright man,"—ever in full command of all his great and various talents, with just enough of genius to preserve them all in due order and subordination—for, with either more or less genius, we may not believe that his endowments could have been so finely, yet so firmly balanced, so powerful both in speculat- ive and practical skill, making him at once, perhaps, on the whole, the most philosophic critic of his age, and, beyond all comparison, the most eloquent orator of his country.

ENGLISH OPIUM-EATER. To much of that eulogium, Mr North, great as my admiration is of Mr Jeffrey's abilities, I must demur.

SHEPHERD. And me too.

TICKLER. And I also.

NORTH. Well, gentlemen, demur away; but such for many years has been my opinion, and 'tis the opinion of all Scotland.

ENGLISH OPIUM-EATER. Since you speak of Mr Jeffrey, and of his achievements in law, literature, and philosophy, in Scotland, and without meaning to include the Southern Intellectual Empire of Britain, why, then, with one exception, (*bowing to Mr North,*) I do most cordially agree with you, though of his law I know nothing, and nothing of his oral eloquence, but judge of him solely from the Edinburgh Review, which, (*bowing again to Mr North,*) with the same conspicuous exception—maugre all its manifold and miserable mistakes—unquestionably stands—or did stand—for I have not seen a number of it since the April number of 1826—at the head of the Periodical Literature of the Age—and that the Periodical Literature of the Age is infinitely superior to all its other philosophical criticism—for example, the charlatanerie of the Schlegels, *et id genus omne,* is as certain—Mr Hogg, pardon me for imitating your illustrative imagery, or attempting to imitate what all the world allows to be inimitable—as that the hotch-potch which you are now swallowing, in spite of heat that seems breathed from the torrid zone——

SHEPHERD. It's no hotch-potch—this platefu's cocky-leeky.

ENGLISH OPIUM-EATER. As that cocky-leeky which, though hot as purgatory, (the company will pardon me for yielding to the influence of the *genius loci,*) your mouth is, and for a quarter of an hour has been, vortex-like engulfing, transcends, in all that is best in animal and vegetable matter,—worthy indeed of Scotland's manly Shepherd—the *soup maigre,* that, attenuated almost to invisibility, drenches the odiously-guttural gullet of some monkey Frenchman of the old school, by the incomprehensible interposition of Providence saved at the era of the Revolution from the guillotine.

OMNES! Bravo! bravo! bravo!—Encore—encore—encore!

SHEPHERD. That's capital—it's just me—gin ye were aye to speak that gate, man, folk wou'd understaun' you. Let's hae a caulker thegether—There's a gurgle—your health, sir—no forgettin' the wife and the weans. It's a pity you're no a Scotchman.

NORTH. John Watson's "Lord Dalhousie" is a noble picture. But John's always great—his works win upon you the longer you study them—and that, after all, is at once the test and the triumph of the art. On some portraits you at once exhaust your admiration; and are then ashamed of yourself for having mistaken the vulgar pleasure, so cheaply inspired, of a staring likeness, for that high emotion breathed from the mastery of the painter's skill—and blush to have doated on a daub.

TICKLER. Duncan's "Braw Wooer," from Burns's

> "Yestreen a braw wooer cam down the lang glen,
>   And sair wi' his love he did deave me;
> I said there was naething I hated like men,—
>   The deuce gang wi' him to believe me,"

is a masterpiece. What a fellow, James! Not unlike yourself in your younger days, perhaps—but without a particle of the light of genius that ever ennobles your rusticity, and makes the plaid on our incomparable Shepherd's shoulders graceful as the poet's mantle—But rather like some son of yours, James, of whom you had not chanced to think it worth your while to take any very particular notice, yet who, by hereditary talents, had made his way in the world up to head-shepherd on a four-thousand acre hill-farm,—his face glowing with love and health like a peony over which a milk-pail had happened to be upset—bonnet cocked as crousely on his hard brow as the comb upon the tappin' o' chanticleer when sidling up, with dropped wing, to a favourite pullet—buckskin breeches, such as Burns used to wear himself, brown and burnished to a most perilous polish—and top-boots, the images of your own, my beloved boy—on which the journey down the lang glen has brought the summer-dust to blend with the well-greased blacking—broad chest, gorgeously apparelled in a flapped waistcoat, manifestly made for him by his great-grandmother, out of the damask-hangings of a bed that once must have stood firm in a Ha' on four posts, though now haply in a hut but a trembling truckle—strong harn shirt, clean as a lily, bleached in the showery sunshine on a brent gowany brae, nor untinged with a faint scent of thyme that, in oaken drawer, will lie odorous for years upon years,—and cravat with a knot like a love-posy, and two pointed depending stalks, tied in the gleam of a water-pail, or haply in the mirror of the pool in which that Apollo had just been floundering like a porpoise, and in which, when drought had dried the shallows, he had lister'd many a fish impatient of the sea;—there, James, he sits on a bank, leaning and leering, a lost and love-sick man, yet not forgetful nor unconscious of the charms so prodigally lavished upon him both by nature and art, the BRAW WOOER, who may not fail in his suit, till blood be wersh as water, and flesh indeed fushionless as grass growing in a sandy desert.

SHEPHERD. Remember, Mr Tickler, what a lee-way you hae to mak up, on the sea o' soup, and be na sae descriptive, for we've a' gotten to windward; you seem to hae drapt anchor, and baith mainsail and foresail are flappin' to the extremity o' their sheets.

TICKLER. And is not she, indeed, James, a queenlike quean? What scorn and skaith in the large full orbs of her imperial eyes! How she tosses back her head in triumph, till the yellow lustre of her locks seems about to escape from the bondage of that riband, the hope-gift of another suitor who wooed her under happier auspices, among last-year's "rigs o' barley," at winter's moonless midnight, beneath the barn-balk where roosts the owl,—by spring's dewy eve on the dim primrose bank, while the lark sought his nest among the green braird, descending from his sunset-song!

SHEPHERD. Confound me—if this be no just perfectly intolerable—Mr North, Mr De Quinshy, Mr Tickler, and a', men, women, and children, imitatin' ma style o' colloquial oratory, till a' that's specific and original about me's lost in universal plagiarism.

TICKLER. Why, James, your genius is as contagious—as infectious as the plague—if, indeed, it be not epidemical—like a fever in the air.

SHEPHERD. You're a' glad to sook up the miasmata. But mercy on us! a' the tureens seem to me amaist dried up—as laigh's wells in mid-summer drought. The vermicelli, especially, is drained to its last worms.

Mr De Quinshy, you've an awfu' appeteet!

ENGLISH OPIUM-EATER. I shall dine to-day entirely on soup,—for your Edinburgh beef and mutton, however long kept, are difficult of mastication,—the sinews seeming to me all to go transversely, thus,—and not longitudinally,—so——

NORTH. Hark! my gold repeater is smiting seven. We allow an hour, Mr De Quincey, to each course—and then——

The Leanders play the "The Boatie Rows,"—the door flies open,— enter Picardy and his clan.

Second Course.—Fish.

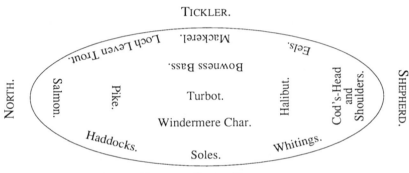

SHEPHERD. I'm sure we canna be sufficiently gratefu' for having got rid o' a' thae empty tureens o' soop—so let us noo set in for serious eatin', and tackle to the inhabitants o' the Great Deep. What's that bit body, North, been about? Daidlin' wi' the mock-turtle. I hate a' things mock—soops, pearls, fawse tails, baith bustles and queues, wigs, cawves, religion, freenship, love, glass-een, rouge on the face o' a woman,—no' excep pin even cork legs, for timmer anes are far better, there bein' nae attempt at deception, which ought never to be practised on ony o' God's reasonable creatures—it's sae insultin'.

ENGLISH OPIUM-EATER. Better open outrage than hidden guile, which——

SHEPHERD. Just sae, sir.—But is't no a bonny instrument, that key-bugle? I've been tryin' to learn't a' this wunter, beginnin' at first wi' the simple coo's-horn. But afore I had weel gotten the gamut, I had nearly lost my life.

TICKLER. What? From mere loss of breath—positive exhaustion? An abscess in the lungs, James?

SHEPHERD. Nothing o' the sort. I hae wund and lungs for ony thing—even for roarin' you doon at argument, whan, driven to the wa', you begin to storm like a Stentor, till the verra neb o' the jug on the dirlin' table regards you wi' astonishment, and the speeders are seen rinning alang the ceilin' to shelter themselves in their corner cobwebs.—(Canna ye learn frae Mr De Quinshy, man, to speak laigh and lown, trustin' mair to sense and less to soun', and you'll find your advantage in't?)—But I allude, sir, to an Adventure.

NORTH. An adventure, James?

SHEPHERD. Aye—an adventure—but as there's nane o' you for cod's-head and shouthers, I'll first fortify mysell wi' some forty or fifty flakes—like half-crown pieces.

TICKLER. Some cod, James, if you please.

SHEPHERD. Help yoursell—I'm unco thrang the noo. Mr De Quinshy, what fish are you devoorin?

ENGLISH OPIUM-EATER. Soles.

SHEPHERD. And you, Mr North?

NORTH. Salmon.

SHEPHERD. And you, Mr Tickler?

TICKLER. Cod.

SHEPHERD. You're a' in your laconics. I'm fear'd for the banes, otherwise, after this cod's dune, I su'd like gran' to gie that pike a yokin'. I ken him for a Linlithgow loun by the length o' his lantern-jaws, and the peacock-neck colour o' his dorsal ridge—and I see by the jut o' his stammach there's store o' stuffin. There'll be naething between him and me, when the cod's dune for, but halibut and turbot—the first the wershest and maist fushionless o' a' swimmin' creturs—and the second owre rich, unless you intend eatin' no other specie o' fish.

TICKLER. Now—for your adventure—my dear Shepherd.

SHEPHERD. Whisht—and you'se hear't. I gaed out, ae day, ayont the knowe—the same, Mr North, that kythes aboon the bit field whare I tried, you ken, to raise a conterband crap o' tobacco—and sat doon on a brae amang the brackens—then a' red as the heavens in sunset—tootin' awa' on the Horn, ettlin first at B flat, and then at A sharp,—when I hears, at the close o' a lesson, what I thocht the grandest echo that ever came frae a mountain-tap—an echo like a rair o' the ghost of ane o' the Bulls o' Bashan, gane mad amang other horned spectres like himsell in the howe o' the cloudy sky——

ENGLISH OPIUM-EATER. Mr North, allow me to direct your attention to that image, which seems to me perfectly original, and, at the same time, perfectly true to nature: Original I am entitled to call it, since I remember nothing resembling it, either essentially or accidentally, in prose or verse, in the literature of antiquity,—in that of the middle, ordinarily, but ignorantly, called the Dark Ages,—in that which arose in Europe after the revival of letters—though assuredly letters had not sunk into a state from which it could be said with any precision that they did revive,—or in that of our own Times, which seem to me to want that totality and unity which alone constitute an Age, otherwise but a series of unconnected successions, destitute of any causative principle of cohesion or evolvement. True to nature, no less am I entitled to call the image, inasmuch as it giveth, not indeed "to airy nothing a local habitation and a name," but to an "airy *something*," namely, the earthly bellowing of an animal, whose bellow is universally felt to be terrific, nay moreover, and therefore, sublime—(for that terror lieth at the root—if not always, yet of verity in by far the greater number of instances—of the true sublime, from early boyhood my intellect saw, and my imagination felt, to be among the great primal intuitive truths of our spiritual frame)—because it giveth, I repeat, to the earthly bellowing of such an animal, an aerial character, which, for the moment, deludes the mind into a belief of the existence of a cloudy kine, spectral in the sky-region, else thought to be the dwelling-place of silence and vacuity, and thus an affecting, impressive,—nay, most solemn and almost sacred feeling, is impressed on the sovereign reason of the immortality of the brute creatures—a doctrine that visits us at those times only when our own being breathes in the awe of divining thought, and, disentangling her wings from all clay encumbrances, is strong in the consciousness of her DEATHLESS ME—so Fichte and Schelling speak——

SHEPHERD. Weel, sir, you see, doon came on my "DEATHLESS ME" the Bonassus, head cavin, tail-tuft on high, hinder legs visible owre his neck and shouthers, and his hump clothed in thunder, louder in his ae single sell than a wheeling charge o' a haill regiment o' dragoon cavalry on the Portobello sands,—doon came the Bonassus, I say, like the Horse Lifeguards takin a park o' French artillery at Waterloo, right doon, Heaven hae mercy! upon me, his ain kind maister, wha had fed him on turnips, hay, and straw, ever syne Lammas, till the monster was as fat's he could lie in the hide o' him—and naething had I to defend mysell wi' but that silly coo's horn. A' the colleys were at hame. Yet in my fricht—deadly as it was—I was thankfu' wee Jamie wasna there lookin' for primroses—for he micht hae lost his judgment. You understand, the Bonassus had mista'en my B sharp for anither Bonassus challengin' him to single combat.

ENGLISH OPIUM-EATER. A very plausible theory.

SHEPHERD. Thank you, sir, for that commentary on ma text—for it has gien me time to plouter amang the chowks o' the cod. Faith it was nae theory, sir, it was practice—and afore I could fin' my feet, he was sae close upon me that I could see up his nostrils. Just at that moment I remembered that I had on an auld red jacket—the ane that was ance sky-blue, you ken, Mr North, that I had gotten dyed—and that made the

Bonassus just an evendoun Bedlamite. For amaist a' horned cattle hate and abhor red coats.

NORTH. So I have heard the army say—alike in town and country.

SHEPHERD. What was to be done? I thocht o' tootin the horn, as the trumpeter did when run aff wi' in the mouth o' a teeger; but then I recollected that it was a' the horn's blame that the Bonassus was there—so I lost no time in that speculation,—but slipping aff my breeks, jacket, waistcoat, shirt, and a', just as you've seen an actor on the stage, I appeared suddenly before him as naked as the day I was born—and sic is the awe, sir, wi' which a human being, *in puris naturalibus*, inspires the maddest of the brute creation, (I had tried it ance before on a mastiff,) that he was a' at aince, in a single moment, stricken o' a heap, just the very same as if the butcher had sank the head o' an aix intill his harn-pan—his knees trummled like a new-dropped lamb's—his tail, tuft and a', had nae mair power in't than a broken thrissle stalk—his een goggled instead o' glowered, a heartfelt difference, I assure you——

ENGLISH OPIUM-EATER. It seems to be, Mr Hogg—but you will pardon me, if I am mistaken—a distinction without a difference, as the logicians say——

SHEPHERD. Aye, De Quinshy, ma man—logician as you are, had you stood in my shoon, you had gotten yoursell on baith horns o' the dilemma.

NORTH. Did you cut off his retreat to the Loch, James, and take him prisoner?

SHEPHERD. I did. Poor silly sumph! I canna help thinkin' that he swarfed; though perhaps he was only pretendin'—so I mounted him, and, putting my worsted garters through his nose—it had been bored when he was a wild beast in a caravan—I keepit peggin' his ribs wi' my heels, till, after gruntin' and graenin', and raisin' his great big unwieldy red bowk half up frae the earth, and then swelterin' doon again, if aince, at least a dizzen times, till I began absolutely to weary o' my situation in life, he feenally recovered his cloots, and, as if inspired wi' a new speerit, aff like lichtnin' to the mountains.

NORTH. What!—without a saddle, James? You must have felt the loss —I mean the want, of leather——

SHEPHERD. We ride a' mainner o' animals bare-backed in the Forest, sir. I hae seen a bairn, no aboon fowre year auld, ridin' hame the Bill at the gloamin'—a' the kye at his tail, like a squadron o' cavalry ahint Joachim Murat King o' Naples.—Mr North, gin ye keep eatin' sae vorawciously at the sawmon, you'll hurt yoursell. Fish is heavy. Dinna spare the vinegar, if you will be a glutton.

NORTH. Ma!

SHEPHERD. But, as I was sayin', awa' went the Bonassus due west. Though you could hardly ca't even a snaffle, yet I soon found that I had a strong purchase, and bore him doun frae the heights to the turnpike-road that cuts the kintra frae Selkirk to Moffat. There does I encounter three gig-fu's o' gentlemen and leddies; and ane o' the latter—a bonny cretur—leuch as if she kent me, as I gaed by at full gallop—and I remembered haein seen her afore, though where I couldna tell; but a' the lave shrieked as if at the visible superstition o' the Water-Kelpie on the Water-Horse mistakin' day for nicht, in the delirium o' a fever—and thinkin' that it had been the moon shining down on his green pastures aneath the Loch, when it was but the shadow o' a lurid cloud. But I soon vanished into distance.

TICKLER. Where the deuce were your clothes all this time, my dear matter-of-fact Shepherd?

SHEPHERD. Aye—there was the rub. In the enthusiasm of the moment I had forgotten them—nay, such was the state of excitement to which I had worked myself up, that, till I met the three gig-fu's o' leddies and gentlemen—a marriage-party—full in the face, I was not, Mr Dequinshy, aware of being so like the Truth. Then I felt, all in a moment, that I was a Mazeppa. But had I turned back, they would have supposed that I had intended to accompany them to Selkirk; and therefore, to allay all such fears, I made a shew of fleeing far awa' aff into the interior—into the cloudland of Loch Skene and the Grey Mare's Tail.

ENGLISH OPIUM-EATER. Your adventure, Mr Hogg, would furnish a much better subject for the painter, or for the poet, than the Mazeppa of Byron. For, it is not possible to avoid feeling, that in the image of a naked man on horseback, there is an involution of the grotesque in the picturesque—of the truly ludicrous in the falsely sublime. But, farther, the thought of bonds—whether of cordage or of leather—on a being naturally free, is degrading to the moral, intellectual, and physical dignity of the creature so constricted; and it ought ever to be the grand aim of poetry to elevate and exalt. Moreover, Mazeppa, in being subjected to the scornful gaze of hundreds—nay, haply of thousands of spectators—the base retinue of a barbarous power—in a state of utter-most nudity, was subjected to an ordeal of shame and rage, which neither the contemplative nor imaginative mind could brook to see applied to even the veriest outcast scum of our race. He was, in fact, placed naked in a moving pillory—and the hissing shower of scornful curses by which he was by those barbarians assailed, is as insupportable to our thoughts as an irregular volley, or street-firing, of rotten eggs, discharged by the hooting rabble against some miscreant standing with his face through a hole in the wood, with his crime placarded on his felon-breast. True, that as Mazeppa "recoils into the wilderness," the exposure is less repulsive to common imagination; but it is not to common imagination that the highest poetry is addressed; and, therefore, though to the fit reader there be indeed some relief or release from shame in the "deserts idle," yet doth not the feeling of degradation so subside as to be merged in that pleasurable state of the soul, essential to the effect of the true and legitimate exercise of poetical power. Shame pursues him faster than the wolves; nor doth the umbrage of the forest-trees, that fly past him in his flight, hide his nakedness, which, in some other conditions, being an attribute of his nature, might even be the source to him and to us of a high emotion, but which here being forcibly and violently imposed against his will by the will of a brutal tyrant, is but an accident of his position in space and time, and therefore unfit to be permanently contemplated in a creature let loose before the Imaginative Faculty. Nor is this vital vice—so let me call it—in anywise cured or alleviated by his subsequent triumph, when he returns—as he himself tells us he did—at the head of "twice ten thousand horse!"—for the contrast only serves to deepen and darken the original nudity of his intolerable doom. The mother-naked man still seems to be riding in front of all his cavalry; nor, in this case, has the poet's art sufficed to reinstate him in his pristine dignity, and to efface all remembrance of the degrading process of stripping and of binding, to which of yore the miserable Nude had been compelled to yield, as helpless as an angry child ignominiously whipt by a nurse, till its mental sufferings may be said to be lost in its physical agonies. Think not that I wish to withhold from Byron the praise of considerable spirit and vigour of execution, in his narrative of the race; but that praise may duly belong to very inferior powers; and I am now speaking of Mazeppa in the light of a great Poem. A great Poem it assuredly is not; and how small a Poem is assuredly is, must be felt by all who have read, and are worthy to read, Homer's description of the dragging, and driving, and whirling of the dead body of Hector in bloody nakedness behind the chariot-wheels of Achilles.

SHEPHERD. I never heard ony thing like that in a' my days. Weel, then, sir, there were nae wolves to chase me and the Bonassus, nor yet mony trees to overshadow us, but we made the cattle and the sheep look about them, and mair nor ae hooded craw and lang-necked heron gat a fricht, as we came suddenly on him through the mist, and gaed thundering by the cataracts. In an hour or twa I began to get as firm on my seat as a Centaur; and discovered by the chasms that the Bonassus was not only as fleet as a racer, but that he could loup like a hunter, and thocht nae mair o' a thirty feet spang than ye wad think o' stepping across the gutter. Ma faith, we were na lang o' being in Moffat!

ENGLISH OPIUM-EATER. In your Flight, Mr Hogg, there were visibly and audibly concentrated all the attributes of the highest Poetry. First, freedom of the will; for self-impelled you ascended the animal: Secondly, the impulse, though immediately consequent upon, and proceeding from, one of fear, was yet an impulse of courage; and courage is not only a virtue, and acknowledged to be such in all Christian countries, but among the Romans—who assuredly, however low they must be ranked on the intellectual scale, were nevertheless morally a brave people—to it alone was given the name *virtus:* Thirdly, though you were during your whole flight so far passive as that you yielded to the volition of the creature, yet were you likewise, during your whole course, so far active, that you *guided*, as it appears, the motions, which it was beyond your power entirely to control; thus vindicating in your own person the rights of the superior order of creation: Fourthly, you were not so subjugated by the passion peculiar and appropriate to your situation, as to be insensible to or regardless of the courtesies, the amenities, and the humanities of civilized life,—as witness that glance of mutual recognition that passed, in one moment, between you and the "bonny creature" in the gig; nor yet to be inattentive to the effect produced by yourself and the Bonassus on various tribes of the inferior creatures,—cattle, sheep, crows, and herons, to say nothing of the poetical delight experienced by you from the influence of the beautiful or august shows of nature,—mists, clouds, cataracts, and the eternal mountains: Fifthly, the constantly accompanying sense of danger interfused with that of safety, so as to constitute one complex emotion, under which, hurried as you were, it may be said with perfect truth that you found leisure to admire, nay, even to wonder at, the strange speed of that most extraordinary animal—and most extraordinary he must be, if the only living representative of his species since the days of Aristotle— nor less to admire and wonder at your own skill, equally, if not more, miraculous, and well entitled to throw into the shade of oblivion the art of the most illustrious equestrian that ever "witched the world with noble horsemanship." Sixthly, the sublime feeling of penetrating, like a thunder-bolt, cloud-land and all the mist-cities that evanished as you galloped into their suburbs, gradually giving way to a feeling no less sublime, of having left behind all those unsubstantial phantom-regions, and of nearing the habitation or tabernacle of men, known by the name of Moffat—perhaps one of the most imaginative of all the successive series of states of your soul since first you appeared among the hills, like Sol entering Taurus: And, Finally, the deep trance of home-felt delight that must have fallen upon your spirit—true still to all the sweetest and most sacred of the social affections—when, the Grey Mare's Tail left streaming far behind that of the Bonassus, you knew from the murmur of that silver stream that your flight was about to cease—till, lo! the pretty village of which you spoke, embosomed in hills and trees—the sign of the White Lion, peradventure, motionless in the airless calm—a snug parlour with a blazing ingle—re-apparelling instant, almost as thought—food both for man and beast—for the Ettrick Shepherd—pardon my familiarity for sake of my friendship—and his Bonassus: Yea, from goal to goal, the entire

Flight is Poetry, and the original idea of nakedness is lost—or say rather veiled—in the halo-light of imagination.

SHEPHERD. Weel, if it's no provokin', Mr De Quinshy, to hear you, who never was on a Bonassus a' your days, analeezin', wi' the maist comprehensive and acute philosophical accuracy, ma complex emotion during the Flight to Moffat far better than I could do mysell——

NORTH. Your genius, James, is synthetical.

SHEPHERD. Synthetical? I houp no—at least nae mair sae than the genius o' Burns or Allan Kinninghame—or the lave—for——

ENGLISH OPIUM-EATER. What is the precise Era of the Flight to Moffat?

SHEPHERD. Mr De Quinshy, you're like a' ither great philosophers, ane o' the maist credulous o' mankind! You wad believe me, were I to say that I had ridden a whale up the Yarrow frae Newark to Eltrive! The haill story's a lee! and sae free o' ony fundation in truth, that I wou'd hae nae objections to tak my bible-oath that sic a beast as a Bonassus never was creawted—and it's lucky for him that he never was, for seeing that he's said to consume three bushel o' ingans to dinner every day o' his life, Noah would never hae letten him intill the Ark, and he would have been found, after the subsiding o' the waters, a skeleton on the tap o' Mount Ararat.

ENGLISH OPIUM-EATER. His non-existence in nature is altogether distinct from his existence in the imagination of the poet—and, in good truth, redounds to his honour—for his character must be viewed in the light of a pure *Ens rationis*—or say rather——

SHEPHERD. Just let him be an *Ens rationis*. But confess, at the same time, that you was bammed, sir.

ENGLISH OPIUM-EATER. I recognise the legitimate colloquial use of the word *Bam*, Mr Hogg, denoting, I believe, "the willing surrendering of belief, one of the first principles of our mental constitution, to any statement made with apparent sincerity, but real deceit, by a mind not previously suspected to exist in a perpetual atmosphere of falsehood."

SHEPHERD. Just sae, sir,—that's a *Bam*. In Glasgow, they ca't a ggegg.—But what's the matter wi' Mr North? Saw ye ever the cretur lookin' sae gash? I wish he may no be in a fit o' apoplexy. Speak till him, Mr De Quinshy.

ENGLISH OPIUM-EATER. His countenance is, indeed, ominously sable,— but 'tis most unlikely that apoplexy should strike a person of his spare habit: Nay, I must sit corrected; for I believe that attacks of this kind have, within the last quarter of a century, become comparatively frequent, and constitute one of the not least perplexing phenomena submitted to the inquisition of Modern Medical Science.—Mr North, will you relieve our anxiety?

SHEPHERD (*starting up, and flying to* MR NORTH.) His face is a' purple.

Confoun' that cravat!—for the mair you pu' at it, the tichter it grows.

ENGLISH OPIUM-EATER. Mr Hogg, I would seriously and earnestly recommend more delicacy and gentleness.

SHEPHERD. Tuts. It's fastened, I declare, ahint wi' a gold buckle,—and afore wi' a gold prin,—a brotch fra Mrs Gentle, in the shape o' a bleedin' heart!—'Twill be the death o' him—Oh! puir fallow, puir fallow!—rax me owre that knife. What's this? You've given me the silver fish-knife, Mr De Quinshy. Na,—that's far waur, Mr Tickler—That swurd for carvin' the round. But here's my ain jockteleg.

SHEPHERD *unclasps his pocket-knife,—and while brandishing it in great trepidation,* MR NORTH *opens his eyes.*

NORTH. Emond! Emond! Emond!—Thurtell—Thurtell—Thurtell!

SHEPHERD. A drap o' bluid's on his brain,—and Reason becomes Raving! What's Man?

TICKLER. Cut away, James. Not a moment to be lost. Be firm and decided, else he is a dead heathen.

SHEPHERD. Wae's me,—wae's me! Nae goshawk ever sae glowered,—and only look at his puir fingers hoo they are workin'! I canna thole the sight,—I'm as weak's a wean,—and fear that I'm gaun to fent. Tak the knife, Tickler. O, look at his hauns,—look at his hauns!

TICKLER (*bending over* MR NORTH.) Yes, yes, my dear sir,—I comprehend you—I——

SHEPHERD (*in anger and astonishment.*) Mr Tickler! are you mad?—fingerin' your fingers in that gate,—as if you were mockin' him!

ENGLISH OPIUM-EATER. They are conversing, Mr Hogg, in that language which originated in Oriental——

SHEPHERD. Oh! they're speakin' on their fingers?—then a's richt,—and Mr North's comin' roun' again until his seven senses. It's been but a dwawm!

TICKLER. Mr North has just contrived to communicate to me, gentlemen, the somewhat alarming intelligence, that the backbone of the pike has for some time past been sticking about half-way down his throat; that being unwilling to interrupt the conviviality of the company, he endeavoured at first to conceal the circumstance, and then made the most strenuous efforts to dislodge it, upwards or downwards, without avail; but that you must not allow yourselves to fall into any extravagant consternation, as he indulges the fond hope that it may be extracted, even without professional assistance, by Mr De Quincey, who has an exceedingly neat small Byronish hand, and on whose decision of character he places the most unfaltering reliance.

SHEPHERD (*in a huff.*) Does he?—Very weel—syne he forgets auld freen's—let him do sae—

NORTH. Ohrr Hogrwhu—chru—u—u—u—Hogruwhuu——

SHEPHERD. Na! I canna resist sic pleadin' eloquence as that—here's the screw, let me try it—Or, what think ye, Mr Tickler,—what think ye, Mr De Quinshy—o' thir pair o' boot-hooks?—Gin I could get a cleik o' the bane by ane o' the vertebræ, I might hoise it gently up, by slaw degrees, sae that ane could get at it wi' their fingers, and then pu' it out o' his mouth in a twinklin'! But first let me look doon his throat—Open your mouth, my dearest sir.

MR NORTH *leans back his head, and opens his mouth.*

SHEPHERD. I see't like a harrow. Rin ben, baith o' ye, for Mr Awmrose.

TICKLER *and* MR DE QUINCEY *obey.*

Weel ackit, sir—weel ackit—I was ta'en in mysell at first, for your cheeks were like coals. Here's the back-bane o' the pike on the trencher—I'll—

Re-enter TICKLER *and* OPIUM-EATER, *with* MR AMBROSE, *pale as death.*

It's all over, gentlemen—It's all over!

AMBROSE. Oh! oh! oh!   [*Faints away into* TICKLER'S *arms.*

SHEPHERD. What the deevil's the matter wi' you, you set o' fules?— I've gotten out the bane.—Look here at the skeleton o' the shark!

ENGLISH OPIUM-EATER. Monstrous!

NORTH (*running to the assistance of* MR AMBROSE.) We have sported too far, I fear, with his sensibilities.

ENGLISH OPIUM-EATER. A similar case of a fish-bone in Germany——

SHEPHERD. Mr De Quinshy, you can really swallow *that?*

Looking at the pike-back, about two feet long.

But the hour has nearly expired.

The Leanders play—"*Hey, Johnnie Cope, are you wauken yet?*"—

MR AMBROSE *starts to his feet—runs off—and re-appears almost instanter at the head of the forces.*

Third Course.—Flesh.

TICKLER.

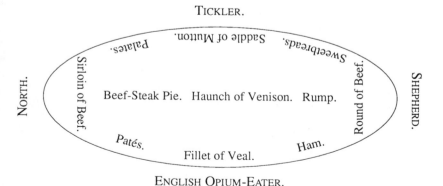

NORTH.

SHEPHERD.

Palates.   Saddle of Mutton.   Sweetbreads.

Sirloin of Beef.   Beef-Steak Pie.   Haunch of Venison.   Rump.   Round of Beef.

Patés.   Fillet of Veal.   Ham.

ENGLISH OPIUM-EATER.

SHEPHERD (*in continuation.*) And do you really think, Mr North, that the kintra's in great and general distress, and a' orders in a state o' absolute starvation?

NORTH. Yes—James—although the Duke cannot see the sufferings of his subjects, I can—and——

SHEPHERD. Certain appearances do indicate national distress; yet I think I cou'd, withouten meikle difficulty, lay my haun the noo on ithers that seem to lead to a different conclusion.

NORTH. No sophistry, James. True, that we are now sitting at a Feast. But remember, James, that All Fool's Day has been duly celebrated by us ever since the commencement of our career, and that one omission of observance of such anniversary might prove fatal to the existence of "The Magazine."

SHEPHERD. At least ominous. For sure aneuch it wou'd be ungratefu' to forget our subscribers.

NORTH. And are we to violate a sacred custom, merely because the country has been brought by an incapable and unprincipled ministry to the brink of ruin?

ENGLISH OPIUM-EATER. Yet, I have seen nothing in the condition of the people, to incline me to doubt the truth of the doctrine—originally stated by Say, afterwards expounded by Ricardo—and, since the death of that illustrious discoverer—(happier than Cooke, who by twice circumnavigating the globe,—for on his third voyage he was cut off by the savage Sandwichers, the problem unsolved—ascertained the non-existence of Terra Incognita Australis;—yea, more felicitous even than Columbus, who, while he indeed found a new world, mistook it for an old one, and dreamt that he beheld isles that of old had been visited for their golden store by the ships of Solomon:)—I say, since the death of David Ricardo unmercifully and laboriously overloaded with a heap of leaden words that love the ground, by Smith and MacCulloch [whose pages are the most arid spots in that desert of Politico-Economical science which the genius of the Jew mapped out, indicating the direction in which all the main caravan roads ought to run by the banks of the rivers, by the wells, and by the oases]—that doctrine, which, being established by arguments *a priori*, would indeed remain in my reason immutable as an axiom in the mathematics, in spite of all the seeming opposition of mere outward facts, or phenomena from which the blind leading the blind, owl-like in mid-day, would seek to draw conclusions at vital enmity with those primal truths subsisting effectually and necessarily in the Relations of Things;—[which relations indeed they are, shadowed or figured out to ordinary apprehension under various names:]—the Doctrine, in short, that Production is the Cause of Production, that Vents create Vents, and thence, that a universal Glut is a Moral and Physical Impossibility, the monster of a sick merchant's dream.

SHEPHERD. That Vents creawte Vents! Do you mean, in plain language, Mr De Quinshy, to say that lums creawte lums—that ae chimley procreawtes anither chimley——

NORTH. My dear James, you know nothing of Political Economy—so hold your——

SHEPHERD. Heaven be praised—for a' them that pretends they do—I mean the farmers—aye break. I ken ae puir fallow, a cock-laird, wi' a pleasant mailin' o' his ain, that had been in the family since Seth, that got his death by studyin' the Stot. "Stimulate Production! Stimulate Production!" was aye puir Watty's cry—"Nae fear o' consumption. The *nati consumere fruges*"—(for the Stot had taught him to quote some rare lines o' Latin)—"will aye be hungry and thirsty, and need to wear claes;"—but Watty drave baith his pigs and his sheep to a laigh market; he fand that the Stot was likewise far wrang in tellin' him that competition cou'd no possibly reduce profits—an apophthegm you would hae thocht aforehaun' that wud hae scunner'd a natural-born idiot—yet still wad Watty study the Stot—for he was a dour cretur—till ae nicht, ridin' hame frae Selkirk, wi' MacCulloch's Principles in the right-haun' pouch o' his big-coat, he was, as you micht easily hae conjectured, thrawn aff his balance, and cowpin' ower till that side, was dragged wi' his fit in the stirrup till he was as dead as the Stot's ain doctrine about Absentees.

NORTH. Besides, gentlemen, remember that our board to-day is chiefly supplied by presents, among which are many love-gifts from the fair——

SHEPHERD. And then, The Fragments——

NORTH. The *Reliquiæ Danaum*——

SHEPHERD. Are the property o' the poor——

NORTH. And will all be distributed to-morrow—by ticket—according to the arrangement of Mrs Gentle——

SHEPHERD. The maist charitable o' God's creturs—exceptin' yoursell, my dear sir—whose haun' is open as day——Oh, man! but there's a heap o' hatefu' meanin' in the epithet, *close-fisted!* I like aye to see the open pawm, for it's amaist as expressive 's the open broo. A greedy chiel—him that's ony way meeserly, aye sits, you'll observe, wi' his nieves crunkled up unconsciously through the power o' habit, or keeps them in the pockets o' his breeks as if fumblin' amang the fardens; and let the conversation be about what it wull, there's aye a sort o' mental reservation in his een, seemin' to say, that if the talk shou'd tak a turn, and ony hint be drapt about a subscription to a droon'd fisherman's widow and weans, or the like, he'll instantly thraw cauld water on't, suggest enquiries intill her character, and ring the bell for his hack.— North, luk at thae twa creturs gutlin'—the tane at the saiddle, and the tither at the fillet!—Awmrose, change the position o' the foure principal dishes answerin' to the Foure Airts.

AMBROSE *makes the saddle exchange places with the fillet,*
the sirloin with the round.

By this dispensation, each o' us gets easy access, feenally, to a' the dishes, sereawtim; can carve in his ain way, and taks his fair chance o' the tid-bits;—but d'ye ken, sirs, that I'm gettin' melancholy—fa'in' into laigh spirits—weary o' life. I houp it's but the reaction frae that daffin'—but really the verra skies seem to ma een as if I were lookin' up to them, lyin' on my back aneath a muddy stream—while, as for this globe, it's naething but glaur! The poetry o' life is dead and buried, sir, and wha can bear to be wadin' frae mornin' till nicht, up to his oxters, in prose? The verra Deevil himsell 's got dull in the haun's o' that Rab Montgomery,—cauld-rifed, as if hell were out o' coals,—a' its blast-furnaces choked up wi' blue silent ashes—and the damned coorin' and chitterin' in corners, as if fire were frost.

NORTH. James! James!

SHEPHERD. Dinna be feared for me bein' blasphemous. Rather than sin sae, micht I cease to breathe, or gang sighin' and sabbin' in insanity through the woods and moors! The Deevil's just as utter a nonentity as ony ither dream; or if no, at the maist, he's but a soap-bubble. Mind ye, I'm speakin' o' an external Deevil—a shaped Satan—a limb'd Lucifer—a Beelzebub wi' a belly—goin' bodily about, wi' cloots and horns, seeking whom he may devour.

NORTH. The saving superstition of the imagination.

SHEPHERD. Just sae—shadows seen by sin movin' atween and the sky in the gloamin', when naebody's near, but some glowerin' and listenin' auld motionless tower—shadows o' its ain thochts, at which it aften gangs demented—nor will they subside awa' intill naething, but, unsubstantial as they are, far mair endurable than substance—just as ghosts continue to glide about for centuries after the bodies have amaist ceased to be even banes, and haunt a' the hills and glens, sunshine and moonlight alike, loun or stormy days;—nor unprivileged are they by conscience to enter—just as if a thunder-cloud were passin' the sky-light windows—into the house o' God—still by the side o' the sinner, even on the Sabbath—and keepin' fixed on his their dismal een, they can frichten the immortal spirit within him, sae that his ears nae mair transmit to it the singin' o' the psalm—unless you ca' that singin', which is mair like the noise o' ever sae mony swarms o' bees a' castin' thegether on a het day on the same sycamore, and murderin' ane anither in the confusion o' queens, by haill hives, till the winged air is in torment, and a' the grun' aneath crawlin' wi' wrathfu' mutilation!

NORTH. Pollok was a true poet—and the Course of Time, though not a poem, overflows with poetry; but the apes of that angel must be bagged, and stifled in the cess-pools of the cities where they——

SHEPHERD. Suppose we begin wi' the Embro' apes. There's that cretur——

NORTH. Let him stand over for a season—one other chatter—and he dies.

SHEPHERD. I cou'd greet—I hae grat—to think o' puir Pollok haein' been ca'd sae sune awa'—but his country may be said to hae bigged a monument ower his remains.

NORTH. Poor Blanco White's London Review—got up among some of the most formal of the Oxford prigs—for Whatley surely could never countenance such a concern—the only number that ever got printed ordered the world to despise Pollok. The Course of Time—Miltonic in design and execution—was tried by the Oriel critic as a prize poem——

SHEPHERD. I recolleck, sir. Yon Number's used at Mount-Benger still, as a stane weight——

NORTH. Each paltry periodical, James, that, born of poorest parents, and fed from the first, as paupers' brats must be, on pap provided by charity, begins soon as it is dropped, drab-and-ditch-delivered, instinctively to caterwaul after the fashion of its progenitors, like a nest o' kittens, snoking about the straw with their little red snub-noses, and sealed swoln eyes, which are plainly doomed never to see the day, except perhaps one single blink on the morning they are all plopped pitilessly into a pond, to be fished out and flung in again, every spring-Saturday, by schoolboys learning the elements of angling——Each paltry periodical, James, weekly, monthly, or quarterly—while like a puddle in a cart-wheel rut, it attempts to reflect the physiognomy of Christopher North—employs the very first moments of its transitory existence in shewing its gums—for time is not given it for teeth—at ME—at Us—at the MAGAZINE—who would not even take the trouble of treating it as a Newfoundland dog has been sometimes seen to treat a troublesome turnspit.

SHEPHERD. Oot they gang, ane after the ither, like sae mony farden candles stickin' intill turnips—and och! what a shabby stink! Ae single sneer frae you, sir, smeeks and smithers them in their ain reek; and yet, sic is the spite o' stupidity, that ae fule taks nae warnin' frae the fate o' the fule afore him, but they are a' like sae mony sheep, jumpin' o' their ain accord into the verra shambles—although the Shepherd—that's me—does a' he can wi' his colleys to keep them out o' the jaws o' destruction, and get them a' safely collected in ae staring squad on the common, whare they may feed on herbage little or nane the waur for the goose-dung.—Hoo's the Embro Review gaun on?

NORTH. Very well indeed, James. Methinks, under the new editor, it hath more pith and smeddum.

SHEPHERD. O' late years it has aye reminded me o' an auld worn-out ram, whom the proprietor does na like either to let dee o' hunger, or a' at aince to pit out o' its meesery—but syne he's of nae use noo, and wunna sell either for woo' or meat, the master flings him noo and then a turnip, and noo and then alloos him a wusp o' strae—as he stauns wi' his tawty sides, speeral horns, and beard that has never been shaven in the memory o' man—the Eemage rather than the Reality o' a Ram.

NORTH. Why, James, the youth of the animal seems in some measure restored, and he butts away with much animation and——

SHEPHERD. Let him tak tent he does na break his horns. Them that's beginning to bud's tender, but them that's dune wi' growin' 's frush; I hae nae faith in the renewal o' youth; and though the Ram, videlicet, the Review, may be better fed noo than for some wunters by-past—puir beast!—yet he can only be patched up. Ye may aiblins fatten his sides— but I'll defy you to harden his horns. Wash him in the Sky-blue Pool, but still wull his woo' be like a specie o' hair on some outlandish dug; and as for continuin' his——

NORTH. Southey's Colloquies are, in the opinion of young Macauley, exceedingly contemptible——

SHEPHERD. And wha's young Macauley?

NORTH. The son of old Macauley.

SHEPHERD. And wha the deevil's auld Macauley?

NORTH. Zachary.

SHEPHERD. What? The Sierra Leone Saint, who has been the means of sendin' sae mony sinners to Satan through that accursed settlement?

NORTH. The same—whom our friend Macqueen has squabashed— and whom that able and accomplished man, Charles M'Kenzie, late consul-general at Hayti——

SHEPHERD. Charles M'Kenzie! I see his Notes on Hayti advertised by Colburn. I'll warrant they'll be gude—for I remember him lang ago, a medical student at the College here, afore he turned himsell to mercantile affairs, and a cleverer young man wasna in a' Embro'.

NORTH. He is about to be sent out by Government to Cuba—one of the judges to enquire——

SHEPHERD. I'm glad to hear't—I houp noo he'll send me hame some rum and limes—wi' a hoghead o' sugar——

NORTH. But, James, as I was saying, Thomas Macauley informs his fellow-creatures that Robert Southey's mind is "utterly destitute of the power of discerning truth from falsehood."

SHEPHERD. Then Thomas Macauley is nather mair nor less than an impertinent puppy for his pains; and Maga should lay him across her knee, doun wi' his breeks, and haun' ower head wi' the tause on his doup, like Dominie Skelp—

NORTH. He adds, "Mr Southey brings to the task two faculties which were never, we believe, vouchsafed in measure so copious to any human being,—the faculty of believing without a reason, and the faculty of hating without a provocation;" and again, "in the mind of Mr Southey, reason has no place at all, as either leader or follower, as either sovereign or slave."

SHEPHERD. I wonner, sir, hoo you can remember sic malignant trash. An' these are the symptoms, sir, are they, that the youth o' the auld Ram is renewed?

NORTH. No doubt seems to have entered the mind of the young gentleman, that, while in fact he was merely attempting, without much point, to stick a pin into the calve of one of Mr Southey's literary legs, he was planting a dagger in the brain of the Laureate.

SHEPHERD. A Lilliputian atween the spauls o' Gulliver. Yet one canna but admire the courage o' the cretur in the inverse ratio o' its impotence. Only suppose Soothey to stir in his sleep—but to gie a sneeze or a snore—and hoo the bit barrister—for I remember what the bit body is noo—would wriggle awa like a worm, and divin' intill some dung, hide himsell amang the grubs.

NORTH. He's a clever lad, James—

SHEPHERD. Evidently, and a clever lad he'll remain, depend ye upon that, a' the days o' his life. A clever lad o' thirty year auld and some odds, is to ma mind the maist melancholy sicht in nature—only think o' a clever lad o' three-score and ten on his death-bed, wha can look back on nae greater achievement than haein' aince—or aiblins ten times—abused Mr Soothey in the Embro' Review!

NORTH. The son of the Saint, who seems himself to be something of a reviewer, is insidious as the serpent, but fangless as the slow-worm.

SHEPHERD. That's the hag or blin-worm?

NORTH. The same. He pretends to admire Mr Southey's poetry, that with its richness he may contrast the poverty of his prose. "His larger poems," quoth he, "though *full of faults*, are nevertheless extraordinary productions. We doubt greatly *whether they will be read fifty years* hence—but that, *if they are read*, they will be admired, we have no doubt whatever." As for his short poems, "they are not generally happy;" and "his odes are for the most part worse than Pye's, and as bad as Cibber's."

SHEPHERD. Puir deevil! hoo envious thochts maun hae been eatin' awa' at his heart like mites in a rotten cheese!

NORTH. All Mr Southey's heroes—says the Templar—"make love either like seraphim or cattle." "No man out of a cloister ever wrote about love so coldly, and at the same time so grossly."

SHEPHERD. A' the young leddies in Britain ken that to be a lee—and the cross-bred puppy o' a mongrel-cur wadna hesitate to ca' themselves limmers, after speakin' o' the coldness and grossness of the love of Thalaba for Oneiza his Arabian Maid, whether breathed in delight in their tent beneath the palm-tree's shade, or groaned in madness amid the tombs, after Azrael the angel of death had left their bridal chamber. What does he mean by cattle?

NORTH. Obscene insolence!

SHEPHERD. Trash like that, sir, wad damn at aince ony new periodical. Tak ma word for't, sir, the auld Ram'll no leeve lang on sic articles o' consumption. He'll tak the rot, and dee a' ae scab, ae carbuncle, "a perfect chrysolite."

NORTH. I had some thoughts of exposing the gross misrepresentations—say the falsehoods—of this article—but——

SHEPHERD. 'Tweel it's no worth your while. The weed's withered, I'se warrant, by this time, though no a month auld—while the flowers o' Mr Soothey's genius, rich and rare, bright and balmy, will breathe and bloom as lang's the sun shines on the earth, and the Seasons keep rinnin', alternately, unwearied alangside o' his chariot wheels. Mr De Quinshy, what for dinna ye speak?

ENGLISH OPIUM-EATER. Mr Southey is, beyond all doubt, one of the most illustrious, just as Mr Macauley is one of the most obscure men, of the age. The abuse lavished upon him in that contemptible critique on his Colloquies—a critique which I have read, and therefore must correct the statement I made about the middle of the last Course, that I had not seen any number of the Edinburgh Review since that for April 1826—is baser than I could have expected even from a Macauley—meaning thereby any Sinner among the Saints—and I do not doubt, Mr Hogg, to use your own amusing image, that it will sicken, if not poison to death, the old Ram—the ancient Aries—a sign into which the sun never enters——

SHEPHERD. That's wutty—I'm a sure judge o' wut—that's wutty!

TICKLER (*aside to the* SHEPHERD.) But so-so—I prefer our admirable friend's logic to his——

SHEPHERD (*aside to* TICKLER.) Na—na—I canna thole his logic.

ENGLISH OPIUM-EATER. But while I reprobate the insolent spirit in which this obscure cipher has chosen to speak of such a good and great man, let it be understood that I not only withhold my sympathy from some of the sentiments expressed by Mr Southey in his Colloquies, but censure them as most erroneous, and most unjust—as, for example, all that he has falsely and foolishly said, in that and other works, respecting the periodical literature of this age. What right had Mr Southey, who gains an honourable livelihood chiefly by his contributions to Reviews, to put into the mouth of Sir Thomas More the following insulting sentence—insulting to many minds of the same order with his own, and as devoted to the truth:—"The waters in which you have now been angling have been shallow enough, if the pamphlet in your hand is, as it appears to be, a Magazine." Nor is his answer to the Ghost more courteous to his contemporaries:—"In publications of this kind, prejudicial as they are to public taste and public feeling, and therefore deeply injurious to the real interests of literature, something may sometimes be found to compensate for the trash, and tinsel, and insolent flippancy, which are now become the staple commodities of such journals."

SHEPHERD. Hut—tut, Mr Soothey; you shouldna hae said that, sir,— for it's no tr——.

ENGLISH OPIUM-EATER. In the first place, Mr Southey ought to have given the name of the pamphlet—that is, the Magazine—from which he chose to extract Kant's Idea of a Universal History on a Cosmopolitical plan. Secondly, he ought to have printed that extract as an extract from that Magazine, and not to have attempted—rather unsuccessfully—to incorporate its substance with his own work. Thirdly, he ought to have given the name of the translator, not unknown to him, when he scrupled not to enrich his Colloquies with some of Kant's thoughts, in the original to him inaccessible, as Mr Southey's knowledge of the language of Germany does not embrace the nomenclature of any of its philosophical schools or sects. Fourthly, to insult publicly the character of all Magazines—that included from which you are at the same time pilfering a jewel, (Mr Southey will—nay, must—ponder the word "pilfer,") is inconsistent with the common courtesies of life, and unworthy of a scholar and gentleman. Fifthly, the Magazine from which Mr Southey makes that extract (which I may mention was translated by me) was the London Magazine, published by Taylor and Hessey, and originally under the editorship of John Scott. Its chief supporters were Charles Lamb, William Hazlitt, Allan Cunningham, Thomas Hood, Reynolds, the most amiable and ingenuous Aytoun, whose beautiful and original Papers were afterwards collected and published in two volumes, and—let me not assume the semblance of that paltry humility which I despise—myself; and how dared Mr Southey to assert, that of any journal so supported, tinsel, trash, and insolent flippancy, were the staple commodities?

SHEPHERD. I cou'dna love as weel as admire ony man, however great and good, and Mr Soothey's baith, and has aye been generous to my genius, gin he hadna his wee bit weaknesses like ither folk—sae on the whole, I'm glad that he has been sae far left to himsell as to sneer at a' the Maggazins, and insult, in a lump, a' their editors, contributors, and subscribers, comprehending, I guess, nine-tenths o' the nation.

ENGLISH OPIUM-EATER. Neither shall a spurious delicacy deter me from declaring, even here, that there is more wit, and more wisdom, in the Periodical over which, Mr North, you preside, and to which there are now present two of the most distinguished contributors——

E

SHEPHERD. Say three, sir—say three, Mr De Quinshy—for when you do write—pity it's sae seldom—ye bang us a'——

ENGLISH OPIUM-EATER. Than in an equal number of any other miscellaneous volumes, the product of this or the preceding century, not excepting on the list all the best of Mr Southey's own, full as they are of wit and wisdom, and placing him deservedly in the first rank of our literature. Tinsel there may be, but it lies lightly over bars of the beaten gold; he must have an instinct for trash who can detect it among the necessaries and luxuries of life, that are monthly distributed to all classes, with most lavish, even prodigal profusion, from that inexhaustible Magazine; and as for insolent flippancy, that cannot be said, without senseless and blindfolded injustice, to be the staple commodity of a Periodical, of which one of the chief claims has long lain in those myriad-minded Dialogues, whose facete benignities, cordialities, and humanities, form a continued era in the philosophy of human life. Need I name, unworthy member as I am of this meeting—the Noctes Ambrosianæ!

OMNES. Hurra—hurra—hurra!

SHEPHERD. Gie me an unce o' opium, Mr De Quinshy——

ENGLISH OPIUM-EATER (*filling up drops of laudanum in the minimeter to 120.*) I give you a small dose to begin with, Mr Hogg——

SHEPHERD. Na—na—I was just jokin—I'm ower auld to begin on the poppy, I'se e'en keep to the maut.

ENGLISH OPIUM-EATER. To recur, for a brief space, to the article on Mr Southey in the Edinburgh Review. The editor, who, I am told, is an able and judicious man, ought not to have admitted it, at this juncture, or crisis, into his work. Mr Jeffrey and Mr Southey were open and avowed foes, Mr Jeffrey having been, beyond all question, the aggressor. The interest of the war was at an end, when that accomplished champion quitted the field; and the public is not prepared to regard, with any satisfaction, the renewal of the attack on Mr Southey, by a combatant whose shield bears no impress of any high emprise. He is, after all, but a mere skirmisher, and could not abide the onset of a man-at-arms.

NORTH. The editor should at least have assured himself, by a perusal of the Colloquies, that the young man's critique, as it is called, contained no such wilful misrepresentations as would disgrace a gentleman in the intercourse of private life.

ENGLISH OPIUM-EATER. Yet several such there are—gross mistatements of facts—to say nothing of the spirit of misinterpretation that pervades the whole article—like envenomed blood, circulated through a body bloated and discoloured by some rank disease. The mention of one will suffice; and, if not dead to shame, let the face of the reviewer blush brass, while he hangs down his head.

NORTH. The volumes are in the saloon-library. I will get them for you in a moment.

Mr NORTH *takes down the Colloquies from the shelf* Cæsar.

ENGLISH OPIUM-EATER. Beautifully bound!—By what artist?

NORTH. By Henderson.

ENGLISH OPIUM-EATER. Now, I will make a complete exposure of this prig—who, in seeking to render Mr Southey ridiculous, has made himself hateful.

SHEPHERD. Here's your health, sir, again, in a caulker.—Let's hear't.

ENGLISH OPIUM-EATER. In the Colloquy entitled—Walla-Crag—Sir Thomas More, having said that the progress of the useful arts, and the application of science to the purposes of common life, warrant the expectation, that whenever a state shall duly exercise its parental duties, there will be no trades which shall either hebetate the faculties or harden the heart,——

SHEPHERD. That, I fear, 's Utopian.

ENGLISH OPIUM-EATER. Not the less characteristic, on that account, Mr Hogg, of Sir Thomas More.

SHEPHERD. Eh?

ENGLISH OPIUM-EATER. Montesinos—the name Mr Southey adopts in these Colloquies—says, "Butchers will continue,"—and then adds, "I cannot but acknowledge, with good John Fox, that the sight of a slaughterhouse or shambles, if it does not disturb this clear conviction," (he is alluding to the mercifulness of cutting off suddenly and violently the existence of animals, who thus suffer less than those who die of disease or inanition,) "excites in me uneasiness and pain, as well as loathing."

SHEPHERD. Natural enough, surely, and likely to happen to a' men unaccustomed to see butchin'——

ENGLISH OPIUM-EATER. "They produce," continues Mr Southey, "a worse effect upon the persons employed on them;" and, again, he says, "perhaps, however, the hardness of heart which this occupation is believed to produce, may, in most cases, have been the cause wherefore it is chosen."

SHEPHERD. I can scarcely agree wi' that——

ENGLISH OPIUM-EATER. Allow me, Mr Hogg, to complete what I have got to say, without interruption. Here the Reviewer falls foul of Mr Southey for an alleged libel on Butchers. "Mr Southey," quoth he, "represents them as men who are necessarily reprobates—as men who must necessarily be reprobates—even in the most improved state of society—even, to use his own phrase, in a Christian Utopia." Here follows a forty-line page of high moral vituperation. Now, the charge is entirely false, and the Reviewer must have known it to be entirely false. For there is an alternation—an interchange of sentiment on this subject between the two interlocutors in the Dialogue. Sir Thomas More corrects this first wholly natural, but partly erroneous impression, made on the mind of Montesinos by the sight of the shambles, and shews him "how he is mistaken." Montesinos represents himself as being set right by the gracious Ghost, and says, "The best answer, however, to what I was unthinkingly disposed to credit, is, that the men engaged in this occupation are not found to furnish more than their numerical proportion of offenders to the criminal list; and that, as a body, they are by no means worse than any other set of men upon the same level." He then quotes Dr Beddoes, and enters somewhat deeper into the philosophy of the matter—observing, "because they are well fed, they are not exposed to the temptation which necessity brings with it, the mother of crime, as well as of arts; and their occupation being constant, they are likewise safe from the dangers of idleness. The relation, too, in which they stand to their customers, places them in a salutary degree of dependence, and makes them understand how much their own welfare depends upon civility and good conduct."

SHEPHERD. Macauley can hae nae principle—that's flat.

ENGLISH OPIUM-EATER. Sir Thomas More is then made to say to Montesinos—"You have thus yourself remarked, that men who exercise the occupation, which of all others at first sight appears most injurious to the human heart, and which inevitably must injure it to some degree, are, in point of fact, no worse than their neighbours, and much better than the vagrant classes of the population, and than those whose employment is casual. They are better, because they fare better, and are more under the influence of order. Improve the condition of others, bring them within the sphere of order, instead of leaving them merely within the reach—the chance reach, almost it may be called—of vindictive law, and the result will be the same."

TICKLER. Your exposure, sir, of the calumniator, is complete.

ENGLISH OPIUM-EATER. Allow me to read one short passage more from the Review—"And what reasons are given for a judgment so directly opposed to every principle of sound and manly morality?— *Merely this*—that he cannot abide the sight of their apparatus—that from certain peculiar associations, he is affected with disgust when he passes by their shops."

SHEPHERD. O man! I wadna be that Macauley for ony money. Hoo sma' he looks! Hoo sma' he sings! and hoo sma' he maun feel in the preevat consciousness, and the public conviction, o' haein deliberately traduced sic a man as Mr Soothey! without ony ither provocation, I jalouse, than the sense o' inferiority, that keeps gnawin like a veeper at the veetals o' the envious, and licks up party spite, or rather party spittle, a foul and fetid foam that drenches the worm's fangs—if it has gotten ony—and a' worms hae organs o' some sort or ither for bitin'—in a poison that only the mair blackens and embitters its ain rotten heart.

NORTH (*glancing over the article in the Review.*) What stuff's this about lawyers and soldiers?

ENGLISH OPIUM-EATER. All of the same kidney—silly sophistry or monstrous misrepresentations—which——

NORTH. The Whigs will chuckle and crow over—but the gentlemen of England tread scornfully under foot, as something smelling of a new kind of Cockneyism, even more offensive to the senses than that which stinks Little Britain.

SHEPHERD. Fling't frae you. Wi' a' your fawtes, sir, you never admit intill Maga ony malignant attacks on Genius, and Virtue, and Knowledge—and when or where were these Three ever united mair gloriously, and mair beautifully, and endearingly, than in Mr Soothey? Had Mr Soothey been a Whig—and had he leev'd in Embro' here—and had you written in that way about him—(a great heap o' maist impossible and contradictory supposes, I alloo—something like supposin' licht darkness, and straught crooked, and honey the jice o' aloes)—what a hullyballoo wou'd hae been raised again you, and what'n an assassin wou'dna ye hae been ca'd, like the Auld Man o' the Mountain! But ye never was an assassin, sir, ony mair than a Sant. O' a' the Great Poets o' the age, whatever their politics or their purity, you have sounded the eulogium, trumpet-tongued, till a' the warld rang wi' their fame. What'n a contrast atween Maga and the Ram!—But whisht, I heard a fisslin in the gallery!

NORTH. Leander!

The Horns sound, and enter ὁι περι AMBROSE.

SHEPHERD (*in continuation.*) Ggemm! and Fools!

Fourth Course.—Fowl.

TICKLER.

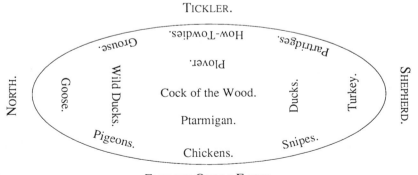

ENGLISH OPIUM-EATER.

SHEPHERD. I fancy the order of the day hauds gude alike through a' the coorses—every man helpin' himsell to the dish neist him;—and then to think hoo the verra seasons themsells accommodate their productions to our Festival!—Soops, Fish, Flesh, and Fool o' a' sorts in perfection, in spite o' the month—it's really curious, and shews hoo folk's the slaves o' habit.—Mr North, ony thing gaun on, up by yonner in Lunnun, in the literary department?

NORTH. I live so entirely out of the literary world, James, that——

SHEPHERD. Ye leeve in a' kind o' warlds, you warlock; and confoun me if I dinna believe you employ spies.

NORTH. None, my dear James, but these two eyes—now waxing somewhat dim—and these two ears, now waxing somewhat deaf—and that general sense of feeling spread by nature all over the surface of the body, all through its frame, and originating in the interior of the soul, by which one is made to feel and know a thousand indescribable things, far beyond the acquisition of the mere understanding, things of which the range grows, so it seems, wider and wider every day as we near the place of our final rest.

SHEPHERD. No—I canna say I do—but what's gaun on in Lunnun in the book-way?

NORTH. Sotheby has published three Specimens of his translation of Homer—The First Book of the Iliad—the Parting between Hector and Andromache—and the Shield of Achilles.

TICKLER. A bold, nay, a rash man, to enter the lists with Pope.

SHEPHERD. Wi' Pop? What for no? I've heard there's a great difference atween Pop's Homer and Homer's Homer, and I can weel believ't——

TICKLER. And so perhaps will there be found to be between Sotheby's Homer and Homer's Homer—James—a great or greater——

NORTH. Sotheby's Georgics stamped him the best translator in Christendom. That was, in my opinion, a more difficult achievement than an equally admirable translation of the Iliad. I have read his Specimens—and in an early Number—perhaps the next—intend to sift them thoroughly, comparing all the fine or difficult passages in the original, with Pope, Hobbes, Chapman, Cowper—and my friend, Mr Sotheby, who will probably be found, in the whole, to have excelled all his predecessors in this great task.

TICKLER. I'll back Pope for a rump and dozen——

NORTH. Done. Have you seen a little volume, James, entitled "Tales in Verse," by the Reverend H. M. Lyte—published by Marsh and Miller, and which seems to have reached a second edition?

SHEPHERD. Na!

NORTH. Now, that is the right kind of religious poetry. Mr Lyte shews how the sins and sorrows of man flow from irreligion, in simple but strong domestic narratives, told in a style and spirit reminding one sometimes of Goldsmith, and sometimes of Crabbe. A volume so humble in its appearance and pretensions runs the risk of being jostled off the highway into bye-paths—and indeed no harm if it should, for in such retired places 'twill be pleasant reading—pensive in the shade, and cheerful in the sunshine. Mr Lyte has reaped

> "The harvest of a quiet eye,
> That broods and sleeps on its own heart"—

and his Christian Tales will be read with interest and instruction by many a fireside. The Brothers is eminently beautiful; and he ought to give us another volume.

SHEPHERD. Wha's she, that Mrs Norton, that wrote the Sorrows o' Rosalie?

NORTH. Daughter of poor dear Tom Sheridan, who was indeed a star. Four generations of genius!—She is, I am told, even more beautiful than——

SHEPHERD. Her poetry? That'll no be easy, sir; for there's a saftness and a sweetness, and a brichtness, and abune a' an indefinite, and indescribable, and undefinable, and unintelligible, general, vague, dim, fleetin' speerit o' feminine sympathy and attraction—na, na, na, these are no the richt words ava—a celestial atmosphere o' the balm o' a thousand flowers, especially lilies and roses, pinks, carnations, violets, honeysuckle, and sweetbriar—an intermingled mawgic o' the sweetest scents in natur—heaven and earth breathin' upon ane anither's faces and breasts—hangin' ower yon bit pathetic poem, Rosalie, that inclines ane to remember the fair young lady that wrote it in his prayers!

NORTH. Good, kind, and true, my dear James. That *is* criticism.

SHEPHERD. It's a story of seduction, nae doot, and the prim-mou'd will purse up their lips at it, as if you were gaun to offer to kiss them—than whilk naething could be farther frae my intentions—however near it might be to their desires.

NORTH.

> "A tale of tears—a mortal story."

SHEPHERD. Oh! sir! hoo delicately virtuous women write about love! Chastity feels her ain sacred character—and, when inspired by genius, isna she a touchin' Muse! Modesty, Chastity's sister, though aiblins at times rather just a wee thocht ower doun-lookin', and as if a red light fell suddenly on a white lily or a white rose, blushin' no that deeply, but wi' a thin, fine, faint, fleetin' tint, sic as you may see within the inside o' a wee bit curled shell when walking on the yellow sea-shore, you haud it up atween you and the licht, and feel hoo perfectly beautifu' is the pearl——

NORTH. Mrs Norton is about to publish another poem—"The Undying One."—I do not like the title——

SHEPHERD. Nor me the noo. But, perhaps, when published, it may be felt to be appropriate; and at a' events, whatever objections there may be to the name, there'll be nane, I'm sure, to the speerit o' the poem.

NORTH. I remember reading, one day last summer, at the foot of Benlomond, a little poem, called Gabrielle, from the pen of Cyrus Redding,—the collaborateur of Campbell, I have heard, in the New Monthly,—which breathed a fine, fresh, free mountain spirit. The scene is laid in Switzerland—and the heroine goes mad with woe on the death of her parents under an avalanche. There are numberless true touches of nature, both in the pathetic and the picturesque, which prove the author to belong to the right breed. He is a Poet.

SHEPHERD. Wha's Bawl?

NORTH. Mr Ball is a young gentleman, at least I hope so, who has modestly avoided the more difficult and extensive subjects of song, and chosen one of the easiest and narrowest—The Creation.

SHEPHERD. Of coorse—in blanks?

NORTH. Yes, James, in blanks.—I see Mr Murray has advertised a "Descent into Hell."

SHEPHERD. That's rather alarmin'—is it to be performed by Mooshy Shawbert? I thocht Mr Murray wou'd hae keepit clear o' sic flams. The Descent into Hell! That's fearsome. You see, sir, as I was sayin' afore, last coorse, a' the pious poets are plageareesin' frae Pollok. They'll a' be forgotten in the Course of Time. Preserve me! there's a pun!

NORTH. And a very fair one, too, James.

SHEPHERD. A' this wark wi' religious poems reminds me o' the shootin' o' a wild swan ae day, about twenty years syne, by a shepherd, on the Loch. It was, indeed, a maist majestic, and, at the same time, beauteous creatur, seeming, as it lay dead on the greensward, baith foreign and indigenous, to belang equally to a' the snaw-mountains o' the earth. Hunders flocked frae a' pairts o' the Forest to gaze on't, and there was some talk o' stuffin't; but ae nicht it unaccountably disappeared—and a lassie, that was comin' by hersell across the moon-licht hills, said she saw something spiritual-like sailing amang the stars, on wings, that, as they winnowed the blue air, were noiseless as a cloud; but the simple thing, at the time, never thocht of a swan. Weel—naething would serve a' the Shepherds in the Forest, but to gang ilka idle day to the Loch a-swan-shootin'!—so they ca'd it—though never anither swan was shotten on't frae that day till this; but then the chiels now and then got a wild guse, and no unfrequently a wild dyuck; and on ae grand occasion, I remember Jock Linton bringin' to Fahope's an auld drake and an auld dyuck, wi' about a dizzen flappers, as he ca'd them, as tame as ony that ever waddled about the dubs o' a farm-yard. The truth is, they were Fahope's ain Quackies, that had stravaiged to the Loch; and daft Jock never doubted they were swans and cygnets. The application, sir, 's obvious. Pollok's poem is the bonny and magnificent wild swan; a' the lave are but geese or goslins, dyucks or dyucklins—yet every Cockney shooter's as proud as puir Jock Linton, and thinks himsell an Apollo— or, as Homer—that's Pop—says—"The God with the silver bow."

NORTH. Yet better even such "dilution of trashiness," than a fashionable novel!

SHEPHERD. Do you ken, sir, I really thocht "The Exclusives" no sae meikle amiss, considerin' that the author's a butler—or rather—I ax his pardon—a gentleman's gentleman, that is to say, a valley-de-sham. To be sure, it was rather derogatory to his dignity, and disgracefu' to the character which he had brocht frae his last place—to marry his master's cast-off kept-mistress; but then, on the other haun', she was a woman o' pairts, and o' some sma' education, and was a great help to him in his spellin' and grammar, and figures o' speech. The style, for that reason, o' the Exclusives, is rather yelegant—and had the limmer, after the loun had made her an honest woman, contributed the maitter too, the trash wou'd hae been far better worth readin', and if nae great favourite in the heart o' toons and cities, micht hae had its ain run amang the sooburbs.

NORTH. Mr Colburn has lately given us two books of a very different character, Richelieu and Darnley—by Mr James. Richelieu is one of the most spirited, amusing, and interesting romances I ever read; characters well drawn—incidents well managed—story perpetually progressive— catastrophe at once natural and unexpected—moral good, but not goody—and the whole felt, in every chapter, to be the work of a— Gentleman.

SHEPHERD. And what o' Darnley?

NORTH. Read, and judge.—The scribes who scrawl the fashionable novels compose a singular class. Reps of both sexes—including kept-mistresses and kept men—fancy men, as they are called in St Giles's;— married women, with stains on their reputations as well as on their gowns, labouring under the imputation of ante-nuptial children; unmarried women, good creatures enough, and really not immodest, but who have been *in*fortunate, and, victorious in literature, have yet met a fatal overthrow from love; gamblers, now billiard-makers in hells; fraudulent bankrupts in the Bench; members once returned and received for a rotten borough; rouès, who, at school and college, were reckoned clever, and, upon town, still cling to that belief, which is fast fading into pity, contempt, or scorn; forgers; borrowers; beggars; thieves; robbers; perhaps a murderer, for Jack Thurtell had a literary turn; and had he not been hanged, would, ere now, have produced a fashionable novel.

SHEPHERD. I wunner, if sic be the constitution o' the clan, that they dinna write better byucks. Blackguards and —— are aften gaily clever. I suspeck you omit, in your philosophical enumeration, the mere sumphs and sumphesses——

NORTH. Two or three men of birth and fashion do wield the pen, such as Lord Normanby, Mr Lister, and Mr Bulwer—they, in their respective styles, write well, and must be horribly annoyed at being brought into contact, by Mr Colburn's indiscriminate patronage, with the scurvy crew of both sexes whose *cacoethes scribendi* is not the worst itch that frets their cuticle.

SHEPHERD. Hoo's Murray's Family Library gettin' on, sir?

NORTH. Swimmingly, soaringly. Allan Cunningham's Lives of the Painters—I know not which of the two volumes is best—are full of a fine and an instructed enthusiasm. He speaks boldly, but reverentially, of genius, and of men of genius; strews his narrative with many flowers of poetry; disposes and arranges his materials skilfully; and is, in few words, an admirable critic on art—an admirable biographer of artists. Have you read Stebbings' History of Chivalry and the Crusades?—No. Then do. 'Tis the last and one of the best of the series in Constable's Miscellany—style clear, sentiments and opinions just, descriptions picturesque, and the stream of narrative strong and flowing. Mr Stebbings is a rising writer.

SHEPHERD. Are there nae mair o' them, sir?

NORTH. Several. The author of the Collegians has much genius. Leitch Ritchie writes powerfully; and Picken's Dominie's Legacy, three volumes of stories chiefly Scottish, well deserves a place in every library that prides itself on its own snug national corner, set apart for worthies born north of the Tweed.

SHEPHERD. I aye prophecied gude things o' that Picken; O but his "Mary Ogilvie" is verra affeckin. But, speakin' o' national corners, read ye that letter, sir, in the Examiner, abusin' a' Scotchmen, and the twa capital anes in answer?

NORTH. I did, James. The Examiner for some years past has been a very able paper—and frequently shews fight, even with the Standard. They are both good swordsmen—and sometimes bleed with mutual but not mortal wounds.

"Thrice is he armed who hath his quarrel just;"

and therefore the Examiner contends at odds. But he is "cunning of fence"—strong and nimble-wristed—and without fear. He is—savage as he sometimes seems, nay truculent—I verily believe an honest and generous man,—and while he propounds his own opinions in his leading columns as an honest man should do, why, it is not to the discredit of a generous man, perhaps now and then to give an obscure corner to some pauper who may have seen better days, that the poor wretch, shivering in rags and filthy in squalor, may have the only comfort of which his miserable condition now admits—for cheap as gin is, it must be purchased—the relief of spitting out his bile, as the diseased drunkard dreams on some object of his insane malignity, while the fetid dregs of his spleen, hawked up in a fit of coughing that crinkles of a galloping consumption, fall down a gob on the sore nakedness of his own unstockinged and shoeless feet.

SHEPHERD. Your defence o' the Examiner's kind, but no sound, sir. He ought to send the pauper to the poor-house. Nay, true charity would alloo him gin and forbid ink.

NORTH. There can be no bad blood in any good heart, when the question is debated, of the comparative glories of England and Scotland.

SHEPHERD. I'm no sure o' that, sir; dang't, the fire flees to my face whenever I articulate the first critical letter o' a syllable about to be uttered against Scotland by a Southron.

ENGLISH OPIUM-EATER. Far be it from me, Mr Hogg, to disallow to such feelings, natural as they are; and, therefore, since right in educated minds is but another name for natural—also right; far be it from me, I repeat——

SHEPHERD. I wasna speakin' o' you, sir, though aiblins I cou'd shew, even in your writins, certain sneering uses o' the word "Scotch," that you micht just as weel hae left to the Cockneys——

ENGLISH OPIUM-EATER. I indignantly deny the charge, Mr Hogg. A sneer is the resource of the illiberal and illogical——

SHEPHERD. And deevil tak me, and you too, sir, gin you belang to either o' thae twa classifications! for, as to liberality, I've seen you walkin' arm in arm wi' an atheist; and as to logic, were Aristotle himsell alive, ye wad sae scarify him wi' his ain syllogisms, as no to leave the silly Stagyrite the likeness o' a dog.

ENGLISH OPIUM-EATER. Of the illiberal and illogical—whereas from the earliest dawn of reason——

SHEPHERD. Nae mair about it, sir. I ax your pardon.

ENGLISH OPIUM-EATER. Mr Hogg, your mind, with all its rich endowments, must be singularly illogical to conclude——

SHEPHERD. Oh! Mr North—Mr North—I'm about to fa' into Mr De Quinshy's hauns, sae come to my assistance, for I canna thole bein' pressed up backwards, step by step, intul a corner, till an argument that's ca'd a clencher, clashes in your face, and knocks your head wi' sic force against the wa', that your croon gets a clour, leavin' a dent in the wainscoat.

ENGLISH OPIUM-EATER. Insulted, sir, by your boorish breakings-in on that continuous integrity of discourse, which must be granted to each speaker, as long as he usurps not either time or turn in conversation, else dialogue loses both its name and its nature, and colloquy ceases to be— the *esse* sunk in the *posse*——

SHEPHERD. I never interruppit a man when he was speakin' in a' my born days, sir. I'm just remarkable for the verra contrar, and for lettin' every body, baith Christian and Cockney, prose awa' till he's tired, sittin' mysell as patient as Job, and as dumb's Diogenes.

ENGLISH OPIUM-EATER. I hesitate not to affirm, that the Scottish intellect is degraded by an odious disputativeness, which truth compels me to denounce as a national depravity or disease, and which it is difficult—nay, I have found it impossible—to reconcile, in belief, with the pure possession of the sovereign reason.

NORTH. A true bill.

ENGLISH OPIUM-EATER. Thus private life, Scotland thorough, is polluted by the froth spurted from argumentative lips, and darkened by the frowns scowled from argumentative foreheads, and deafened by the noise grinded and grated from argumentative teeth——

SHEPHERD. Capital—capital—carry on, Mr De Quinshy, I'll no interrupt ye——

ENGLISH OPIUM EATER. While public life—witness Bar, Bench, and Pulpit—what is it but one eternal, harsh, dull debate, in which the understanding, a self-sufficient All-in-All, swallows feeling and imagination up—so that when the shallow and muddy waters have at nightfall been run off, lo! the stony channel dry, and the meadows round—irrigated say not—but corrugated with mud-seams—and the hopes of the husbandman or shepherd buried beneath an unseemly and unsavoury deposit of——

SHEPHERD. Stop. I say, stop. Heard ye e'er o' Dr Chawmers, or Dr Thamson, or Dr Gordon?—Oh ho! ma man—that froon on your face says no; but I'm no feared for your froons—no me indeed—and I just tell you, that like a' the ither lakers, you pheelosopheeze in the face o' facts—try to bend till they break in your verra hands a' practicals that staun in the way o' your ain theories—begin biggin' gran' steadins without ever diggin' ony foundation—which maist likely were ye to attempt doin', you would sune be smothered in a rush o' water and san'—an' feenally, delude yoursell intill the belief that it's a dwallin'-house or mansion o' granite or freestane, while all the rest o' mankind see wi' half an ee that it's composed o' clouds and mist, a mere castle in the air, and that, payin' nae taxes, it'll be flaffered awa to the Back o' Beyond outower the mountain-taps, whenever Lord Raise-the-Wind gets into the government, and the Duke o' Stormaway becomes Prime Minister.

NORTH. Noble—noble,—my dear James. Yet Mr De Quincey's charge against the prevailing character of the national mind holds, with some illustrious exceptions, good. We dig deep wells in dry places—with costly enginery and a pompous display of buckets; when, by using the divining rod of instinct, we might have detected many springs a few feet beneath the gowany greensward—nay, by observing "that inward eye that is the bliss of solitude," have seen flowing on the unsuspected waters of everlasting life!

SHEPHERD. Tickler! What for are ye no speakin'?

TICKLER. Bu!

SHEPHERD. What'n sort o' an answer's that, man, to a ceevil question?

TICKLER. Mu!

SHEPHERD. Curious mainners!—they may suit Southside, where ye're a kind o' king, or three-tailed Bashaw; but here, in Northside, they dinna answer, for here every man's every inch a king, and he that plays the tyrant yonner must here submit to sit the slave.

TICKLER. Whu! toothach—toothach!

SHEPHERD. A thoosan' pardons, my dear sir! Let me get a red-het skewer frae the kitchen, and burn the nerve.

ENGLISH OPIUM-EATER. Neither, Mr Hogg, can I bring my mind to assent to the proposition with which you ushered in the subject of our present discussion; *to wit,* that Englishmen are prone, as a people, to underrate the national virtues of Scotchmen. This allegation I hold to be the polar opposite of what is true; nor can I refrain from affirming, that manifold as are the excellencies of the Scottish character, there is a tendency, which philosophy may not approve, in the English mind—say rather the English imagination—monstrously and enormously to magnify their proportions—till of the entire frame and limbs thereof, thus rendered more than colossal, it may be said, in the language of Milton, "its stature reached the sky;" but reason recoils from all such dim delusions of dream-land, and sees in a Scotchman—no offence, I hope, gentlemen—a being apparently human, with sandy hair—high cheek-bones—light-blue eyes—wide mouth——

SHEPHERD. Aiblins wi' buck-teeth like mine—and oh! pray, do tell us, sir, for we're verra ignorant, and it's a subject o' great importance, what sort o' a nose?

ENGLISH OPIUM-EATER. The entire face acute, but coarse—intelligent, but not open——

SHEPHERD. Like North's, there—or Tickler's. Confound me gin I think there are twa sic auld men in a' England, whuther for face or feegur,—as for mainners, when Tickler's out o' the toothach, and North no in the gout or rudiments, they're perfect paragons, sic as never were seen in the South—and as for mind, ma faith if ye come to that, where's their match in a' your twal millions, though our poppilation's scarcely twa, wi' women and weans out o' a' proportion?

ENGLISH OPIUM-EATER. Nor can I imagine a charge—at once more false and loathsome—than one which I have heard even you, Mr Hogg, more than once utter against the English—as a people—that they are slaves to the passion of the palate—epicures and gluttons in one—or as the Scotch call it, sneeringly and insultingly—accompanying the reproach with a vulgar laugh, of which the lowest birth would be incapable but for the lowest breeding—"fond of good eating:"—whereas I appeal to the whole history, not of England alone, but of the world, in proof of this simple proposition—"that there exists not, nor ever did exist, a people comparable to the English, in the ascendency in their national character of the spirituous over the sensuous, in the due ordination of the correlates"——

SHEPHERD. I grant a' that—but still I manteen that the English are fonder—prooder they canna be—o' rost-beef and plumm-pudden, than the Scotch o' brose and haggis—that they speak mair and think mair—and muse and meditate atween meals mair—and when at meals, eat mair—and drink mair—and wipe the sweat aff their foreheads mair—and gie every kind o' proof mair o' a fu' stammach—than the Scotch;—and in proof o' that proposition, alloo me, sir, also to make an appeal, no to the haill history o' the warld, but to the pot-bellies ane sees waddlin' out frae front-doors as he spins through English toons and villages on the top o' a licht cotch—pot-bellies, Mr De Quinshy, o' a' sizes, frae the bouk o' my twa hauns expanded upon ane anither's finger-nebs—sae—up till, moderately speaking, the girth o' a hoghead—and no confined to the men, but extendin' to the women—and, pity me, even to the weans—na, to the verra infants (what sookers!) that a' look as they were crammed—instead o' wee piggies—for the second coorse o' the denner o' the King o' the Cannibals.

ENGLISH OPIUM-EATER (*suavely.*) Though I pity your prejudices, my dear Shepherd, I cannot but smile with pleasure at your quaint and humorous illustrations.

SHEPHERD. Argument and illustration, sir, a' in ane. Here's anither doobler. Nae fat wean born in Scotland o' Scotch parents, was ever exhibited as a show in a caravan. Answer me that—and confute the deduction? You canna. Again—there never was a Scotch Lambert. Mercy on us—a Scotchman fifty-seven stane wecht! Feenally, a' great eatin' fates hae been performed in England—sic as a beggar devourin' at ae meal, for a wager, atween twa sportin' characters, twal poun' o' lichts and livers, ae pail o' tripe, and anither o' mashed turnip peelin's,—or a farmer an equal wecht o' beef-steaks, a peck plumm-pudden, and a guse, washin' a' ower wi' twa imperial gallons—that's twal' bottles—o' yill.

ENGLISH OPIUM-EATER. A man worthy to be admitted—by acclamation—member of that society whose sittings are designated by the celebrated sound—Noctes Ambrosianæ!

SHEPHERD. Oh! Mr De Quinshy, Mr De Quinshy! can it be that ye ken sae little o' human natur, o' Scotland, and o' yoursell, as no to ken that this denner—which you wud bring forrit as a cowp-de-grace argumentum at ony man in proof o' the Scotch bein' fonder o' gude eatin' than the English—was provided wi' a' its Coorses—no abune the half o' them's come yet—entirely, though no exclusively—FOR YOU?

ENGLISH OPIUM-EATER. For me! Most monstrous!

NORTH. Poor people in Scotland, sir—I do not mean paupers—of whom, in ordinary times, there are few—live almost on nothing—meal and water—nor do they complain of a hard lot. The labouring classes in general, who are not in the same sense poor people, feed not so fully, believe me, in Scotland as in England.

SHEPHERD. Nor sae frequently in ae day. Five times is common in England. In Scotland, never mair nor three—often but twa—and never nane o' your pies and puddens! rarely flesh-meat, except——

NORTH. And thus, Mr De Quincey, as the appetites are very much habits, "good eating," among the lower orders in Scotland, is an indulgence or enjoyment never thought of, beyond the simple pleasure of the gratification of hunger, and of the restoration of strength and spirits so supplied. Believe me, my dear sir, it is so; whereas in England it assuredly is otherwise—though not to any degrading pitch of sensuality;—there the labouring man enjoys necessaries which here we should reckon luxuries of life.

SHEPHERD. Pies! pies! raised crust pies! Puddens! puddens! rice, bread, and egg puddens!

NORTH. The whole question lies in a nutshell. England has long been a great, powerful, rich, highly-civilized country, and has equalled, if not excelled, all the countries of modern Europe in all the useful and fine arts, in all the sciences, in all literature, and in all philosophy. Her men, as Campbell, himself a glorious Scotchman, has nobly exulted to declare, "are of men the chief,"—as Wordsworth, himself a glorious Englishman, has nobly exulted to declare,

"Are sprung
Of earth's first blood, have titles manifold."

During her long course of glory, she has produced from her celestial soil children of celestial seed—unequalled names—Shakspeare, Spenser,

Milton, Newton, Bacon, and other giants who scaled heaven not to storm it, but to worship and adore. Scotland has enjoyed but a single century, it may be said, of full intellectual light. She has not slept nor slumbered beneath the "rutili spatia ampla diei," but uplifted her front in inspiration to the auspicious heavens. Genius, too, has sprung fair and stately from her soil, and eyed the stars shining in fitful beauty through her midnight storms. She too has had, and has, her poets and philosophers—"a glorious train attending;"—transfigured by the useful arts, her old mountains shout aloud for joy—the fine arts have wreathed round the brows of her cities a towery diadem, and filled with lovely imagery her halls and temples. "Science has frowned not on her humble birth,"— while Religion, the source of the highest inspiration, loves her blue skies and green fields with an especial love.

SHEPHERD. Stop. Ye canna impruv' that—and it's God's truth, every word o't—is na't, Mr De Quinshy?

ENGLISH OPIUM-EATER. Will you accept from me, Mr North, an essay, to be entitled, "Comparative Estimate of the English and Scotch Character?"

NORTH. My dear sir, when did I ever decline an article of yours?

SHEPHERD. Faith he seldom gies ye an opportunity—about twice, may be, in the three years.

NORTH. Why, Scotland is making great strides even in Sculpture. Gibson and Campbell are the most eminent young sculptors now in Rome. Scoular and Steele are following in their footsteps. At home, Fletcher shews skill, taste, and genius—and Lawrence Macdonald, equal to any one of them, if not, indeed, superior to them all—after displaying in groups or single figures, of children, "boys and virgins," and maidens in their innocent prime, a finest sense of beauty and of grace, that kindles human tenderness by touches of the ideal and divine—has lately nobly dared to take a flight up to a higher sphere, and, in his Ajax and Patroclus, his Thetis and Achilles, essayed, and with success that will soon spread wide his fame, the Heroic in Art, such as gave visible existence in Greece to her old traditions—and peopled the groves and gardens, and pillared porticoes of Athens, with gods and demigods, the tutelary genii of the Acropolis on her unconquered hill.

SHEPHERD. That's beautifu'. You maun gie us an article on Sculpture.

NORTH. I will—including a critical account of those extraordinary works of two original, self-taught geniuses, Thom and Greenshields— Tam o' Shanter and Souter Johnny—and the Jolly Beggars. The king-doms of all the Fine Arts have many provinces—why not Sculpture?

SHEPHERD. Aye, why no?

NORTH. The Greek Tragedy, James, was austere, in its principles, as the Greek Sculpture. Its subjects were all of ancestral and religious consecration; its style, high, and heroic, and divine, admitted no intermixture even of mirth, or seldom and reluctantly,—much less of grotesque and fantastic extravagancies of humour,—which would have marred the consummate dignity, beauty, and magnificence of all the scenes that swept along that enchanted floor. Such was the spirit that shone on the soft and the stately Sophocles. But Shakspeare came from heaven—and along with him a Tragedy that poured into one cup the tears of mirth and madness; shewed Kings one day crowned with jewelled diadems, and another day with wild wisps of straw; taught the Prince who, in single combat,

> "Had quench'd the flame of hot rebellion
> Even in the rebels' blood,"

to moralize on the field of battle over the carcass of a fat buffoon wittily simulating death among the bloody corpses of English nobles; nay, shewed the son—and that son, prince, philosopher, paragon of men—jocularly conjuring to rest his Father's Ghost, who had revisited earth "by the glimpses of the moon, making night hideous."

SHEPHERD. Stop—stop—sir. That's aneuch to prove your pint. Therefore, let the range o' sculpture be extended, so as to comprehend sic subjects as Tam O'Shanter and Souter Johnny—The Jolly Beggars——

NORTH. Well, James—Of this more hereafter. You see my drift.

SHEPHERD. Isna Galt's Lowrie Todd indeed maist amusin'?

NORTH. It is indeed;—our friend's genius is as rare and original as ever—the field, too, he treads, is all his own—and it has yielded a rich harvest. By the bye, the Editor of the Monthly Review is a singular person. He thinks Sir Walter Scott's History of Scotland meagre, feeble, and inaccurate; John Bowring no linguist, and a mere quack of no talents; Galt he declares he never, till very lately, heard of; and the Double Number of Blackwood's Magazine for February was, in his opinion, dull, stupid, and——

SHEPHERD. O the coof! Wha is he?

NORTH. For fourteen years, James, he was Hermit to Lord Hill's Father.

SHEPHERD. Eh?

NORTH. He sat in a cave in that worthy Baronet's grounds, with an hour-glass in his hand, and a beard once belonging to an old goat—from sunrise to sunset—with strict injunctions to accept no half-crowns from visitors—but to behave like Giordano Bruno.

SHEPHERD. That's curious. Wha had the selection o' him—think ye?—But what's this I was gaun to say?—Ou, aye—heard ye ever Knowles's Lectures on Dramatic Poetry?

NORTH. I have—They are admirable—full of matter—elegantly written, and eloquently delivered. Knowles is a delightful fellow—and a man of true genius.

The Horns sound for the Fifth Course—"The Gloomy Nicht is gatherin' fast." Enter Picardy, &c. The Pipe is obstructed—the Gas Orrery extinguished—and a strange hubbub heard in the mirk.—Finis.

Extracts.

1. Odoherty's Song of the Ettrick Shepherd
(from Noctes 7: March 1823)

ODOHERTY. (*Sings, accompanying himself on the trombone.*)

I.

Greek and Latin
Will come pat in
Our Chaldean Shepherd's page.
With geology,
And petrology,
Sans apology,
He, he alone is born to cram our age. (*bis.*)

II.

'Tis He will tickle ye
With Molliculi,
Pouzzolanum, Schorl, and Schist;
'Tis he will bristle,
With cone and crystal,
His shepherd's whistle
Is now, in loathing and high scorn, dismist. (*bis.*)

III.

Show your glory
In shells and scoriæ!
Pour your lava, drop your spar!—
With Stalactites,
And Pyrites,
And Zeolites,
Hogg now will make thee stare, prodigious Parr! (*bis.*)

IV.

When he prints it out,
The French Institute
Will enrol one Scotchman more;—
How we'll caper,
When Supplement Napier,
For a physical paper,
Bows low, nor bows in vain, by Altrive's shore! (*bis.*)

V.

Grasp your slate, sir,
Scratch your pate, sir,
You must speak—the world is dumb!
Logic, Rhet'rick,
Chemic, Metric,
Fresh from Ettrick,
With glorious roar, and deaf'ning deluge come! (*bis.*)

2. Mullion Takes Opium
(from Noctes 12: October 1823)

MULLION. Never, never, never, in all my born days, did I eat such a glorious platefull of kidneys as that which Mr Opium-Eater lately transmitted to me through the hands of our Ambrose. I feel as if I could bump my crown against the ceiling. I hae eaten the apple o' the tree of knowledge. I understand things I never had the least ettling of before. Will ony o' ye enter into an argument? Chuse your subject, and I'm your man, in theology, morality, anatomy, chemistry, history, poetry, and the fine arts. My very language is English, whether I will or no, and I am overpowered with a power of words.

THE OPIUM-EATER, (*aside to* TICKLER.) I fear that Mr Mullion's excessive animation is owing to a slight mistake of mine. I carelessly allowed a few grains of opium to slide out of my box into the plate of kidneys which Mr Hogg sent for my delectation; and ere I could pick them out, Mr Ambrose wafted away the poisoned dish to Mr Mullion, at a signal, I presume, understood between the parties.

MULLION. I say, Opium-Eater, or Opossum, or what do they call you, did you ever see an unicorn? What signifies an Egyptian ibis, or crocodile of the Nile—I have an unicorn at livery just now in Rose-Street. Tickler, will you mount? Noble subject for John Watson. No man paints an unicorn better.

NORTH. John Watson paints everything well. But (*aside to* THE

SHEPHERD) saw ye ever such extraordinary eyes in a man's head as in Mullion's?

MULLION. Francis Maximus Macnab's Theory of the Universe is the only sensible book I ever read. Mr Ambrose—Mr Ambrose—bring me the Scotsman.

THE SHEPHERD, (*to* NORTH.) I have heard there was something wrang wi' Mullion at school; and it's breaking out you see noo. He's gaen clean wud. I wus he mayna bite.

TICKLER. Sell your unicorn to Polito, Mullion.

MULLION. Polito!—ay, a glorious collection of wild beasts—a perfect House o' Commons; where each tribe of beasts has its representative. Mild, majestic, towzy-headed, big-pawed, lean-hurdied lion, saw ye ever Mungo Park? Tiger, tiger, royal tiger—jungle-jumping, son-o'-Sir-Hector-Munro-devouring tiger! (*Rises.*)

THE SHEPHERD. Whare are you gaun?—Wait an hour or twa, and I'll see ye hame.

MULLION. I am off to the Pier of Leith. What so beautiful as the sea at midnight! A glorious constellation art thou, O Great Bear! Hurra! hurra!
Exit, without his hat.

THE OPIUM-EATER. I must give this case, in a note, to a new edition of my Confessions. If Mr Mullion did really eat all the kidneys, he must now have in his stomach that which is about equal to 570 drops of laudanum.

THE SHEPHERD. Eat a' the kidneys!—That he did, I'll swear.

THE OPIUM-EATER. Most probably, Mr Mullion will fall into a state of utter insensibility in a couple of hours. Convulsions may follow, and then—death.

THE SHEPHERD. Deevil the fears. Mullion 'ill dee nane. I'll wauger he'll be eating twa eggs to his breakfast the morn, and a shave o' the red roun'; luking fra him a' the time wi' een as sharp as darnin' needles, and paunin' in his cup for mair sugar.

3. The Shepherd Swallows a Fly
(from Noctes 14: April 1824)

NORTH. ... But what were we talking about a little ago?

THE SHEPHERD. Never ask me siccan a like question. Ye ken weel aneuch that I never remember a single thing that passes in conversation. But may I ask gin you're comin' out to the fishing this season?

NORTH. Apropos. Look here, James. What think you of these flies? Phin's, of course. Keep them a little farther off your nose, James, for they are a dozen of devils, these black heckles. You observe,—dark yellow body—black half heckle, and wings of the mallard, a beautiful brown—

gut like gossamer, and the killing Kirby.

THE SHEPHERD. I'll just put them into my pouch. But, first, let me see how they look sooming.

Draws out a fly, and trails it slowly along the punch in his tumbler,
which he holds up to the argand lamp—a present to Mr Ambrose
from Barry Cornwall.

O, man! that's the naturallest thing ever I saw in a' my born days. I ken whare theres a muckle trout lying at this very moment, below the root o' an auld birk, wi' his great snout up the stream, drawing in slugs and ither animalculas, into his vortex, and no caring a whisk o' his tail for flees; but you'se hae this in the tongue o' you, my braw fallow, before May-day. He'll sook't in saftly, saftly, without shewing mair than the lip o' him, and then I'll streck him, and down the pool he'll gaung, snoring like a whale, as gin he were descending in a' his power to the bottomless pit, and then up wi' a loup o' lightning to the verra lift, and in again into the water wi' a squash and a plunge, like a man gaun in to the douking, and then out o' ae pool into anither, like a kelpie gaun a-coorting, through alang the furds and shallows, and ettling wi' a' his might at the waterfa' opposite Fahope's house. Luk at him! luk at him! there he glides like a sunbeam strong and steady, as I give him the butt, and thirty yards o' the pirn—nae stane to stumble, and nae tree to fankle—bonnie green hills shelving down to my ain Yarrow—the sun lukin' out upon James Hogg, frae behint a cloud, and a breeze frae St Mary's Loch, chaunting a song o' triumph down the vale, just as I land him on the gowany edge of that grassy-bedded bay,

> Fair as a star, when only one
> Is shining in the sky.

NORTH. Shade of Isaac Walton!

THE SHEPHERD. I'm desperate thirsty—here's your health. Oh, Lord! What's this? what's this? I've swallowed the flee!

NORTH. (*starting up in consternation.*) Oh, Lord! What's this? what's this? I've trodden on a spike, and it has gone up to my knee-pan!—O my toe! my toe! But, James—James—shut not your mouth—swallow not your swallow—or you are a dead man. There—steady—steady—I have hold of the gut, and I devoutly trust that the hook is sticking in your tongue or palate. It cannot, must not be in your stomach, James. Oh!——

THE SHEPHERD. Oh! for Liston, wi' his instruments!

NORTH. Hush—hush—I see the brown wings.

Enter AMBROSE. Here, here is a silver spoon—I am all in a fluster. O dear, Mr North, will this do to keep dear Mr Hogg's mouth open, while you are—

NORTH. It is the soup-ladle, sir. But a sudden thought strikes me. Here is my gold ring.—I shall let it down the line, and it will disentangle the hook. Don't swallow my crest, my dear Shepherd. There—all's right—the black heckle is free, and my dear poet none the worse.

THE SHEPHERD, (*coughing out Mr North's gold ring.*) That verra flee shall grip the muckle trout. Mr Ambrose, quick,—countermand Liston. (*Mr Ambrose vanishes.*) I'm a' in a poor o' sweat—Do you hear my heart beating?

NORTH. Mrs Phin's tackle is so excellent that I felt confident in the result. Bad gut, and you were a dead man. But let us resume the thread of our discourse.

THE SHEPHERD. I have a sore throat, and it will not be weel till we soop. Tak my arm, and we'se gang into the banquetting-room. Hush—there's a clampering in the trance. It's the rush o' critics frae the pit o' the Theatre. They're coming for porter—and let's wait till they're a' in the tap-room, or ither holes. In five minutes you'll hear nae ither word than "Vandenhoff," "Vandenhoff."

NORTH. The shower is over, let us go; and never, James, would old Christopher North desire to lean for support on the arm of a better man.

THE SHEPHERD. I believe you noo—for I ken when you're serious and when you're jokin', and that's mair than every ane can say.

NORTH. Forgive, James, the testy humours of a gouty old man. I am your friend.

THE SHEPHERD. I ken that fu' brawly. Do you hear the sound o' that fizzing in the pan? Let's to our wark. But, North, say naething about the story of the flee in that wicked Magazine.

NORTH. Mum's the word. *Allons.*

4. The Age of Revolution
(from Noctes 15: June 1824)

TICKLER. Listen to me one moment more, ODoherty. The fact, sir, stands simply thus:—It is obvious to any one who is capable of casting a comprehensive eye over things, that there are three different great veins of thought and sentiment prevalent in this age of the world; and I hold it to be equally clear, that England has furnished at least one great poetical expositor and interpreter for each of the three. This, sir, is the Age of Revolution. It is an age in which earth rocks to and fro upon its foundations—in which recourse is had to the elements of all things—in which thrones, and dominations, and principles, and powers, and opinions, and creeds, are all alike subjected to the sifting of the winds of Intellect, and the tossing and lashing of the waves of Passion.—Now, there are three ways in which the mind of poetic power *may* look at all this—there are three parts among which it may choose. First, there is the spirit of scorn of that which is old—of universal distrust and derision, mingled up with a certain phrenzy of indignation and innovating fury— Here is Byron—Then there is the high heroic spirit of veneration for that which has been—that still deeper, that infinitely more philosophical distrust, which has for its object this very rage and storm of coxcombical innovation which I have been describing—This is Scott—the noble bard of the noble—the prop of the venerable towers and temples, beneath which our fathers worshipped and did homage in the days of a higher, a purer, a more chivalric race.—This is the voice that cries—*In defence—!*

> "Faster come, faster come,
>   Faster and faster,—
> Page, vassal, squire, and groom,
>   Tenant and master:
> Come as the winds come,
>   When forests are rending;
> Come as the waves come,
>   When navies are stranding!"

And there is yet a third spirit—the spirit of lonely, meditative, high-souled, and yet calm-souled men—of him who takes no part in sounding or obeying the war-pipe of either array—the far-off, philosophic contemplator, who, turning from the turmoil, out of which he sees no escape, and penetrated with a profound loathing of all this mighty clamour, about things, at the best, but fleeting and terrestrial, plunges, as it were, into the quiet, serene ocean-depths of solitary wisdom, there to forget the waves that boil upon the surface—there to brood over the images of eternal and undisturbed truth and beauty.—This is Wordsworth;—hear how *he* describes a poet's tomb.—

> "A convent—even a hermit's cell—
> Would break the silence of this dell.
> It is not quiet—is not ease,
> But something deeper far than these.
> The separation that is here
> Is of the grave—and of *austere*
> *And happy feelings of the dead:*
> And therefore was it rightly said,
> That Ossian, last of all his race,
> Lies buried in this lonely place."

5. Hogg, Byron, and Wordsworth
(from Noctes 17: November 1824)

MULLION. Well, well, James. But you and Byron took to each other famously, it seems?

HOGG. We were just as thick as weavers in no time. Ye see I had been jauntin aboot in that country for tway three weeks, seeing Wulson and Soothey, and the rest of my leeterary friends there. I had a gig with me— John Grieve's auld yellow gig it was—and as I was standing by mysell afore the inn door that evening, just glowring frae me, for I kent naebody in Ambleside, an be not the minister and the landscape painter, out comes a strapping young man frae the house, and off with his hat, and out with his hand, in a moment like. He seemed to think that I would ken him at ance; but seeing me bamboozled a thocht, (for he wasna sae very dooms like the capper-plates,) Mr Hogg, quo' he, I hope you will excuse me—my name is Byron—and I cannot help thinking that we ought to hold ourselves acquaintance.

MULLION. So you shook hands immediately, of course?

HOGG. Shook! Od! he had a good wrist of his ain; yet, I trow, I garred the shackle-bane o' him dinnle.

MULLION. August moment! Little did you then foresee either Don Juan or the Chaldee. What was your potation?

HOGG. Potation!—we had everything that was in the house—Claret, and Port, and ale, and ginger-beer, and brandy-wine, and toddy, and twist, an' a'; we just made a night on't. O, man, wasna this a different kind of behaviour frae that proud Don Wordsworth's? Od! how Byron leuch when I tell'd him Wordsworth's way wi' me!

MULLION. What was this?—I don't recollect to have heard it, Hogg.

HOGG. Toots! a'body has heard it—I never made ony concealment of his cauld, dirty-like behaviour. But, to be sure, it was a' naething but envy—just clean envy. Ye see I had never forgathered wi' Wordsworth before, and he was invited to dinner at Godswhittles, and down he came; and just as he came in at the east gate, De Quuncey and me cam in at the west; and says I, the moment me and Wordsworth were introduced, "Lord keep us a'!" says I, "Godswhittle, my man, there's nae want of poets here the day, at ony rate." Wi' that Wordsworth turned up his nose, as if we had been a' carrion, and then he gied a kind of a smile, that I thought was the bitterest, most contemptible, despicable, abominable, wauf, narrow-minded, envious, sneezablest kind of an attitude that I ever saw a human form assume—and "*Poet*S!" quo' he, (deil mean him!)— "PoetS, Mr Hogg?—Pray, where are they, sir?" Confound him!—I doubt if he would have allowed even Byron to have been a poet, if he had been there. He thinks there's nae real poets in our time, an it be not himself, and his sister, and Coleridge. He doesna make an exception in favour of Southey—at least to ony extent worth mentioning. Na, even Scott—would ony mortal believe there was sic a donneration of arrogance in this waurld?—even Scott I believe's not a *pawet,* gin you take his word—or at least his sneer for't.

MULLION. Pooh! we all know Wordsworth's weaknesses—the greatest are not without something of the sort. This story of yours, however, is a curious *pendant* to one I have heard of Wordsworth's first meeting with Byron—or rather, I believe, his only one.

HOGG. They had never met when Byron and me were thegither; for I mind Byron had a kind of a curiosity to see him, and I took him up to Rydallwood, and let him have a glimpse o' him, as he was gaun staukin up and down on his ain backside, grumblin out some of his havers, and glowering about him like a gawpus. Byron and me just reconnattred him for a wee while, and then we came down the hill again, to hae our laugh out. We swam ower Grasmere that day, breeks an a'. I spoilt a pair o' as gude corduroys as ever cam out of the Director-General's for that piece of fun. I couldna bide to thwart him in onything—he did just as he liket wi' me the twa days we staid yonder: he was sic a gay, laughing, lively, wutty fallow,—we greed like breether. He was a grand lad, Byron—nane of your blawn-up pompous laker notions about him. He took his toddy brawly.

MULLION. D—n the Lakers!

6. Skating at Duddingston
(from Noctes 24: February 1826)

TICKLER. Try the anchovies. I forget if you skate, Hogg?

SHEPHERD. Yes, like a flounder. I was at Duddingston Loch on the great day. Twa bands of music kept chearing the shade of King Arthur on his seat, and gave a martial character to the festivities. It was then, for the first time, that I mounted my cloak and spurs. I had a young leddie, you way weel guess that, on ilka arm; and it was pleasant to feel the dear timorous creturs clinging and pressing on a body's sides, every time their taes caught a bit crunkle on the ice, or an embedded chucky-stane. I thocht that between the twa they wad never hae gei'n ower till they had pu'd me doun on the bread o' my back. The muffs were just amazing, and the furbelows past a' enumeration. It was quite Polar. Then a' the ten thousand people (there could na' be fewer) were in perpetual motion. Faith, the thermometer made them do that, for it was some fifty below zero. I've been at mony a bonspeil, but I never saw such a congregation on the ice afore. Once or twice it cracked, and the sound was fearsome,—

a lang, sullen growl, as of some monster starting out o' sleep, and raging for prey. But the bits o' bairns just leuch, and never gied ower sliding; and the leddies, at least my twa, just gied a kind o' sab, and drew in their breath, as if they had been gaun in naked to the dooken on a cauld day; and the mirth and merriment were rifer than ever. Faith, I did make a dinner at the Club-house.

TICKLER. Was the skating tolerable?

SHEPHERD. No; intolerable. Puir conceited whalps! Gin you except Mr Tory o' Prince's Street, wha's a handsome fallow, and as good a skaiter as ever spread-eagled; the lave a' deserved drowning. There was Henry Cowburn, like a dominie, or a sticket minister, puttin' himself into a number o' attitudes, every ane clumsier and mair ackward than the ither, and nae doubt flatterin himself that he was the object o' universal admiration. The hail loch was laughing at him. The cretur can skate nane. Jemmy Simpson is a feckless bodie on the ice, and canna keep his knees straught. I couldna look at him without wondering what induced the cretur to write about Waterloo. The Skatin' Club is indeed on its last legs.

TICKLER. Did you skate, James?

SHEPHERD. That I did, Timothy—but ken you hoo? You will have seen how a' the newspapers roosed the skatin' o' an offisher, that they said lived in the Castle. Fools!—it was me—naebody but me. Ane o' my two leddies had a wig in her muff, geyan sair curled on the frontlet, and I pat it on the hair o' my head. I then drew in my mouth, puckered my cheeks, made my een look fierce, hung my head on my left shouther, put my hat to the one side, and so, arms a-kimbo, off I went in a figure of 8, garring the crowd part like clouds, and circumnavigating the frozen ocean in the space of about two minutes. "The curlers quat their roaring play," and every tent cast forth its inmates, with a bap in the ae haun' and a gill in the ither, to behold the Offisher frae the Castle. The only fear I had was o' my long spurs;—but they never got fankled; and I finished with doing the 47th Proposition of Euclid, with mathematical precision. Jemmy Simpson, half an hour before, had fallen over the *Pons assinorum*.

TICKLER. Mr Editor, I fear that if in your articles you follow the spirit that guides your conversation, you will be as personal as Mr North himself. No intrusion on private character.

SHEPHERD. Private character! If Mr James Simpson, or Mr Henry Cockburn, or myself, exhibit our figures or attitudes before ten thousand people, and cause all the horses in the adjacent pastures to half-die of laughter, may I not mention the disaster? Were not their feats celebrated in all the newspapers? There it was said that they were the most elegant and graceful of volant men. What if I say in the next Number of the Magazine, that they had the appearance of the most pitiful prigs that ever exposed themselves as public performers? Besides, they are by far too old for such nonsense. They are both upwards of fifty, and seem much older. At that time of life they should give their skates to their boys.

7. Haggises, and the Old Town
(from Noctes 26: June 1826)

SHEPHERD. ... Tell me about the Haggis-Feast.

TICKLER. A dozen of us entered our Haggises for a sweepstakes—and the match was decided at worthy Mrs Fergusson's, High Street. My Haggis (they were all made, either by our wives or cooks, at our respective places of abode) ran second to Meg Dods's. The Director General's (which was what sporting men would have called a roarer) came in third—none of the others were placed.

SHEPHERD. Did ony accident happen amang the Haggises? I see by your face that ane at least amang the dizzen played the deevil. I recollec' ance the awfu'est scene wi' a Haggis, in auld Mr Laidlaw's house. It was a great muckle big ane, answering to Robert Burns's description, wi' its hurdies like twa distant hills, and occupied the centre o' the table, round whilk sat about a score o' lads and lasses. The auld man had shut his een to ask a blessing, when some evil speerit put it into my head to gie the bag a slit wi' my gulley. Like water on the breakin' o' a dam, out rushed, in an instantawneous overflow, the inside o' the great chieftain o' the Pudding race, and the women-folk brak out into sic a shriek, that the master thocht somebody had drapped down dead. Meanwhile, its contents didna stop at the edge o' the table, but gaed ower wi' a sclutter upon the lads' breeks and the lassies' petticoats, burnin' the wearers to the bane; for what's hetter than a haggis?

TICKLER. Nothing on this side of the grave.

SHEPHERD. What a skirlin'! And then a' the colleys began yelpin' and youffin', for some o' them had their tauted hips scalded, and ithers o' them could na see for the stew that was rinnin' down their chafts. Glee'd Shooshy Dagleish fell a' her length in the thickest part o' the inundation, wi' lang Tommy Potts aboon her, and we thocht they would never hae foun' their feet again, for the floor was as sliddery as ice—and——

NORTH. Now, James, were you to write that down, and give it to the world in a book, it would be called coarse.

SHEPHERD. Nae doubt. Everything nat'ral, and easy, and true, is ca'd coarse—as I think I hae observed afore noo in this verra room—and what has been the consequence o' sic puling criticism? Wishy washy water-colours, sae faint that you canna tell a tree frae a tether, or a doug frae a soo, or a fish frae a fule, or a man frae a woman. Why, Mr North, I'd lay my lugs, that gin our conversation here were a' taen doon in short hand, and prented in the Magazine, there wadna be wantin' puir cheepin' fuizenless cretures to ca't coorse.

NORTH. Theocritus has been blamed, James, on the same score.

SHEPHERD. The Allan Ramsay o' Sicily, as I hae heard; and the best pastoral poet o' the ancient warld. Thank God, Mr North, the fresh airs o' heaven blaw through your shepherd's hut, and purify it frae a' pollution. Things hae really come to a queer pass when towns' bodies, leevin' in shops and cellars, and garrets and common stairs, and lanes and streets that, wi' a' their fine gas lamp-posts, are pestilential wi' filth and foulzie; and infested wi' lean, mangy dowgs, ruggin' out stinkin' banes frae the sewers; and wi' auld wives, like broken-backed witches, that are little mair than bundles o' movin' rags, clautin' among the bakiefu's o' ashes; and wi' squads o' routin' or spewin' bullies o' chiels, staggerin' hame frae tripe-soopers, to the disturbance o' the flaes in their yellow-tinged-lookin' blankets; and wi' anes, and twas, and threes, o' what's far waur than a' these, great lang-legged, tawdry, and tawpy limmers, standin' at closes, wi' mouths red wi' paint, and stinkin' o' gin like the bungs o' speerit-casks, when the speerit has been years in the wudd; while far and wide ower the city (I'm speakin' o' the Auld Town) you hear a hellish howl o' thieves and prostitutes carousin' on red herrings and distillery-whusky, deep down in dungeons aneath the verra stanes o' the street; and faint far-aff echoes o' fechts wi' watchmen, and cries o' "murder, murder—fire, fire" drowned in the fiercer hubbub o' curses, endin' in shouts o' deevilish lauchter—I say—What was I gaun to say, sir? something about the peace and pleasantness o' Mount Benger, was't no? and o' the harmless life and conversation o' us shepherds amang the braes, and within the murmurs o' the sheep-washing Yarrow.

NORTH. I hope it was so—for that dark picture needs relief.

8. The Hackney Coach
(from Noctes 27: July 1826)

SHEPHERD. ... as for the hackney-cotch——

TICKLER. The meanest of miseries!

SHEPHERD. It's waur than sleepin' in damp sheets. You haena sat twa hunder yards till your breeks are glued to the clammy seat, that fin's saft and hard aneath you, at ane and the same time, in a maist unaccountable manner. The auld, cracked, stained, faded, tarnished, red leather lining stinks like a tan-yard. Gin' you want to let down the window, or pu't up, it's a' alike; you keep ruggin' at the lang slobbery worsted till it cums aff wi' a tear in your haun', and leaves you at the mercy o' wind and weather—then what a sharp and continual ratttle o' wheels! far waur than a cart; intolerable aneuch ower the macadam, but, Lord hae mercy on us, when you're on the causeway! you cou'd swear the wheels are o' different sizes; up wi' the tae side, down wi' the tither, sae that nae man can be sufficiently sober to keep his balance. Puch! puch! what dung-like straw aneath your soles; and as for the roof, sae laigh, that you canna keep on your hat, or it'll be dunshed down atower your eebrees; then, if there's sax or eight o' you in ae fare——

9. The Guse-Dubs of Glasgow
(from Noctes 28: October 1826)

SHEPHERD. If you interrup me, Mr North, I'll no scruple to interrup you, in spite o' a' my respect for your age and endowments. But was ye ever in the Guse-dubs o' Glasgow? Safe us a', what clarty closses, narrowin' awa' and darkening down, some stracht, and some serpentine, into green middens o' baith liquid and solid matter, soomin' wi' dead cats and auld shoon, and rags o' petticoats that had been worn till they fell aff and wad wear nae langer, and then ayont the midden, or say, rather surrounding the great central stagnant flood o' fulzie, the wundows o' a coort, for a coort they ca'd, some wi' panes o' glass and panes o' paper time about, some wi' what had ance been a hat in this hole, and what had been a pair o' breeks in that hole, and some without lozens athegether; and then siccan fierce faces o' lads that had enlisted, and were keeping themselves drunk night and day on the bounty money, before ordered to join the regiment in the Wast Indies, and die o' the yellow fever! And what fearsome faces o' limmers, like she-demons, dragging them down into debauchery, and haudin' them there, as in a vice, when they hae gotten them down,—and, wad ye believe't, swearin' and dammin' ane anithers' een, and then lauchin', and tryin' to look lo'esome, and jeerin' and leerin' like Jezabels.

TICKLER. Hear! hear! hear!

SHEPHERD. Dive down anither close, and you hear a man murderin' his wife, up stairs in a garret. A' at ance flees open the door at the stairhead, and the mutchless mawsey, a' dreepin' wi' bluid, flings herself frae the tap-step o' the flicht to the causeway, and into the nearest changehouse, roaring in rage and terror, twa emotions that are no canny when they chance to forgather, and ca'in' for a constable to tak haud o' her gudeman, who has threatened to ding out her brains wi' a hammer, or cut her throat wi' a razor.

NORTH. What painting, Tickler! What a Salvator is our Shepherd!

SHEPHERD. Down anither close, and a battle o' dugs! A bull-dug and a mastiff! The great big brown mastiff mouthin' the bull-dug by the verra hiunches, as if to crunch his back, and the wee white bull-dug never seemin' to fash his thoomb, but stickin' by the regular set teeth o' his under-hung jaw to the throat o' the mastiff, close to the jugular, and no to be drawn aff the grip by twa strong baker-boys puin' at the tail o' the tane, and twa strong butcher-boys puin' at the tail o' the tither—for the mastiff's maister begins to fear that the veeper at his throat will kill him outright, and offers to pay a' betts and confess his dug has lost the battle. But the crood wush to see the fecht out—and harl the dugs that are noo worryin' ither without ony growlin'—baith silent, except a sort o' snortin' through the nostrils, and a kind o' guller in their gullets—I say, the crood harl them out o' the midden ontil the stanes again—and "Weel dune, Cæsar."—"Better dune, Veeper."—"A mutchkin to a gill on whitey."—"The muckle ane canna fecht."—"See how the wee bick is worryin' him now, by a new spat on the thrapple."—"He wud rin awa' 'gin she wud let him loose."—"She's just like her mither that belanged to the caravan o' wild beasts."—"Oh man, Davie, but I wud like to get a breed out o' her, by the watch-dug at Bell-meadow bleachfield, that killed, ye ken, the Kilmarnock carrier's Help in twunty minutes, at Kingswell——"

10. The Fish-Wives of Edinburgh
(from Noctes 29: November 1826)

NORTH. What think ye, James, of this plan of supplying Edinburgh with living fish?

SHEPHERD. Gude or bad, it sall never hae my countenance. I cudna thole Embro without the fish-wives, and gin it succeeded, it would be the ruin o' that ancient race.

TICKLER. Yes, James, there are handsome women among these Nereids.

SHEPHERD. Weel-faured hizzies, Mr Tickler. But nane o' your winks— for wi' a' their fearsome tauk, they're decent bodies. I like to see their well-shaped shanks aneath their short yellow petticoats. There's some- thing heartsome in the creak o' their creeshy creels on their braid backs, as they gang swinging up the stey streets without sweatin', with the leather belt atower their mutched heads, a' bent laigh down against five stane load o' haddocks, skates, cods, and flounders, like horses that never reest—and, oh man, but mony o' them hae musical voices, and their cries afar aff make my heart-strings dirl.

NORTH. Hard-working, contented, cheerful creatures, indeed, James, but unconscionable extortioners, and——

SHEPHERD. Saw ye them ever marchin' hamewards at nicht, in a baun of some fifty or threescore, down Leith Walk, wi' the grand gas lamps illuminating their scaly creels, all shining like silver? And heard ye them ever singing their strange sea-sangs—first half a dizzin o' the bit young anes, wi' as saft vices and sweet as you could hear in St George's Kirk on Sabbath, half singin' and half shoutin' a leadin' verse, and then a' the mithers, and granmithers, and ablins great-granmithers, some o' them wi' vices like verra men, gran' tenors and awfu' basses, joinin' in the chorus, that gaed echoing roun' Arthur's Seat, and awa ower the tap o' the Martello Tower, out at sea ayont the end o' Leith Pier? Wad ye believe me, that the music micht be ca'd a hymn—at times sae wild and sae mournfu'—and then takin' a sudden turn into a sort o' queer and outlandish glee? It gars me think o' the saut sea-faem—and white mew-wings wavering in the blast—and boaties dancin' up and down the billow vales, wi' oar or sail—and waes me—waes me—o' the puir fishing smack, gaun down head foremost into the deep, and the sighin' and the sabbin' o' widows, and the wailin' o' fatherless weans!

11. A Military Execution
(from Noctes 31: March 1827)

SHEPHERD. ... ance—it's a lang time syne—I saw a sodger shot—dead, sir, as a door-nail, or a coffin-nail, or ony ither kind o' nail.

NORTH. Was it in battle, James?

SHEPHERD. In battle?—Na, na; neither you nor me was ever fond o' being in battle at ony time o' our lives.

NORTH. I was Private Secretary to Rodney when he beat Langara, James.

SHEPHERD. Haud your tongue!—What a crowd on the Links that day! But a' wi' fixed whitish faces—nae speakin'—no sae muckle as a whisper—a frozen dumbness that nae wecht could break!

NORTH. You mean the spectators, James.

SHEPHERD. Then the airmy appeared in the distance; for there were three hail regiments, a' wi' fixed beggonets; but nae music—nae music for a while at least, till a' at ance, mercy on us! we heard, like laigh sullen thunder, the soun' o' the great muffled drum, aye played on, ye ken, by a black man; in this case, an African neegger, sax feet four; and what bangs he gied the bass—the whites o' his een rowin' about as if he was glad, atween every stroke!

NORTH. I remember him—the best pugilist then going, for it was long before the days of Richmond and Molineaux—and nearer forty than thirty years ago, James.

SHEPHERD. The tread of the troops was like the step o' ae giant—sae perfate was their discippleen—and afore I weel kent that they were a' in the Links, three sides o' a square were formed—and the soun' o' the great drum ceased, as at an inaudible word of command, or wavin' o' a haun, or the lowerin' o' a banner. It was but ae man that was about to die—but for that ae man, had their awe no hindered them, twenty thousan' folk wad at that moment hae broken out into lamentations and rueful cries—but as yet not a tear was shed—not a sigh was heaved—for had a' that vast crowd been sae mony images, or corpses raised up by cantrip in their death-claes, they couldna hae been mair motionless than at that minute, nor mair speechless than that multitude o' leevin' souls!

NORTH. I was myself one of the multitude, James.

SHEPHERD. There, a' at ance, hoo or whare he cam frae nane could tell, there, I say, a' at ance stood the Mutineer. Some tell't me afterwards that they had seen him marchin' along, twa three yards ahint his coffin, wi' his head just a wee thocht inclined downwards, not in fear o' man or death, but in awe o' God and judgement, keepin' time wi' a military step that was natural to him, and no unbecoming a brave man on the way to the grave, and his een fixed on the green that was fadin' awa for ever and ever frae aneath his feet; but that was a sicht I saw not—for the first time I beheld him he was standin', a' unlike the ither men, in the middle o' that three-sided square, and there was a shudder through the hail multitude, just as if we had been a' standin', haun in haun, and a natural philosopher had gien us a shock o' his electrical machine. "That's him—that's him— puir, puir fallow!—Oh! but he's a pretty man!"—Such were the ejaculations frae thousan's of women, maist o' them young anes, but some o' them auld, and grey-headed aneath their mutches, and no a few wi' babies sookin' or caterwailin' at their breasts.

NORTH. A pretty girl fainted within half-a-dozen yards of where I stood.

SHEPHERD. His name was Lewis Mackenzie—and as fine a young man he was as ever stepped on heather. The moment before he knelt down on his coffin, he seemed as fu' o' life as if he had stripped aff his jacket for a game at foot-ba', or to fling the hammer. Ay, weel micht the women-folk gaze on him wi' red weeping een, for he had loed them but ower weel, and mony a time, it is said, had he let himsel down the Castle-rock at night, God knows hoo, to meet his lemans—but a' that, a' his sins, and a' his crimes acted and only meditated, were at an end noo—puir fallow—and the platoon, wi' fixed beggonets, were drawn up within ten yards, or less, o' whare he stood, and he himsel having tied a handkerchief ower his een, dropped down on his knees on his coffin, wi' faulded hands, and lips movin' fast, fast, and white as ashes, in prayer!

NORTH. Cursed be the inexorable justice of military law! he might have been pardoned.

SHEPHERD. Pardoned! Hadna he disarmed his ain captain o' his sword, and ran him through the shouther—in a mutiny of which he was himsel the ringleader? King George on the throne durstna hae pardoned him—it would hae been as much as his crown was worth—for hoo could King, Kintra, and Constitution thole a standing army, in which mutiny was not punished wi' death?

NORTH. Six balls pierced him—through head and heart—and what a shriek, James, then arose!

SHEPHERD. Ay, to hae heard that shriek, you wad hae thought that the women that raised it wad never hae lauched again; but in a few hours, as sune as nightfall darkened the city, some o' them were gossipin' about the shootin' o' the sodger to their neighbours, some dancin' at hops that shall be nameless, some sitting on their sweethearts' knees wi' their arms roun' their necks, some swearin like troopers, some doubtless sitting thochtfu' by the fireside, or awa' to bed in sadness an hour sooner than usual, and then fast asleep.

NORTH. I saw his old father, James, with my own eyes, step out from the crowd, and way being made for him, he walked up to his son's dead body, and embracing it, kissed his bloody head, and then with clasped hands, looked up to heaven.

SHEPHERD. A strang and stately auld man, and ane too that had been a soldier in his youth. Sorrow, not shame, somewhat bowed his head, and ance he reel'd as if he were faint on a sudden—But what the deevil's the use o' me haverin' awa' this way about the shootin' o' a sodger thretty years sin syne, and mair too—for didna I see that auld silvery-headed father o' the mutineer staggering alang the Grass-Market, the verra next day after the execution, as fou' as the Baltic, wi' a heap o' mischievous weans hallooin' after him, and him a' the while in a dwam o' drink and despair, maunderin' about his son Lewis, then lyin' a' barken'd wi' blood in his coffin, six feet deep in a fine rich loam.

NORTH. That very same afternoon, I heard the drums and fifes of a recruiting party, belonging to the same regiment, winding away down towards Holyrood; and the place of Lewis Mackenzie, in the line of bold sergeants with their claymores, was supplied by a corporal, promoted to a triple bar on his sleeve, in consequence of the death of the mutineer.

SHEPHERD. It was an awfu' scene yon, sir; but there was naething humiliating to human nature in it,—as in a hangin'; and it struck a wholesome fear into the souls o' many thousan' sodgers.

NORTH. The silence and order of the troops, all the while, was sublime.

SHEPHERD. It was sae, indeed.

12. Sarah Siddons as Lady Macbeth
(from Noctes 32: April 1827)

NORTH. ... Sarah was a glorious creature. Methinks I see her now in the sleep-walking scene!

SHEPHERD. As Leddy Macbeth! Her gran' high straicht-nosed face, whiter than ashes! Fixed een, no like the een o' the dead, yet hardly mair like them o' the leevin'; dim, and yet licht wi' an obscure lustre through which the tormented sowl looked in the chains o' sleep and dreams wi' a' the distraction o' remorse and despair,—and oh! sic an expanse o' forehead for a warld o' dreadfu' thochts, aneath the braided blackness o' her hair, that had nevertheless been put up wi' a steady and nae uncarefu' haun' before the troubled Leddy had lain doon, for it behoved ane so high-born as she, in the middle o' her ruefu' trouble, no to neglect what she owed to her stately beauty, and to the head that lay on the couch of ane o' Scotland's Thanes—noo, likewise about to be, during the short space o' the passing o' a thunder-cloud, her bluidy and usurping King.

NORTH. Whisht—Tickler—Whisht—no coughing.

SHEPHERD. Onwards she used to come—no Sarah Siddons—but just Leddy Macbeth hersel'—though through that melancholy masquerade o' passion, the spectator aye had a confused glimmerin' apprehension o' the great actress—glidin' wi' the ghostlike motion o' nicht-wanderin' unrest, unconscious o' surroundin' objects,—for oh! how could the glazed, yet gleamin' een, see aught in this material world?—yet, by some mysterious power o' instinct, never touchin' ane o' the impediments that the furniture o' the auld castle micht hae opposed to her haunted footsteps,—on she came, wring, wringin' her hauns, as if washin' them in the cleansin' dews frae the blouts o' blood,—but wae's me for the murderess, out they wad no be, ony mair than the stains on the spat o' the floor where some midnicht-slain Christian has groaned out his soul aneath the dagger's stroke, when the sleepin' hoose heard not the shriek o' departing life.

TICKLER. North, look at James's face. Confound me, under the inspiration of the moment, if it is not like John Kemble's!

SHEPHERD. Whether a' this, sirs, was natural or not, ye see I dinna ken, because I never beheld ony woman, either gentle or semple, walkin' in her sleep after having commited murder. But, Lord safe us! that hollow, broken-hearted voice, "out, damned spot," was o' itsell aneugh to tell to a' that heard it, that crimes done in the flesh during time will needs be punished in the spirit during eternity. It was a dreadfu' homily yon, sirs; and wha that saw't would ever ask whether tragedy or the stage was moral, purging the soul, as she did, wi' pity and wi' terror?

13. Edinburgh in Summer and Winter
(from Noctes 40: December 1828)

NORTH. Where were we, James?

SHEPHERD. I was abusin' Embro' in simmer.

NORTH. Why?

SHEPHERD. Whey? a' the lumms smokeless! No ae jack turnin' a piece o' roastin' beef afore ae fire in ony ae kitchen in a' the New Toon! Streets and squares a' grass-grown, sae that they micht be mawn! Shops like bee-hives that hae de'ed in wunter! Coaches settin' aff for Stirlin', and Perth, and Glasgow, and no ae passenger either inside or out—only the driver keepin' up his heart wi' flourishin' his whup, and the guard, sittin' in perfect solitude, playin' an eerie spring on his bugle-horn! The shut-up play-house a' covered ower wi' bills that seem to speak o' plays acted in an antediluvian world! Here, perhaps, a leevin' creter, like ane emage, staunin' at the mouth o' a close, or hirplin' alang, like the last relic o' the plague. And oh! but the stane-statue o' the late Lord Melville, staunin' a' by himsell up in the silent air, a hunder-and-fifty feet high, has then a ghastly seeming in the sky, like some giant condemned to perpetual imprisonment on his pedestal, and mournin' ower the desolation of the city that in life he loved so well, unheeded and unhonoured for a season in the great metropolitan heart o' the country which he ance rejoiced to enrich and beautify, telling and teaching her how to hold up her head bauldly among the nations, and like a true patriot as he was, home and abroad caring for the greatest—and the least of all her sons!

NORTH. He was the greatest statesman ever Scotland produced, James; nor is she ungrateful, for the mutterings of Whig malice have died away like so much croaking in the pouchy throats of drought-dried toads, and the cheerful singing and whistling of Industry all over the beautifully cultivated Land, are the hymns perpetually exhaled to heaven along with the morning dews, in praise and commemoration of the Patriots who loved the sacred soil in which their bones lie buried.

SHEPHERD. That's weel said, sir. Let there be but a body o' Truth, and nae fear but imagery will crood around it, just like shadows and sunbeams cast frae the blue sky, the white clouds, and the green trees round about the body o' some fair maid,—that is some bonnie Scotch lassie, bathin' in a stream as pure as her ain thochts.

TICKLER. There again, James!

SHEPHERD. But to return to the near approch o' wunter. Mankind hae again putten on worsted stockins, and flannen drawers—white jeans and yellow nankeen troosers hae disappeared—dooble soles hae gotten a secure footen ower pumps—big coats wi' fur, and mantles wi' miniver, gie an agreeable rouchness to the picturesque stream o' life eddyin' alang the channel o' the streets—gloves and mittens are sae general that a red hairy haun' looks rather singular—every third body ye meet, for fear o' a sudden blash, carries an umbrella—a' folk shave noo wi' het water—coal-carts are emptyin' theirsells into ilka area—caddies at the corners o' streets and drivers on coach-boxes are seen warmin' themsells by blawin' on their fingers, or whuskin' themsells wi' their open nieves across the shoothers—skates glitter at shop-wundows prophetic o' frost—Mr Phin may tak' in his rod noo, for nae mair thocht o' anglin' till spring,—and wi' spring hersell, as wi' ither o' our best and bonniest friens, it may be said, out o' sicht out o' mind,—you see heaps o' bears hung out for sale—horses are a' hairier o' the hide—the bit toon-bantam craws nane, and at breakfast you maun tak tent no to pree an egg afore smellin' at it—you meet hares carryin' about in a' quarters—and ggem-keepers proceedin' out into the kintra wi' strings o' grews—sparrows sit silent and smoky wi' ruffled feathers waitin' for crumbs on the ballustrawds—loud is the cacklin' in the fowl-market o' Christmas geese that come a month at least afore the day, just like thae Annuals the Forget-me-Nots, Amulets, Keepsakes, Beejoos, Gems, Anniversaries, Souvenirs, Friendship's Offerings, and Wunter-Wreaths——

TICKLER. Stop, James—stop. Such an accumulation of imagery absolutely confounds—perplexes——

14. Another Haggis
(from Noctes 40: December 1828)

Enter MR AMBROSE *with a hot roasted Round of Beef*—KING PEPIN *with a couple of boiled Ducks*—SIR DAVID GAM *with a trencher of Tripe, a la Meg Dods—and* TAPITOURIE *with a Haggis. Pickled Salmon, Welch Rabbits, &c. &c.—and, as usual, Oysters, raw, stewed, scolloped, roasted, and pickled, of course—Gizzards, Finzeans, Red Herrings.*

SHEPHERD. You've really served up a bonny wee neat bit sooper for three, Mr Awmbrose. I hate, for my ain pairt, to see a table overloaded. It's sae vulgar. I'll carve the haggis.

NORTH. I beseech you, James, for the love of all that is dear to you, here and hereafter, to hold your hand. Stop—stop—stop!—

The SHEPHERD *sticks the Haggis, and the Table is instantly overflowed.*

. SHEPHERD. Heavens and earth! Is the Haggis mad? Tooels! Awmrose—tooels! Safe us—we'll a' be drooned!

Picardy and his Tail rush out for towels.

NORTH. Rash man! what ruin have you wrought! See how it has

overflown the deck from stem to stern—we shall all be lost.

SHEPHERD. Sweepin' every thing afore it! Whare's the puir biled dyucks? Only the croon-head o' the roun' visible! Tooels—tooels—tooels! Send roun' the fire-drum through the city.

Re-enter Picardy and "the Rest" with napery.

MR AMBROSE. Mr North, I look to you for orders in the midst of this alarming calamity. Shall I order in more strength?

SHEPHERD. See—see—sir! it's creepin' alang the carpet! We're like men left on a sand-bank, when the tide's comin' in rampaugin'. Oh! that I had insured my life! Oh! that I had learned to soom! What wull become o' my widow and my fatherless children!

NORTH. Silence! Let us die like men.

SHEPHERD. O, Lord! it's ower our insteps already! Open a' the doors and wundows—and let it find its ain level. I'll up on a chair in the meantime.

The SHEPHERD *mounts the back of The Chair, and draws*
MR NORTH *up after him.*

Sit on my shoothers, my dear—dear—dearest sir. I insist on't. Mr Tickler, Mr Awmrose, King Pepin, Sir David, and Tappitourie—you wee lazy deevil—help Mr North up—help Mr North up on my shoothers!

MR NORTH *is elevated, Crutch and all, astride on the*
SHEPHERD'S *shoulders.*

NORTH. Good God! Where is Mr Tickler?

SHEPHERD. Look—look—look, sir,—yonner he's staunin' on the brace-piece—on the mantel! Noo, Amrose, and a' ye waiters, make your escape, and leave us to our fate. Oh! Mr North, gie us a prayer.—What for do you look so meeserable, Mr Tickler? Death is common—'tis but "passing through Natur' to Eternity!" And yet—to be drooned in haggis 'll be waur than Clarence's dream! Alack, and alas-a-day! it's up to the ring o' the bell-rope! Speak, Mr Tickler—O speak, sir—Men in our dismal condition—Are you sittin' easy, Mr North?

NORTH. Quite so, my dear James, I am perfectly resigned. Yet, what is to become of Maga—

SHEPHERD. O my wee Jamie!

NORTH. I fear I am very heavy, James.

SHEPHERD. Dinna say't, sir—dinna say't. I'm like the pious Æneas bearin' his father Ancheeses through the flames o' Troy. The similie does na haud gude at a' points—I wish it did—Oh, haud fast, sir, wi' your arms roun' my neck, lest the cruel tyrant o' a haggis swoop ye clean awa under the sideboard to inevitable death!

NORTH. Far as the eye can reach it is one wide wilderness of suet!

TICKLER. Hurra! hurra! hurra!

SHEPHERD. Do you hear the puir gentleman, Christopher? It's

affeckin' to men in our condition to see the pictur we hae baith read o'
in accounts o' shipwrecks realeezed! Timothy's gane mad! Hear till him
shoutin' wi' horrid glee on the brink o' eternity!

TICKLER. Hurra! hurra! hurra!

NORTH. Horrible! most horrible!

TICKLER. The haggis is subsiding—the haggis is subsiding! It has
fallen an inch by the sabbase since the Shepherd's last ejaculation.

SHEPHERD. If you're teilin' a lee, Timothy, I'll wade ower to you, and
bring you doon aff the mantel wi' the crutch.—Can I believe my een? It
is subseedin'. Hurraw! hurraw! hurraw! Nine times nine, Mr North, to
our deliverance—and the Protestant ascendency!

OMNES. Hurra! hurraw! hurree!

SHEPHERD. Noo, sir, you may dismunt.

Re-enter the Household, with the immediate neighbourhood.

SHEPHERD. High Jinks! High Jinks! High Jinks! The haggis has puttin'
out the fire, and sealed up the boiler—

The SHEPHERD *descends upon all fours, and lets* MR NORTH
off gently.

15. The Shepherd's Skating Marathon
(from Noctes 41: March 1829)

SHEPHERD. An English bagman, you see,—he's unco fond o' poetry
and the picturesque, a traveller in the soft line—paid me a visit the day
just at denner-time, in a yellow gig, drawn by a chestnut blude meer; and
after we had discussed the comparative merits o' my poems and Lord
Byron's, and Sir Walter's, he rather attributin' to me, a' things considered,
the superiority over baith; it's no impossible that my freen got rather
fuddled a wee, for, after rousin' his meer to the skies, as if she were fit for
Castor himsell to ride upon up and doun the blue lift, frae less to mair he
offered to trot her in the gig into Embro, against me on the best horse in a'
my stable, and gie me a half hour's start before puttin' her into the shafts;
when, my birses being up, faith I challenged him, on the same condition,
to rin him intil Embro' on shank's naiggie.

NORTH. What! biped against quadruped?

SHEPHERD. Just. The cretur, as sune as he came to the clear understandin' o' my meanin', gied ane o' these but creenklin' cackles o' a
Cockney lauch, that can only be forgiven by a Christian when his soul is
saften'd by the sunny hush o' a Sabbath morning.

NORTH. Forgotten perhaps, James, but not forgiven.

SHEPHERD. The bate was committed to black and white; and then on
wi' my skites, and awa' like a reindeer.

TICKLER. What? down the Yarrow to Selkirk—then up the Tweed.

SHEPHERD. Na—na! naething like keepin' the high road for safety in a skiting-match. There it was—noo stretchin' straught afore me, noo serpenteezin' like a great congor eel, and noo amaist coilin' itself up like a sleepin' adder; but whether straught or crooked or circlin', ayont a' imagination sliddery, sliddery!

TICKLER. Confound me—if I knew that we had frost.

SHEPHERD. That comes o' trustin' till a barometer to tell you when things hae come to the freezin' pint. Frost! The ice is fourteen feet thick in the Loch—and though you hae nae frost about Embro' like our frost in the Forest, yet I wadna advise you, Mr Tickler, to put your tongue on the airn-rim o' a cart or cotch-wheel.

NORTH. I remember, James, being beguiled—sixty-four years ago!—by a pretty little, light-haired, blue-eyed lassie, one starry night of black frost, just to touch a cart-wheel for one moment with the tip of my tongue.

SHEPHERD. What a gowmeril!

NORTH. And the bonny May had to run all the way to the manse for a jug of hot water to relieve me from that bondage.

SHEPHERD. You had a gude excuse, sir, for gi'en the cutty a gude kissin'.

NORTH. How fragments of one's past existence come suddenly flashing back upon—

SHEPHERD. Hoo I snuved alang the snaw! Like a verra curlin' stane, when a dizzen besoms are soopin' the ice afore it, and the granite gangs groanin' gloriously alang, as if instinct wi' spirit, and the water-kelpie below strives in vain to keep up wi' the straight-forrit planet, still accompanied as it spins wi' a sort o' spray, like the shiverin' atoms of diamonds, and wi' a noise to which the hills far and near respond, like a water-quake—the verra ice itself seemin' at times to sink and swell, just as if the loch were a great wide glitterin' tin-plate, beaten out by that cunnin' whitesmith, Wunter,—and——

TICKLER. And every month, in spite of frost, thaws to the thought of corned beef and greens.

SHEPHERD. Hoo I snuved alang! Some colleys keepit geyan weel up wi' me as far's Traquair manse—but ere I crossed the Tweed my canine tail had drapped quite away, and I had but the company of a couple of crows to Peebles.

NORTH. Did you dine on the road, James?

SHEPHERD. Didn't I tell you I had dined before I set off? I ettled at a cauker at Eddlestone—but in vain attempted to moderate my velocity as I neared the village, and had merely time to fling a look to my worthy friend the minister, as I flew by that tree-hidden manse and its rill-divided garden, beautiful alike in dew and in cranreuch!

TICKLER. Helpless as Mazeppa!

SHEPHERD. It's far worse to be ridden aff wi' by ane's ain sowle than by the wildest o' the desert-born.

NORTH. At this moment, the soul seems running away with the body,— at that, the body is off with the soul. Spirit and matter are playing at fast and loose with each other—and at full speed, you get sceptical as Spinoza.

SHEPHERD. Sometimes the ruts are for miles thegither regular as rail-roads—and your skite gets fitted intil a groove, sae that you can haud out ane o' your legs like an opera dancer playin' a peeryette; and on the ither glint by, to the astonishment o' toll-keepers, who at first suspect you to be on horseback—then that you may be a bird—and feenally that you must be a ghost.

TICKLER. Did you upset any carriages, James?

SHEPHERD. Nane that I recollect—I saw severals—but whether they were coming or going—in motion or at rest, it is not for me to say—but they, and the hills, and woods, and clouds, seemed a' to be floatin' awa' thegither in the direction o' the mountains at the head o' Clydesdale.

TICKLER. And where all this while was the bagman?

SHEPHERD. Wanderin', nae doubt, a' afoam, leagues ahint; for the ches-nut meer was weel cauked, and she ance won a king's plate at Doncaster. You may hae seen, Mr North, a cloud-giant on a stormy day striding alang the sky, coverin' a parish wi' ilka stretch o' his spawl, and pausin', aiblins, to tak' his breath now and then at the meetin' o' twa counties—if sae, you hae seen an image o' me—only he was in the heavens and I on the yerth—he an unsubstantial phantom, and I twal stane wecht—he silent and sullen in his flight, I musical and merry in mine——

TICKLER. But on what principle came you to stop, James?

SHEPHERD. Luckily the Pentland Hills came to my succour. By means of one of their ridges I got gradually rid of a portion of my velocity—subdued down into about seven miles an hour, which rate got gradually diminished to about four; and here I am, gentlemen, after having made a narrow escape from a stumble, that in York Place threatened to set me off again down Leith Walk, in which case I must have gone on to Portobello or Musselburgh.

16. Thirst
(from Noctes 49: May 1830)

SHEPHERD. Hunger's naething till Thrust. Ance in the middle o' the muir o' Rannoch I had near dee'd o' thrust. I was crossing frae Loch Ericht fit to the heed o' Glenorchy, and got in amang the hags, that for leagues and leagues a' round that dismal region seem howked out o' the black moss by demons doomed to dreary days-dargs for their sins in the wilderness. There was naething for't but lowp—lowp—lowpin' out o' ae pit intil anither—hour after hour—till, sair forfeuchen, I feenally gied mysel' up for lost. Drought had sooked up the pools, and left their cracked bottoms barken'd in the heat. The heather was sliddery as ice, aneath that torrid zone. Sic a sun! No ae clud on a' the sky glitterin' wi' wirewoven sultriness! The howe o' the lift was like a great cawdron pabblin' into the boil ower a slow fire. The element o' water seem'd dried up out o' natur, a' except the big draps o' sweat that plashed doon on my fever'd hauns that began to trummle like leaves o' aspen. My mouth was made o' cork cover'd wi' dust—lips, tongue, palate, and a', doon till my throat and stammack. I spak—and the arid soun' was as if a buried corpse had tried to mutter through the smotherin' mouls. I thocht on the tongue of a parrot. The central lands o' Africa, whare lions gang ragin' mad for water, when cheated out o' blood, canna be worse— dreamed I in a species o' delirium—than this dungeon'd desert. Oh! but a drap o' dew would hae seem'd then pregnant wi' salvation!—a shower out o' the windows o' heaven, like the direct gift o' God. Rain! Rain! Rain! what a world o' life in *that* sma' word! But the atmosphere look'd as if it would never melt mair, entrenched against a' liquidity by brazen barriers burnin' in the sun. Spittle I had nane—and when in desperation I sooked the heather, 'twas frush and fusionless, as if withered by lichtenin', and a' sap had left the vegetable creation. What'n a cursed fule was I—for in rage I fear I swore inwardly, (heev'n forgie me,) that I did na at the last change-house put into my pooch a bottle o' whisky! I fan' my pulse—and it was thin—thin—thin—sma'—sma'—sma'—noo nane ava'—and then a flutter that tel't tales o' the exhausted heart. I grat. Then shame came to my relief—shame even in that utter solitude. Somewhere or ither in the muir I knew there was a loch, and I took out my map. But the infernal idewit that had planned it had na alloo'd a yellow circle o' about six inches square for a' Perthshire. What's become o' a' the birds—thocht I—and the bees—and the butterflees—and the dragons?—a' wattin' their bills and their proboscisces in far-off rills, and rivers, and lochs! O blessed wild-dyucks, plouterin' in the water, strieckin' theirsells up, and flappin' their flashin' plumage in the pearly freshness! A great big speeder, wi' a bag-belly, was rinnin' up my leg, and I crushed it in my fierceness—the first inseck I ever wantonly murdered syne I was a wean. I kenna whether at last I swarfed or slept— but for certain sure I had a dream. I dreamt that I was at hame—and that a tub o' whey was staunin' on the kitchen dresser. I dook'd my head intil't, and sooked it dry to the wood. Yet it slokened not my thrust, but aggravated a thousan' fauld the torment o' my greed. A thunder-plump or water-spout brak amang the hills—and in an instant a' the burns were on spate; the Yarrow roarin' red, and foaming as it were mad,—and I thocht I cou'd hae drucken up a' its linns. 'Twas a brain fever ye see, sirs, that had stricken me—a sair stroke—and I was conscious again o' lyin' broad awake in the desert, wi' my face up to the cruel sky. I was the verra personification o' Thrust! And felt that I was ane o' the Damned Dry, doom'd for his sins to leeve beyond the reign o' the element to a' Eternity. Suddenly, like a man shot in battle, I bounded up into the air— and ran off in the convulsive energy o' dyin' natur—till doon I fell—and felt that I was about indeed to expire. A sweet saft celestial greenness cooled my cheek as I lay, and my burnin' een—and then a gleam o' something like a mighty diamond—a gleam that seemed to comprehend within itsel' the haill universe—shone in upon and through my being—I gazed upon't wi' a' my senses—mercifu' heaven! what was't but—a WELL in the wilderness,—water—water—water,—and as I drank—I prayed!

17. A Swarm of Bees
(from Noctes 50: June 1830)

ENGLISH OPIUM-EATER. ... But I rather suspect, Mr North, that I am this moment stung by one of those insects, behind the ear, and in among the roots of the hair, nor do I think that the creature has yet disengaged— or rather disentangled itself from the nape—for I feel it struggling about the not—I trust—immedicable wound—the bee being scarcely distinguishable, while I place my finger on the spot, from the swelling round the puncture made by its sting, which, judging from the pain, must have been surcharged with—nay, steeped in venom. The pain is indeed most acute—and approaches to anguish—I had almost said, agony.

NORTH. Bruise the bee "even on the wound himself has made." 'Tis the only specific.—Any alleviation of agony?

ENGLISH OPIUM-EATER. A shade. The analysis of such pain as I am now suffering—or say rather, enduring——

TICKLER *and the* SHEPHERD, *after having in vain sought shelter among the shrubs, come flying demented towards the Arbour.*

TICKLER AND SHEPHERD. Murder!—murder!—murder!

NORTH.
　　　　"Arcades ambo,
　　　　Et cantare pares, et respondere parati!"

ENGLISH OPIUM-EATER. Each encircled, as to his forehead, with a living crown—a murmuring bee-diadem worthy of Aristæus.

NORTH. Gentlemen, if you mingle yourselves with us, I will shoot you both dead upon the spot with this fowling-piece.

SHEPHERD. What'n a foolin'-piece? Oh! sir, but you're cruel!

TICKLER *lies down, and rolls himself on a plat.*

NORTH. Destruction to a bed of onion-seed! James! into the tool-house.

SHEPHERD. I hae tried it thrice—but John and Betty hae barred themselves in against the swarm—oh! dear me—I'm exhowsted—sae let me lie down and dee beside Mr Tickler!

The SHEPHERD *lies down beside* MR TICKLER.

ENGLISH OPIUM-EATER. If any proof were wanting that I am more near-sighted than ever, it would be that I do not see in all the air, or round the luminous temples of Messrs Tickler and Hogg, one single bee in motion or at rest.

NORTH. They have all deserted their stations, and made a simultaneous attack on O'Bronte. Now, Cyprus, run for your life!

SHEPHERD (*raising his head.*) Hoo he's devoorin' them by hunders!—Look, Tickler.

TICKLER. My eyes, James, are bunged up—and I am flesh-blind.

SHEPHERD. Noo they're yokin' to Ceeprus! His tail's as thick wi' pain and rage as my arm. Hear till him caterwaulin' like a haill roof-fu'! Ma stars, he'll gang mad, and O'Bronte 'll gang mad, and we'll a' gang mad thegither, and the garden 'll be ae great madhouse, and we'll tear ane anither to pieces, and eat ane anither up stoop and roop, and a' that'll be left o' us in the mornin' 'll be some bloody tramplin' up and doon the beds, and that'll be a catastrophe waur—if possible—than that o' Sir Walter's Ayrshire Tragedy—and Mr Murray 'll melodramateeze us in a peece ca'd the "Bluidy Battle o' the Bees;" and pit, boxes, and gallery 'll a' be crooded to suffocation for a hunder nichts at haill price, to behold swoopin' alang the stage the LAST O' THE NOCTES AMBROSIANÆ!!!

ENGLISH OPIUM-EATER. Then indeed will the "gaiety of nations be eclipsed," sun, moon, and stars may resign their commission in the sky, and old Nox re-ascend, never more to be dislodged from the usurpation of the effaced, obliterated, and extinguished universe.

SHEPHERD. Nae need o' exaggeration. But sure eneuch, I wudna', for anither year, in that case, insure the life o' the Solar System.—(*Rising up.*) Whare's a' the bees?

NORTH. The hive is almost exterminated. You and Tickler have slain your dozens and your tens of dozens—O'Bronte has swallowed some scores—Cyprus made no bones of his allowance—and Mr De Quincey put to death—one. So much for the killed. The wounded you may see crawling in all directions, dazed and dusty; knitting their hind legs together, and impotently attempting to unfurl their no longer gauzy wings. As to the missing, driven by fear from house and home, they will continue for days to be picked up by the birds, while expiring on their backs on the tops of thistles and binweeds—and of the living, perhaps a couple of hundreds may be on the combs, conferring on state-affairs, and——

SHEPHERD. Mournin' for their queen. Sit up, Tickler.

TICKLER *rises, and shakes himself.*

What'n a face!

NORTH. 'Pon my soul, my dear Timothy, you must be bled forthwith—for in this hot weather inflammation and fever——

SHEPHERD. Wull soon end in mortification—then coma—and then death. We maun lance and leech him, Mr North, for we canna afford, wi' a' his failin's, to lose Southside.

TICKLER. Lend me your arm, Kit——

NORTH. Take my crutch, my poor dear fellow. How are you now?

SHEPHERD. Hoo are you noo?—Hoo are you noo?

ENGLISH OPIUM-EATER. Mr Tickler, I would fain hope, sir, that notwithstanding the assault of these infuriated insects, which in numbers without number numberless, on the upsetting——

TICKLER. Oh! oh!—Whoh! whoh!—Whuh! whuh!

SHEPHERD. That comes o' wearin' nankeen pantaloons without drawers, and thin French silk stockin's wi' open gushets, and nae neck-cloth, like Lord Byron. I fin' corduroys and tap-boots impervious to a' mainner o' insecks, bees, wasps, hornets, ants, midges, clegs, and warst o' a'—the gad. By the time the bite reaches the skin, the venom's drawn oot by ever so mony plies o' !eather, linen, and wurset—and the spat's only kitly. But (*putting his hand to his face*) what's this?—Am I wearin' a mask?—a fawse face wi' a muckle nose? Tell me, Mr North, tell me, Mr De Qunshy, on the honours o' twa gentlemen as you are, am I the noo as ugly as Mr Tickler?

NORTH. 'Twould be hard to decide, James, which face deserves the palm; yet—let me see—let me see—I think—I think, if there be indeed some slight shade of—What say you, Mr De Quincey?

ENGLISH OPIUM-EATER. I beg leave, without meaning any disrespect to either party, to decline delivering any opinion on a subject of so much delicacy, and——

TICKLER *and* SHEPHERD (*guffawing.*) What'n a face! what'n a face! O! what'n a face!

ENGLISH OPIUM-EATER. Gentlemen, here is a small pocket-mirror, which, ever since the year——

SHEPHERD. Dinna be sae chronological, sir, when a body's sufferin'. Gie's the glass, (*looks in,*) and that's ME? Blue, black, ochre, gambooshe, purple, pink, and—*green!* Bottle-nosed—wi' een like a piggie's! The Owther o' the Queen's Wake! I maun hae my pictur ta'en by John Watson Gordon, set in diamonds, and presented to the Empress o'

Russia, or some ither croon'd head. I wunner what wee Jamie wad think! It is a phenomena o' a fizzionamy—An' hoo sall I get oot the stings?

NORTH. We must apply a searching poultice.

SHEPHERD. O' raw veal?

TICKLER (*taking the mirror out of the* SHEPHERD'S *hand.*) Aye!

NORTH. 'Twould be dangerous, Timothy, with that face, to sport Narcissus.

> "Sure such a pair were never seen,
> So aptly form'd to meet by nature!"

Ha! O'Bronte?

O'Bronte enters the Arbour, still under the influence of opium.

What is your opinion of these faces?

O'BRONTE. Bow—wow—wow—wow—Bow—wow—wow—wow!

SHEPHERD. He taks us for Eskymaws.

NORTH. Say rather seals, or sea-lions.

O'BRONTE. Bow—wow—wow—wow—Bow—wow—wow—wow!

SHEPHERD. Laugh'd at by a dowg!—Wha are ye?

> JOHN *and* BETTY *enter the Arbour with basins and towels,*
> *and a phial of leeches.*

NORTH. Let me manage the worms.—Lively as fleas.

> *Mr* NORTH, *with tender dexterity, applies six leeches*
> *to the* SHEPHERD'S *face.*

SHEPHERD. Preens—preens—preens—preens!

NORTH. Now, Tickler.

> *Attempts, unsuccessfully, to perform the same kind*
> *office to* TICKLER.

Your sanguineous system, Timothy, is corrupt. They wont fasten.

SHEPHERD. Wunna they sook him? I fin' mine hangin' cauld frae temple to chaft, and swallin—there's ane o' them played plowp intill the baishin.

NORTH. Betty—the salt.

SHEPHERD. Strip them, Leezy. There's anither.

NORTH. Steady, my dear Timothy, steady; aye! there he does it, a prime worm—of himself a host. Sir John Leech.

SHEPHERD. You're no feared for bluid, Mr De Qunshy?

ENGLISH OPIUM-EATER. A little so—of my own.

SHEPHERD. I wuss Mr Wordsworth's auld leech-gatherer was here to gie us his opinion o' thae worms. It's a gran' soobjeck for a poem—Leech-Gatherin'! I think I see the body gaun intill the pool, knee-deep in mud, and bringin' them out stickin' till his taes. There's whiles mair genius in the choice o' a soobjeck, than in the execution. I wunner Mr

Wordsworth never thocht o' composin' a poem in the Spenserian stanza, or Miltonic blanks, on a "Beggar sitting on a stane by the road-side crackin' lice in the head o' her bairn." What's in a name?

> "A louse
> By any other name would bite as sharp;"

and he micht ca't—for he's fond o' soundin' words,—see the Excursion *passim*—"The Plague o' Lice," and the mother o' the brat would personify the ministering angel. Poetry would shed a halo round its pow— consecrate the haunted hair, and beautify the very vermin.

ENGLISH OPIUM-EATER. I observe that a state of extreme languor has succeeded excitement, and that O'Bronte has now fallen asleep. Hark! a compressed whine, accompanied by a slight general convulsion of the whole muscular system, indicates that the creature is in the dream-world.

SHEPHERD. In dookin'! or fechtin'—or makin' up to a——

NORTH. Remove the apparatus.

JOHN *and* BETTY *carry away the basins, pitchers, phial, towels,*
&c. &c.

SHEPHERD. Hoo's my face noo?

NORTH. Quite captivating, James. That dim discoloration sets off the brilliancy of your eyes to great advantage; and I am not sure if the bridge of your nose as it now stands be not an improvement.

SHEPHERD. Weel, weel, let's say nae mair aboot it. That's richt, Mr Tickler, to hang your silk handkerchy ower your face, like a nun takin' the veil. Whare were we at?

NORTH. We were discussing the commercial spirit, James, which is now the ruling—the reigning spirit of our age and country.

SHEPHERD. The Fable o' the Bees was an Episode.

18. John Ballantyne
(from Noctes 53: January 1831)

SCENE—*The Snuggery.—Time, seven o'clock.—Members present—*
NORTH, SHEPHERD, O'BRONTE.

SHEPHERD. The wee bit cozzie octagon Snuggery metamorphosed, I declare, intil a perfeck paragon o' a leebrary, wi' glitterin' brass-wired rosewood shelves, through whilk the bricht-bunn' byeuckies glint splendid as sunbeams, yet saftened and subdued somehow or ither, doun to a specie o' moonlicht, sic as lonely shepherd on the hill lifts up his hauns to admire alang the fringed edges o' a fleecy mass o' clouds, when the orb is just upon the verra comin' out again intil the blue, and the entire nicht beautifies itsell up, like a leevin' being, to rehail the stainless apparition!

NORTH. Homeric!

SHEPHERD. Ay, Homer was a shepherd like mysell, I'se warrant him, afore he lost his een, in lieu o' whilk, Apollo, the Great Shepherd o' a' the Flocks o' the Sky, gied him—and wasna't a glorious recompense, sir?— for a' the rest o' his days, the gift o' immortal sang.

NORTH. 'Tis fitted up, James, after a fancy-plan of our poor, dear, old, facete, feeling, ingenious, and most original friend—Johnny Ballantyne.

SHEPHERD. Johnny Ballantyne!

NORTH. Methinks I see him—his slight slender figure restless with a spirit that knew no rest—his face so suddenly changeful in its expression from what a stranger might have thought habitual gravity, into what his friends knew to be native there—glee irrepressible and irresistible—the very madness of mirth, James, in which the fine ether of animal spirits seemed to respire the breath of genius, and to shed through the room, or the open air, a contagion of cheerfulness, against which no heart was proof, however sullen, and no features could stand, however grim—but still all the company, Canters and Covenanters inclusive, relaxed and thawed into murmurs of merriment, even as the strong spring sunshine sends a-singing the bleak frozen moor-streams, till all the wilderness is alive with music.

SHEPHERD. He was indeed a canty cretur—a delichtfu' companion.

NORTH. I hear his voice this moment within my imagination, as distinct as if it were speaking. 'Twas exceedingly pleasant.

SHEPHERD. It was that. Verra like Sandy's—only a hue merrier, and a few beats in the minute faster. Oh, sir! hoo he wou'd hae enjoyed the Noctes, and hoo the Noctes woud hae enjoyed him!

NORTH. In the midst of our merriment, James, often has that thought come over me like a cloud.

SHEPHERD. What'n a lauch!

NORTH. Soul-and-heart-felt!

SHEPHERD. Mony a strange story fell down stane-dead when his tongue grew mute. Thoosands o' curious, na, unaccountable anecdotes, ceased to be, the day his een were closed; for he tel't them, sir, as ye ken, wi' his een mair than his lips; and his verra hawns spak, when he snapped his forefinger and his thoomb, or wi' the hail five spread out—and he had what I ca' an elegant hawn' o' fine fingers, as maist wutty men hae— manually illustrated his soobjeck, till the words gaed aff, murmuring like bees frae the tips, and then Johnny was quate again for a minute or sae, till some ither freak o' a fancy came athwart his genie, and instantly loupt intil look, lauch, or speech—or rather a' the three thegither in ane, while Sir Walter himsell keckled on his chair, and leanin' wi' thae extraordinar' chowks o' his, that aften seem to me amaist as expressive as his pile o' forehead, hoo wou'd he fix the grey illumination o' his een on his freen Johnny, and ca' him by that familiar name, and by the sympathy o' that maist capawcious o' a' sowles, set him clean mad—richt doon wudd a'thegither—till really, sir, he got untholeably divertin', and folk compleen'd o' pains in their sides, and sat wi' the tears rinnin' doon their cheeks, praying him for gudeness to haud his tongue, for that gin he didna, somebody or ither wou'd be fa'in doon in a fit, and be carried out dead.

19. A Crack-Steamer
(from Noctes 57: August 1831)

TICKLER. Well, dear, only conceive of this room being partitioned into some score of sections answering in shape and dimensions to the cabin, lady's cabin, state-rooms, steerage, &c. &c. &c. of a crack-steamer, and people these *domiciliuncula* with such an omnigatherum of human mortals as Captain Macraw or Captain Maclaver is in the habit of transporting from Leith to London, or *vice versa*.

NORTH. God forbid!—the half payers, milliners' apprentices, and all?

TICKLER. Yes—every soul of them—shut them all up here together for three days and nights, more or less, to eat, drink, sleep, snore, walk, strut, hop, swagger, lounge, shave, brush, wash, comb, cough, hiccup, gargle, dispute, prose, declaim, sneer, laugh, whisper, sing, growl, smile, smirk, flirt, fondle, preach, lie, swear, snuff, chew, smoke, read, play, gasconize, gallivant, etcetera, etceterorum.

NORTH. Stop, for God's sake——

TICKLER. Not I—cage your Christians securely, give them at discretion great big greasy legs of Leicestershire mutton; red enormous rounds of Bedford beef; vast cold thick inexpugnable pies of Essex veal; broad, deep, yellow, fragrant Cheshire cheeses; smart, sharp, white acidulous ginger beer,—strong, heavy, black double X—new rough hot port in pint bottles; the very élite of Cape sherry "of the earth earthy;" basketfuls of cracked biscuits; slices of fat ham piled inch thick on two feet long blue and white *ashets;* beautiful round dumpy glazed jugs of tepid Thames water, charming whitey-brown porringers of nutty-brown soft sugar, corpulent bloated seedy lemons, with green-handled saw-edged steel knives to bisect them; gills of real malt whisky, the most genuine Cognac brandy, the very grandest of old antique veritable Jamaica rum, and Schiedam Hollands—tall, thin, glaring tallow candles in dim brazen candlesticks, planted few and far between on deal tables covered with freeze tablecloths, once green and nappy, now bare, tawny, and speckled with spots of gravy, vinegar, punch, toddy, beer, oil, tea, treacle, honey, jam, jelly, marmalade, catsup, coffee, capellaire, soda-water, seidlitz draughts, cocoa, gin twist, Bell's ale, heavy wet, blue ruin, max, cider, rhubarb, Eau de Cologne, chocolate, onion sauce, tobacco, lavender, peppermint, sneeze, slop, barley-sugar, soy, liquorice, oranges, peaches, plums, apricots, cherries, geans, apples, pears, grosets, currants, turnips, lozenges, electuaries, abstersives, diuretics, eau-medicinale, egg, bacon, milk punch, herring, sausage, fried tripe, toasted Dunlop, livers, lights, soap, caudle, cauliflower, tamarinds, potted char, champagne, lunelle, claret, hock, purl, perry, saloop, tokay, gingerbread, scalloped oysters, milk, ink, butter, jalap, pease-pudding, blood——

NORTH. Oh! horrible—most horrible—enough, enough.

SHEPHERD. Hae dune, hae dune, man—od' ye're eneugh to gar a sow scunner——

TICKLER. You agree, then, with my original position. The only circumstances that render the concern in any shape or sort tolerable, are the very things you set out with abusing. The locomotion, the sea blast, the rocking of the waves, the creaking and hissing of the machinery—in short, whatever has a direct and constant tendency to remind us that our misery is but for a certain given number of hours—in other words, that you are not in hell, but only in purgatory. And I have said nothing as to the night-work—the Kilmarnocks—the flannels, the sights and the sounds——

20. Tennyson
(from Noctes 60: February 1832)

NORTH. ... Heavens! Tickler, what a burst of literature there will be after the burial of the Reform Bill! All the genius of the land has been bottled up for a year and more—and must be in a state of strong fermentation. Soon as the pressure has been removed by the purification of the atmosphere, the corks will fly up into the clouds, and the pent-up spirit effervesce in brilliant aspiration.

TICKLER. Not poetry. "The wine of life is on the lees," in that department. We must wait for the vintage.

NORTH. All the great schools seem effete. In the mystery of nature, the number of births by each mind is limited—and we must wait for fresh producers. Scott, Wordsworth, Southey, Coleridge—all the Sacred Band—have done their best—their all—but on the horizon I see not the far-off coming light of the foreheads of a new generation of poets. That dawn will rise over our graves—perhaps not till the forlorn "*hic jacet*" on our tombstones is in green obliteration. The era has been glorious—that includes Cowper and Wordsworth, Burns and Byron. From what region of man's spirit shall break a new day-spring of Song? The poetry of that long era is instinct with passion—and, above all, with the love of nature. I know not from what fresh fountains the waters may now flow—nor can I imagine what hand may unlock them, and lead them on their mazy wanderings over the still beautified flowers and herbage of the dædal earth—the world of sense and of soul. The future is all darkness.

TICKLER. Mighty fine. But how should you? In that case you were the very poet whose advent has not yet been predicted—and which may not be—haply—for a hundred years. Are there no younkers?

NORTH. A few—but equivocal. I have good hopes of Alfred Tennyson. But the cockneys are doing what they may to spoil him—and if he suffers them to put their bird-lime on his feet, he will stick all the days of his life on hedge-rows, or leap fluttering about the bushes. I should be sorry for it—for though his wings are far from being full-fledged, they promise now well in the pinions—and I should not be surprised to see him yet a sky-soarer. His "Golden Days of good Haroun Alraschid" are extremely beautiful. There is feeling—and fancy—in his Oriana. He has a fine ear for melody and harmony too—and rare and rich glimpses of imagination. He has—*genius.*

TICKLER. Affectations.

NORTH. Too many. But I admire Alfred—and hope—nay trust—that one day he will prove himself a poet. If he do not—then am I no prophet.

21. Standing Firm
(from Noctes 60: February 1832)

A NEW SONG, TO BE SUNG BY ALL LOYAL AND TRUE SUBJECTS.

NORTH.
Ye good honest Englishmen, loyal and true,
That, born in Old England, look not for a New,
And your fathers' old principles love to pursue,
Join, join in our chorus, while yet we may sing,
Spite of treason and blasphemy—"God save the King!"

TICKLER.
Priests, Prelates, and Churchmen, who honour the creed
For which martyrs have bled, for which martyrs may bleed,
When Atheists and Papists your flocks shall mislead;
Join, join in our chorus, and loyally sing,
From fiendish conspiracy—"God save the King!"

NORTH.

Ye that mean to stand firm by a Protestant throne,
Nor would see Church or King be deprived of their own;
Nor for bread to the poor would but give them a stone;
Join, join in our chorus, and resolute sing,
With the true voice of loyalty—"God save the King!"

TICKLER.

Ye that know well the plots of fool, knave, and profane,
That the very first act of the Devil's own reign
Would episcopize Cobbett, and canonize Paine;
Join, join in our chorus defiance to fling
At their blasphemous rage, and cry—"God save the King!"

NORTH.

Ye that know when Whig Radical Orators shine,
And bewilder the mobs whom they urge to combine,
What mischievous devils get into the swine;
Join, join in our chorus, and give them a ring,
To keep them from delving—so, "God save the King!"

TICKLER.

Ye that honour the laws that our forefathers made,
And would not see the laurels they twined for us fade,
Nor would yield up your wealth to the cant of "free trade;"
Join, join in our chorus, and let the world ring
With our commerce and glory—and "God save the King!"

NORTH.

All ye that are foes to mean quibbles and quirks,
And twopenny statesmen, well known by their works,
That have used the poor Greeks ten times worse than the Turks;
Join, join in our chorus, and manfully sing,
With good English honesty—"God save the King!"

TICKLER.

Defend us from hypocrites, save us from quacks,
From saintly Macauleys, and some other Macs,
And from white sugar said to be made by free blacks;
Join, join in our chorus, and still let us cling
To our ships and our colonies—"God save the King!"

NORTH.

From, of all the vile humbugs that ever was known,
That vilest and direst, Sierra Leone,
That makes savages howl, and poor Englishmen groan;
Join, join in our chorus, the downfall to sing
Of malice and slander—and "God save the King!"

TICKLER.

Ye nobles, stand forth, and defend us, ye great,
From political sophists, their jargon and prate,
Defend Church and King, and keep both in their state;
Join, join in our chorus, a blessing to bring
On the land of our fathers—and "God save the King!"

NORTH.

Defend us once more from the Regicide Bill,
And the Bedlamite Whigs, that have caused so much ill,
And would bind our bold King to their absolute will;
Join, join in our chorus, and still let us cling
To the laws of Old England—and "God save the King!"

TICKLER.

From Lord Chancellors save us, who flop on their knees,
And pretend to give up, while they bargain for fees,
And sneer about Bishops, and envy their sees;
Join, join in our chorus, and loyally sing,
From scheming hypocrisy—"God save the King!"

NORTH.

That give friendly advice to the Lords they should shun,
That keep the King's conscience, and let him have none,
And strip him of all his tried friends one by one;
Join, join in our chorus, and faithfully sing,
From evil advisers all—"God save the King!"

TICKLER.

From a new House of Peers, that shall put the old down,
And recruit from the Tinkers of Brummagem town,
And set a *mob*ility over the Crown;
Join, join in the chorus, and let the rogues swing,
And thus be exalted—so "God save the King!"

NORTH.

From national robbers, call'd "National Guards,"
That for pike and for gun quit their thimbles and yards,
To hunt down the gentry, proscribed in placards;
Join, join in our chorus, and roar as we sing,
From Frenchified villainy—"God save the King!"

TICKLER.

From a Citizen King, and a new La Fayette,
With his sword in the scales to weigh down a just debt,
And beggar the world for the whims of Burdett;
Join, join in our chorus—all ready to spring
To the rescue from tyranny—"God save the King!"

NORTH.

From a dastardly Ministry, cringing and mean
To their sovereign mob, and reserving their spleen
To insult and to bully—a woman—a Queen!
Join, join in our chorus—true homage we bring
To the wife of our Monarch—and "God save the King!"

TICKLER.

Emancipate Ireland once more from the thirst
Of rapine and murder, with which she is cursed,
From Prime-Minister Shiel, and O'Connell the First;
Join, join in our chorus, and spurn all who wring
From the beggar his pittance—here's "God save the King!"

NORTH.

From defiance of law, and from Catholic rent,
On open sedition by demagogues spent,
And from Parliaments held without England's consent;
Join, join in our chorus—a downfall we sing
To all turbulent scoundrels—so "God save the King!"

TICKLER.

Brave William, stand forth from your radical rout,
And trust your old Peers, that still stand you about;
And, oh! above all, kick your Ministers out!
And hark to our chorus—for that's the true thing,
Hurrah for our country—and "God save the King!"

NORTH.

And if they cling fast, wrest them off like a winch,
Though they bully and storm with their mobs, never flinch,
Be the King of Old England, ay, every inch;
And fear not, your people will thankfully sing
With true hearts and harmony—"God save the King!"

22. The Theatre Royal, Glasgow
(from Noctes 64: November 1832)

TICKLER. Our provincial theatres, compared with the great London ones, are all small—yet——

NORTH. Except that in Glasgow. It is of the same class as Covent-Garden, but of a peculiar construction. It may be divided into three parts; in one you cannot hear, in another you cannot see, and in the third you can neither see nor hear. I remember once sitting alone in the third division—and never before or since have I had such a profound feeling of the power of solitude.

23. Morning
(from Noctes 66: July 1834)

NORTH *(ringing the silver bell.)* Too bad, James! Peter, let off the gas.
Peter lets off the gas.

SHEPHERD. Ha! the bleeze o' Morn! Amazin'! 'Twas shortly after sunset when the gas was let on—and noo the gas is let aff, lo! shortly after sunrise!

BULLER. With us there has been no night.

SHEPHERD. Yesterday was the Twunty First o' June–the Langest Day. We cou'd hae dune without artificial licht—for the few hours o' midnicht were but a gloamin'—and we cou'd hae seen to read prent.

BULLER. A deep dew.

NORTH. As may be seen by the dry lairs in the wet grass of those cows up and at pasture.

SHEPHERD. Naebody else stirrin'. Luik there's a hare washin' her face like a cat wi' her paw. Eh man! luik at her three leverets, like as mony wee bit bears.

BULLER. I had no idea there were so many singing birds so near the suburbs of a great city.

SHEPHERD. Had na ye? In Scotland we ca' that the skriech o' day.

NORTH. What has become of the sea?

SHEPHERD. The sea! somebody has opened the sluice, and let aff the water. Na—there it's—fasten your een upon yon great green shadow— for that's Inchkeith—and you'll sune come to discern the sea waverin' round it, as if the air grew glass, and the glass water, while the water widens oot intil the Firth, and the Firth awa' intil the Main. Is yon North Berwick Law or the Bass—or baith—or neither—or a cape o' cloodlaun, or a thocht?

NORTH.
      "Under the opening eyelids of the morn."

SHEPHERD. See! Specks—like black water-flees. The boats o' the Newhaven fishermen. Their wives are snorin' yet wi' their heads in mutches—but wull sune be risin' to fill their creels. Mr Buller, was you ever in our Embro Fish Market?

BULLER. No. Where is it, sir?

SHEPHERD. In the Parliament Hoose.

BULLER. In the Parliament House?

SHEPHERD. Are you daft? Aneath the North Brigg.

BULLER. You said just now it was in the Parliament House.

SHEPHERD. Either you or me has been dreamin'. But, Mr North, I'm desperate hungry—are ye no intendin' to gi'e us ony breakfast?

NORTH (*ringing the silver bell.*) Lo! and behold!
      Enter Peter, Ambrose, King Pepin, Sir David Gam, and
            Tappietourie, with trays.

SHEPHERD. Rows het frae the oven! Wheat scones! Barley scones! Wat and dry tost! Cookies! Baps! Muffins! Loaves and fishes! Rizzars! Finnans! Kipper! Speldrins! Herring! Marmlet! Jeely! Jam! Ham! Lamb! Tongue! Beef hung! Chickens! Fry! Pigeon pie! Crust and broon aside the Roon'—but sit ye doon—no—freens, let's staun—haud up your haun—bless your face—North, gie's a grace—(*North says grace.*) Noo let's fa' too—but hooly—hooly—hooly—what vision this! What vision this! An Apparition or a Christian Leddy! I ken, I ken her by her curtshy—did that face no tell her name and her nature.—O deign, Mem, to sit doon aside the Shepherd.—Pardon me—tak the head o' the table, ma honour'd Mem—and let the Shepherd sit down aside YOU—and may I mak sae bauld as to introduce Mr Buller to you, Mem? Mr Buller, clear your een—for on the Leads o' the Lodge, in face o' heaven, and the risin' sun, I noo introduce you till MRS GENTLE.

NORTH (*starting and looking wildly round*). Ha!

SHEPHERD. She's gane!

NORTH (*recovering some of his composure*). Too bad, James.

SHEPHERD. Saw you nocht? Saw naebody ocht?

OMNES. Nothing.

SHEPHERD. A cretur o' the element! Like a' the ither loveliest sichts that veesit the een o' us mortals—but the dream o' a dream! But, thank heaven, a's no unsubstantial in this warld o' shadows. Were ony o' us to say sae, this breakfast wou'd gie him the lee! Noo, Gurney, mind hoo ye exten' your short haun.

SMALL STILL VOICE. Aye, aye, sir.

BULLER. "O Gurney! shall I call thee bird, or but a wandering voice!"

NORTH.

> "O blessed Bird! the world we pace
> Again appears to be,
> An unsubstantial faery-place,
> That is fit home for Thee!"

24. An Eagle's Nest
(from Noctes 68: November 1834)

SHEPHERD. I was ance in an eagle's nest.

TICKLER. When a child?

SHEPHERD. A man—and no sae very a young ane. I was let down the face o' the red rocks o' Loch Aven, that affront Cairngorum, about a quarter o' a mile perpendicular, by a hair rape, and after swingin' like a pendulum for some minutes back and forret afore the edge o' the plat-form, I succeeded in establishin' mysel in the eyrie.

TICKLER. What a fright the poor eaglets must have got!

SHEPHERD. You ken naething about eaglets. Wi' them fear and anger's a' ane—and the first thing they do, when taken by surprise amang their native sticks by man or beast, is to fa' back on their backs, and strike up wi' their talons, and glare wi' their een, and snap wi' their beaks, and yell like a couple o' hell-cats. Providentially their feathers werena fu' grown, or they wou'd hae flown in my face and driven me ower the cliff.

TICKLER. Were you not armed?

SHEPHERD. What a slaughter-house!—What a cemetery! Hale hares, and halves o' hares, and lugs o' hares, and fuds o' hares, and tatters o' skins o' hares, a' confused wi' the flesh and feathers o' muirfool and wild dyeucks, and ither kinds o' ggemm, fresh and rotten, undevoor'd and digested animal maitter mixed in blue-mooldy or bloody-red masses— emittin' a strange charnel-hoose, and yet lardner-smell—thickenin' the air o' the eyrie—for though a blast cam sughin' by at times, it never was able to carry awa' ony o' the stench, which I was obliged to breathe, till I grew sick, and feared I was gaun to swarf, and fa' into the loch that I saw, but couldna hear, far doon below in anither warld.

TICKLER. No pocket-pistol?

SHEPHERD. The Glenlevit was ma salvation. I took a richt gude wullie-waught—the mistiness afore my een cleared awa'—the waterfa' in my lugs dried up—the soomin' in my head subsided—my stamach gied owre bockin'—and takin' my seat on a settee, I began to inspect the premises wi' mair preceesion, to mak a verbal inventory o' the furnitur', and to study the appearance or character o' the twa guests that still continued lyin' back on their backs, and regardin' me wi' a malignity that was fearsome, but noo baith mute as death.

NORTH. They had made up their minds to be murdered.

SHEPHERD. I suspect it was the ither way. A' on a sudden doon comes a sugh fae the sky—and as if borne each on a whurlwund—the yell and the glare o' the twa auld birds! A mortal man daurin' to invade their nest! And they dashed at me as if they wud hae dung me intil the rock—for my back was at the wa'—and I was haudin on wi' my hauns—and aff wi' my feet frae the edge o' the ledge—and at every buffet I, like an insect, clang closer to the cliff. Dazed wi' that incessant passing to and fro o' plumes, and pennons, and beaks, and talons, rushin' and rustlin' and yellin', I shut my een, and gied mysell up for lost; when a' at ance a thocht struck me that I woud cowp the twa imps owre the brink, and that the parent birds wou'd dive doon after them to the bottom o' the abyss.

TICKLER. What presence of mind!

NORTH. Genius!

SHEPHERD. I flang mysell on them—and I hear them yet in the gullerals. They were eatin' intil my inside; and startin' up wi' a' their beaks and a' their talons inserted, I flang aff my coat and waistcoat, and them stickin' til't, owre the precipice!

TICKLER. Whew!

SHEPHERD. Ay—ye may weel cry whew! Dreadfu' was the yellin', for ae glaff and ae glint; far doon it deaden'd; and then I heard nocht. After a while I had courage to lay mysell doon on my belly, and look owre the brink—and I saw the twa auld eagles wheelin' and skimmin', and dashin' amang the white breakers o' the black loch, madly seekin' to save the drownin' demons, but their talons were sae entangled in the tartan, that after floatin' awhile wi' flappin' wings in vain, they gied owre strugglin', and the wreck drifted towards the shore wi' their dead bodies.

TICKLER. Pray, may I ask, my dear Shepherd, how you returned to the top?

SHEPHERD. There cam the rub, sirs. My freens abune, seeing my claes, wi' the eaglets flaffing, awa doon the abyss, never doobted that I was in them—and they set up sic a shriek! Awa roon they set to turn the right flank o' the precipice by the level o' the Aven that rins out sae yellow frae the dark-green loch, because o' the colour o' the blue slates that lie shivered in heaps o' strata in that lovely solitude—hardly howpin' to be able to yield me ony assistance, in case they sould observe me attemptin' to soom ashore—nor yet to recover the body gin I was droon'd. Silly cretars! there was I for hours on the platform, while they were waitin' for my corp to come ashore. At last, ashore cam what they supposed to be my corp, and stickin' tilt the twa dead eaglets, and dashin' doon upon't, even when it had reached the shingle the twa savage screamers wi' een o' lichtenin'!

TICKLER. We can conjecture their disappointment, James, on findin' that there was no corpse.

SHEPHERD. I shooted—but nature's self seemed deaf—I waved my bannet—but nature's self seemed blin'. There stood the great deaf, blin', stupid mountains—and a' that I coud hear was ance a laigh echolike lauchter frae the airn heart o' Cairngorum.

TICKLER. At last they recognised the Mountain Bard?

SHEPHERD. And awa' they set again to the tap to pu' me up; but the fules in their fricht had let the rape drap, and never thocht o' lookin' for't when they were below. By this time it was wearin' late, and the huge shadows were stalkin in for the nicht. The twa auld eagles cam back, but sae changed, I could na help pityin' them, for they had seen the feathers o' them they loo'd sae weel wrapt up, a' drookit wi' death, in men's plaids—and as they keep't sailin' slowly and disconsolately before the eyrie in which there was naebody sittin' but me, they werena like the same birds!

NORTH. No bird has stronger feelings than the eagle.

SHEPHERD. That's a truth. They lay but twa eggs.

NORTH. You are wrong there, James.

SHEPHERD. Twa young ones, then, is the average, for gin they lay mair eggs, ane's aften rotten, and I'm mista'en if ae eagle's no nearer the usual nummer than fowre for an eyrey to send forth to the sky. Then they marry for life—and their annual families bein' sma', they concentrate on a single sinner or twa, or three at the maist, a' the passion o' their instinct, and savage though they be, they fauld their wide wings oure the down in their "procreant cradle" on the cliff, as tenderly as turtle-doves on theirs, within the shadow o' the tree. For beautiful is the gracious order o' natur, sirs, and we maunna think that the mystery o' life hasna its ain virtues in the den o' the wild beast and the nest o' the bird o' prey.

TICKLER. And did not remorse smite you, James, for the murder of those eaglets?

SHEPHERD. Aften and sair. What business had I to be let doon by a hair rape intil their birth-place? And, alas! how was I to be gotten up again—for nae hair rape cam' danglin' atween me and the darkenin' weather-gleam. I began to doot the efficacy of a death-bed repentance, as I tried to tak' account o' my sins a' risin' up in sair confusion—some that I had clean forgotten, they had beeen committed sae far back in youth, and never suspected at the time to be sins ava', but noo seemin' black, and no easy to be forgiven—though boundless be the mercy that sits in the skies. But, thank Heaven, there was an end—for a while at least—o' remorse and repentance—and room in my heart only for gratitude—for, as if let doon by hands o' angels, there again dangled the hair-rape wi' a noose-seat at the end o't, safer than a wicker-chair. I stept in as fearless as Lunardi, and wi' my hauns aboon my head glued to the tether—and my hurdies, and a' aneath my hurdies, interlaced wi' a net-wark o' loops and knots, I felt mysell ascendin' and ascendin' the wa's, till I heard the voices o' them hoistin'. Launded at the tap, you may be sure I fell doon on my knees—and while my heart was beginnin' to beat and loup again, quaked a prayer.

NORTH. Thank ye, James; I have heard you tell the tale better and not so well, but never before at a Noctes. Another tureen?

TEXTUAL NOTE AND LIST OF EMENDATIONS
TO THE BASE-TEXT

The only authoritative source for the text of the noctes in this selection is their original appearance in *Blackwood's Edinburgh Magazine*. This text is accordingly reproduced, with the correction of a few typographic and other clear errors. The forms of proper names in Maga sometimes differ from the standard spellings, but they have normally been retained as integral to the world of literary gossip, and because spelling of names in the early nineteenth century was more flexible than it was soon to become. The eccentric handling of French accents is a hallmark of *Blackwood's* and has been preserved as an historical curiosity. Inset verse generally has no inverted commas up to Noctes 36. The change in convention thereafter has been accepted rather than regularised in the present selection, but otherwise the positioning and styling of inset verse has been silently standardised. The distinction in the original between short and long dashes has been preserved, though they were not wholly consistently differentiated. Other eccentricities and inconsistencies of punctuation and spelling have been retained except where they might confuse the reader: exceptions are noted below. Some changes to the style and position of speakers' names and stage directions have been silently introduced to suit the modern page make-up.

The reading of the present text precedes the slash; that of the Maga base-text (Aberdeen University Library copy) follows it.

2.7	Let's hear it! / Let's hear it?
3.30	picked up? / picked up.
4.10	Eclectic / Ecclectic
4.11	Eclectic / Ecclectic
	The word is correctly spelt in Alaric Watts's source letter.
6.2	covers for two. / covers for two
8.3	Review. / Review
8.25–10.24	[The ottava rima stanzas are here printed in the normal manner: in the original they are run together, except for a break after the fourth stanza.]
15.13	[The sixth line of the sonnet, beginning 'D'Amsted', is not set in in the original.]
15.17	apparente /appanente
17.11	BENTHAM, / BENTHAM
19 (gloss)	three recommendeth / three; recommendeth
22.13/14	Revenge." [new speech] EDITOR. The superstitous / Revenge." The superstitious
	To avoid two consecutive speeches by Odoherty, the division most probably intended has been made.
23 (song)	roaring I-rishman. / roaring I-rishman

26.30   these Italian inns/ those Italian inns
             The manuscript was almost certainly misread.
29.13   still? / still.
31.41   heart," / heart;"
36.25   donum. / donum
37.4   house? / house.
38.1   styles / stlyes
42.23   3. / 4.
45.2   V. / VI.
47.6   King" / King'
50.39   enemy. / enemy?
51.27   Bunting? / Bunting.
52.24   Esq., / Esq.
52.43–53.1   *flinging it over to Buller* / flinging it over to Buller
53.13   loudly / louldly
54.37   Pier. / Pier?
55.37   Dilettanti / Dilletanti
64.27   May I ask, sir, who / May I ask, sir who
78.43   a' silent / a silent
91.21   thinkin' / thinkin
             In these two cases there is space for the apostrophes.
108.27   gloamin', / gloamin,'
121.24   James / Jones
             The manuscript was probably misread.
126.16   correlates"——— / correlates———
153.3   desert-born / desert loon
             The manuscript was almost certainly misread.
154.32   butterflees—— / butterflees'——
162.8   lights / llghts

EXPLANATORY NOTES

References to *Blackwood's Edinburgh Magazine* (*BM*) are to volume and page. The following are the dates of the early volumes: **1** April–September 1817; **2** October 1817–March 1818; **3** April–September 1818; **4** October 1818–March 1819; **5** April–September 1819; **6** October 1819–March 1820; **7** April–September 1820; **8** October 1820–March 1821; **9** April–August 1821; **10** August–December 1821. After this regularisation in 1821 there were two volumes per year, January –June and July–December, as follows: **11, 12** (1822); **13, 14** (1823); **15, 16** (1824); **17, 18** (1825); **19, 20** (1826); **21, 22** (1827); **23, 24** (1828); **25, 26** (1829); **27, 28** (1830); **29, 30** (1831); **31, 32** (1832); **33, 34** (1833); **35, 36** (1834).

When it has proved impossible to identify a quotation, or to provide an appropriate explanatory note, this is stated. Readers are invited to let the editor know of any solutions or possible solutions of such problems.

When a note is followed by '(Cartmell)' the editor has been particularly helped by Claire Cartmell's 1974 Leeds University Ph.D. thesis, 'The Age of Politics, Personalities and Periodicals: The Early Nineteenth Century World of the "Noctes Ambrosianae" of *Blackwood's Edinburgh Magazine*'.

Single words are normally defined in the glossary; phrases are normally defined in these notes. To save space, dates are normally given only for people who died before the year of the relevant noctes, the place of publication of books is omitted unless other than London, and the number of volumes in publications is not given. Accurate quotations are identified by a simple reference to the original; quotations differing from the original are normally indicated by a 'from' or 'see' preceding the identification.

1.7   Ebony   a nickname for William Blackwood, derived from the Chaldee Manuscript (see Introduction, ix).

1.11   The Fleet   the debtors' prison in London.

1.19–22   Milman's new tragedy ... one of these days   *The Martyr of Antioch* by Henry Hart Milman, published in London in March 1822, was not in fact reviewed in the *Quarterly Review*. Milman did not become editor of the *Quarterly*, William Gifford being succeeded in 1825 by John Taylor Coleridge, and Lockhart taking over in 1826.

1.26   Procter   *Dramatic Scenes* (1819) and *A Sicilian Story* (1821) by Bryan Waller Procter, writing under his pseudonym of Barry Cornwall, were praised, possibly by Lockhart, in *BM* 5.310–16 and by Wilson in *BM* 6.643–50; but he had been savaged by an unknown hand in *BM* 10.732, and Alaric Watts (for whom see Introduction, ix) warned Blackwood that Procter should not be attacked, partly because of the offence caused 'to many persons whose opinions are worth attending to' (National Library of Scotland MS 4009, f. 250r): this first noctes seems not to have taken the warning on board.

1.31–2   I wrote all Day and Martin's poetry ... blacking   it was actually Byron who was accused of earning £500 'by writing puffs for Day and Martin's blacking' (*Sardanapalus ... The Two Foscari ... Cain* (December 1821), 325).

The 44th was Ensign Odoherty's original regiment (*BM* 2.566): they would be kept in blacking or boot polish, different brands of which were promoted with jocular parodistic verses.

1.33   you wrote the World   Watts wrote (MS 4009, f. 254v): 'There is a wretched creature about town a Hugh Doherty who *assumes* the style and bearings of your *Ensign and Adjutant Odoherty*. This fellow formerly conducted a stupid paper called *the World* which has been at an end long ago.' The reference is probably to *The World*, 38 issues of which appeared between 4 January and 4 October 1818.

2.1   sporting false colours   displaying misleading signs of identification.

2.2   Set a thief to catch a thief   proverbial (*ODEP*, 810).

2.3   You've been writing in Colbourn   Henry Colburn's *New Monthly Magazine and Literary Journal*, begun in 1814. Alaric Watts edited this publication briefly in 1819; it was now under the titular editorship of Thomas Campbell.

2.10–13   Colbourn, Campbell ... Possession   this epigram was contributed by Watts, in a somewhat different form (MS 4009, f. 257v). Campbell published his poem *The Pleasures of Hope* in 1799.

2.19–22   Hazlitt does the drama better ... that table-talk   William Hazlitt was drama critic for the *Morning Chronicle* in 1813–14, the *Champion* later in 1814, the *Examiner* in 1815–17, and the *Times* in 1817. The theatre critic for Colburn's *New Monthly Magazine* was Thomas Noon Talfourd. Some of Hazlitt's *Table Talk* was originally published in irregular monthly numbers in Colburn's magazine in 1822–3, having been transferred from the *London Magazine* for which he had also written articles on contemporary drama in 1820.

2.24   the Cockneys   the London writers so denominated by Maga, the figurehead being Leigh Hunt.

2.25   Murray's, Ridgeway's   the London publishing houses of John Murray and James Ridgway, Piccadilly, meeting places for literati and politicians of Tory and Whig allegiance respectively.

2.35–6   they call Murray ... Divan   Murray's office was (and is) at 50 Albemarle Street in the West End; his rival Longman, Hurst, Rees, Orme and Brown was at 39 Paternoster Row in the City, a street noted for publishers: a *divan* is an Oriental council of state.

2.36–7   Mother Rundell's book upon cookery   *A New System of Domestic Cookery*, by Maria Eliza Rundell, originally edited and published anonymously by Murray in 1808, was a best-seller. Rundell offered an improved version to Longman in 1821, but after litigation she accepted Murray's offer for the copyright the following year and he continued to publish the book.

2.37–9   Kitchener ... cut it up   William Kitchiner, Doctor of Medicine of Glasgow University, published the highly successful *Apicius Redivivus; or, The Cook's Oracle* anonymously in 1817. It was handled with mock severity, perhaps by Lockhart, in *BM* 10.563–9.

2.41–3.1   a black rose in my hat   such a rosette in the hat was a badge of the English clergy.

3.1–3   the famous mistake ... first two volumes   Watts told the story of Murray's failure to recognise George Pretyman Tomline, Bishop of Winchester, in the 'George Winton' who offered him his *Life of Pitt* (MS 4009, ff. 202r–

203r). The blunder was made good, and Murray published the two quarto volumes successfully in April 1821.

3.3   not quite the potato   not the real thing, not very good.

3.6   Horace Walpole's Memoirs   *Memoires of the Last Ten Years of the Reign of George II*, by Horace Walpole (1717–97), edited by Lord Holland (1822).

3.10–11   half your best contributors are Whigs   the claim is no doubt exaggerated, but at least one prominent early contributor, John Herman Merivale, wrote specifically as a 'liberal whig' (6.288–90, 492–3), and other prominent contributors with Whig sympathies were Thomas Doubleday and Peter George Patmore. The Preface to Volume 11 was to observe: 'We have among them [the "true old English Whigs"] many fast friends, nay, many admirable and valuable contributors; and these are every day increasing' (v).

3.13   the Scotch Kangaroo Canaille   the erratic mob of the *Edinburgh Review* Whigs.

3.16   little Jeffrey   Francis Jeffrey, editor of the *Edinburgh Review*.

3.20   the Tumbledowns   derived from a contemporaneous application of *tumble-down* to horses, meaning 'falling down habitually' (Cartmell).

3.21   The Holland-house gentry   Holland House, the London home of Lord and Lady Holland, was the centre for moderate Whig aristocrats.

3.23   the "Irish Advent"   'To the Irish Avatar', a poem written by Byron in September 1821, criticising the enthusiastic reception of George IV in Ireland, was privately circulated.

3.29   the Royal Progress   a lampoon on George IV's visit to Ireland in 1821 by the Whig Sir Thomas Charles Morgan, who had married the novelist Sydney Owenson in 1812 after a long association.

3.32   Taylor and Hessey   the publishers who took over the *London Magazine* from Baldwin, Cradock and Joy after John Scott, editor from its commencement in 1820, was killed in a duel in February 1821. Watts wrote (MS 4009, f. 259v) that John Taylor edited the magazine himself, thus saving money.

3.33   Colburn pays like a hero   Watts wrote (MS 4009, f. 259r) that Colburn paid fifteen guineas per sheet for articles which Blackwood would reject if they were offered to him free of charge.

3.34   the European   in the spring of 1822 Lupton Relfe became the publisher of the *European Magazine*, acquiring it on the death of its former proprietor James Asperne.

3.37   old Sir Richard   Richard Phillips (1767–1840), knighted in 1808, was the proprietor of the liberal *Monthly Magazine* from its foundation in 1796 until 1824.

3.40   matter of cover   advertisements printed on the cover of an issue; *also* ground cover for game.

4.1–2   Nicholls ... Gentleman's Magazine   John Nichols edited the venerable *Gentleman's Magazine* (1731–1907) in collaboration and individually between 1778 and his death in 1826.

4.4   the Gazette of Fashion   the only recorded copy (British Library) of this periodical, edited by C.M. Westmacott, in four parts, covers 2 February 1822 to 11 January 1823. Watts wrote (MS 4009, f. 254r–v) that it was patronised by John Murray, and that it was 'filled with vulgar personal abuse of Sir Walter

G

Scott': it attacked Scott as a political trimmer (1:7 (16 March 1822), 111) and a second-rate poet (1:13 (27 April 1822), 210). Murray had been one of Scott's publishers, and Scott was a leading supporter of his *Quarterly Review*: Murray's connection with the *Gazette of Fashion* is suggested by his advertising there (presumably on the covers, since no advertisements occur on the surviving numbered pages), and by the fact that Byron's letter to him on *Cain* (for which see note to 7.36) was originally published there (1:6 (9 March 1822), 89).

4.5 the Literary Gazette a literary weekly founded in 1817, owned by Henry Colburn and edited by William Jerdan.

4.9 Hercles' vein 'a tyrant's vein', according to Bottom in *A Midsummer Night's Dream*, 1.2.43.

4.9–10 the Eclectic the *Eclectic Review*, founded in 1805, was a liberal nonconformist monthly, edited in 1814–36 by Josiah Conder. Among its contributors were the poet James Montgomery and the essayist John Foster.

4.12–13 Snuffle and Whine pious cant. The phrase is used by Watts (MS 4009, f. 258v).

4.19 Coleridge's did not pay Rest Fenner, the publisher of Coleridge's *Biographia Literaria* (1817), went bankrupt in 1819.

4.21 the proper man presumably William Blackwood: compare 6.11.

4.22 my Armenian Grammar Lockhart may have had in mind Byron's collaboration at Venice on an Armenian Grammar published in 1817 (*BM* 7.186, 11.92), but advertising non-existent works was one of Maga's stock tricks (Cartmell).

4.27 old Scioppius Scioppius, or Caspar Schoppe (1576–1649), was a learned but notoriously irritable German Latin scholar.

4.29 Dr Chalmers in *The Application of Christianity to the Commercial and Ordinary Affairs of Life, in a Series of Discourses* (delivered at the Tron Kirk, Glasgow, in the presence of the Town Council and academics and published in 1820) the Rev. Thomas Chalmers, DD, attacks the city's merchants for setting a bad moral example to the young (see especially Discourses 6 and 7).

4.31–4 Do many clergymen contribute? ... Jocular topics Lockhart is probably thinking primarily of the Rev. Thomas Gillespie and the Rev. Francis Wrangham, both regular contributors of entertaining material.

4.34–5 'Twas an arch-deacon sent me the Irish Melodies a series of Irish Melodies, purporting to be sent by 'Morty Macnamara Mulligan' of Dublin, but really written by Maginn, was published, with music and words, in *BM* 10.613–22.

4.40 Hope to be Anastasius *Anastasius; or, Memoirs of a Greek*, a popular novel published in 1819, was at first attributed to Byron (*BM* 10.200–6), but Thomas Hope acknowledged it in 10.312. Hope was the author of books on household furniture, architecture, and costume.

5.4–5 Sir William Chambers ... monotonous the celebrated architect reported this Chinese complaint in *A Dissertation on Oriental Gardening* (1779), 14.

5.8 Tom Magrath unidentified, but (if historical) possibly the Thomas Magrath who emigrated from Ireland to Canada in 1827 and as T.W. Magrath wrote some of the *Authentic Letters from Upper Canada* (Dublin, 1833).

5.10–11 Bishop Walmesley Charles Walmesley, DD, a Roman Catholic prelate, wrote, under the pseudonym of Signor Pastorini, *The General History of the Christian Church* (1771). This prophesied the end of the Protestant heresy between 1821 and 1826, giving rise to the rhyme: 'In the year eighteen hundred twenty-five,/ There will not be a Protestant alive.'

5.14 Buonaparte Napoleon died in May 1821. Several prophecies of his death at various dates, based on astrological predictions, were published during the early years of the century, but the Ayrshire squire and his book have not been identified.

5.16–17 a new hour's Tete-a-tete with the public Wilson had written 'An Hour's Tete-a-Tete with the Public' in *BM* 8.78–105, and this was followed up with a second by Maginn in 8.529–35.

5.22–3 Judge Blackstone ... commentaries Sir William Blackstone wrote *Commentaries on the Laws of England* (1765–9).

5.24–8 Addison ... Essay on the Evidences ... Cato Joseph Addison, remembered chiefly as an essayist, also wrote *Evidences of the Christian Religion* (published posthumously in 1721) and a tragedy *Cato* (1713): the *Evidences* were composed at Holland House, the London home of his friend the Countess of Warwick; *black strap* is thick, sweet port.

5.30 Nemo bene potest scribere jejunus no one can write well if he is hungry. This recalls a line in the medieval Archpoet's *Confession* (10.62), in translation 'I could never write if I was hungry'.

5.33 Experto crede Roberto see Virgil, *Aeneid*, 11.283: *literally* believe one who has tried something (with 'Robert' added); I'll take your word for it.

5.34–5 humbug articles on German Plays the 'Horae Germanicae' series lasted from November 1819 until August 1828, but only one number appeared between August 1821 and August 1822 (no. 13, January 1822).

5.35–9 Kempferhausen ... the Tent Odoherty put down the young German Kempferhausen (based on Robert Pearce Gillies, who was to contribute translations to the 'Horae Germanicae' series) in *BM* 5.609, 654, and 666; for 'The Tent' see Introduction, ix.

5.40 Ambrose see Introduction, vii.

6.8 the bishop of Winchester see note to 3.1–3.

6.11 Ebony see note to 1.7.

6.12–13 a worthy young man done up 'done up' means financially ruined. Watts wrote, referring to the London publisher John Warren: 'Warren's failure [in late 1821] is not much to be wondered at. What little money he had was sucked out of him by Procter Hazlitt Reynolds and other cockneys of less import. He gave that arch-cockney Reynolds 100 guineas for a farrago called the Garden of Florence of which he sold in all somewhere about 30 copies! His business is now adjusted and he is about to begin again' (MS 4009, f. 253r). *The Garden of Florence and Other Poems* by John Hamilton [Reynolds] was published in May 1821.

6.18 mind your hits look to your chances.

6.18–19 the slang lines *probably* showy, rakish types of writing.

6.21–2 Egan ... Boxiana Pierce Egan the elder wrote *Life in London* (issued in monthly numbers from 1820, and as a complete book in 1821), illustrated by George and Robert Cruickshank. Egan also wrote *Boxiana; or, Sketches of Antient and Modern Pugilism* (issued in parts 1812–13, and extended in 5 vols

1815–29), on which the 'Boxiana' series (perhaps by Wilson) in *BM* between July 1819 and October 1822 was based.

6.24 Hogg's, or Haggart's Hogg's 'Memoir of the Author's Life' was prefixed to *The Mountain Bard* (Edinburgh and London, 1807), and revised in 1821 and 1832. David Haggart (1801–21), thief and homicide, wrote and dictated his autobiography between his trial and execution at Edinburgh: *The Life of David Haggart ... Written by Himself* (Edinburgh, 1821).

6.31 the author of Waverley Scott did not publicly acknowledge the authorship of the Waverley novels until 1827, though it was increasingly an open secret.

6.31 Anastasius see note to 4.40.

6.36 shoot potatoes i.e. fire potatoes, rather than bullets, at each other.

6.37 rum ones ... to go in carriage racing slang a *rum one* is a 'strange looking animal', and *to go* is used of a pair of carriage horses getting along together; but 'devils to go' may just mean 'fast runners'.

6.40 Mrs Macwhirter Odoherty's story and that of 'the fair Irish widow whom the Ensign had loved in Philadelphia' (*BM* 5.710) are told in Thomas Gillespie's anonymous and fictitious 'Some account of the Life and Writings of Ensign Odoherty', *BM* 2.564, 686. Two more accounts appeared in April and December 1818. Mrs Macwhirter also appears in 'The Tent', married to Dr Magnus Oglethorpe (*BM* 5.710).

7.6–7 Sidney Smith's article about missionaries the articles 'Indian Missions' and 'Methodists and Missions', *Edinburgh Review*, 12 (April 1808), 151–81 and 14 (April 1809), 40–50, written by the Rev. Sydney Smith, attack Methodists in the mission field somewhat flippantly rather than indecently.

7.9 Gifford William Gifford, editor of the *Quarterly Review* from its inception in 1809 until 1824.

7.14–15 the Corsair ... Juan ... Richelieu Conrad, hero of Byron's poem *The Corsair* (1814); Juan, protagonist of his *Don Juan* (1819–24); and Louis François Armand du Plessis, Duke of Richelieu (1696–1788), noted for profligacy as well as valour.

7.17–19 Dame Norna ... filius carnalis see Scott's novel *The Pirate* (dated 1822 but published in December 1821), Ch. 19; '*filius carnalis*' means 'fleshly son', illegitimate son.

7.20–4 Kenilworth ... get up the references are to the character of Queen Elizabeth and to Ch. 7 in Scott's novel *Kenilworth* (1821).

7.24–5 the Sorrows of Werter Goethe's *Die Leiden des jungen Werthers* (Leipzig, 1774): an English translation from a French version was published in 1779.

7.25 Julia de Roubigné a novel by Henry Mackenzie published in 1777.

7.26–9 Milman ... Fall of Jerusalem Henry Hart Milman published *The Fall of Jerusalem: A Dramatic Poem* in 1820. The bridal songs, which fall short of the erotic, are on pages 107–8, 112, 116, and 120.

7.31 old P——'s sale the fine library which had belonged to James Perry (1756–5 December 1821), editor of the *Morning Chronicle*, was auctioned shortly after his death.

7.33–4 the Facetiæ ... Poggio the earliest edition of the *Facetiae* by Poggio Bracciolini (1380–1459) was published in Venice *c*. 1470.

7.36 Lord Byron's Mystery Byron's *Cain: A Mystery* was published in December 1821 by John Murray, who was temporarily refused an injunction on 9 February 1822 by the Lord Chancellor, Lord Eldon, against a cheap pirated edition published by William Benbow: a jury later granted the injunction.

7.38–42 The Parsons ... Cockney crew the implication is that the clerical contributors to the *Quarterly Review* spared such works as Byron's *Don Juan* and *Beppo: A Venetian Story* (1818) because Murray published both Byron and that periodical. In fact none of the main articles on the major poets were by clerics, though Shelley was reviewed by William Sidney Walker, fellow of Trinity College Oxford, who declined to take orders because of doubts.

8.10 The Society Watts noted (MS 4009, f. 260r) that the Constitutional Association, a conservative pressure group founded in March 1821, was threatening to prosecute Murray (as publisher of *Cain*). The prosecution did not proceed.

8.16 in the papers Byron's letter was widely published: initially on 9 March in the *Gazette of Fashion* (see note to 4.4), and then e.g. in the *Examiner* on 11 March and the *Edinburgh Weekly Journal* on 13 March.

8.39–40 the Oxford Gentleman an attack on *Cain* by 'Oxoniensis' (the Rev. Henry John Todd) was entitled *A Remonstrance Addressed to Mr. John Murray, Respecting a Recent Publication* (early 1822). Todd says (18–19) that Byron has dared to adopt Satan's words in Milton's *Paradise Lost* 4.110.

9.10 the old one Lucifer (Old Nick).

9.12 Doctor Blair Hugh Blair (1718–1800), author of *Lectures on Rhetoric and Belles Lettres* (1783).

9.23 Milton does in *Paradise Lost.*

9.30 Gibbon's, Hume's, Priestley's, and Drummond's publishers four theologically unorthodox writers: Edward Gibbon (1737–94), David Hume (1711–76), Joseph Priestley (1733–1804), and Sir William Drummond (1770?–1828).

9.34 Me—me adsum qui feci on me,—here I stand who did the deed,—[on me turn your steel]: Virgil, *Aeneid*, 9.427.

9.37–8 Mr Gifford ... Mr Hobhouse William Gifford was Murray's chief adviser. John Cam Hobhouse, Byron's friend, was apprehensive about the reception of *Cain*.

10.2 The Times the London newspaper, founded in 1785 and adopting its present title in 1788, was an independent organ, but some of its views (for example its support of the radical Leigh Hunt) struck Maga as dangerously liberal.

10.4 priestly Playfair's crimes the Rev. John Playfair (1748–1819) was attacked (as Professor Laugner) by Lockhart (as Baron von Lauerwinkel) for abetting the allegedly infidel *Edinburgh Review* (as the *Köningsberg Review*) in *BM* 3.689–95.

10.5 Drummond Sir William Drummond spent the last years of his life abroad.

10.7 Piso the Roman family to whom Horace addresses his *Ars Poetica.*

10.13 In me ... converte telum the concluding phrase (adapted) of the quotation noted at 9.34.

10.13–14 great Sharpe ... Doctor Sewell Sir John Sewel was President of the Constitutional Association; its Secretary Joseph Budworth Sharp is seen wielding an axe against a printing press on behalf of the Association in a cartoon in William Hone's four page broadsheet *A Slap at Slop and the Bridge-Street Gang* (1821), [2] (Cartmell).

10.18–19 your Bull-dog ... My Jackall Gifford and Hobhouse.

10.24 John Bull a scandalous London Tory weekly periodical, edited by Theodore Hook: it first appeared in December 1820.

10.28–31 Colonel Stewart's History ... next Number *Sketches of the Character, Manners, and Present State of the Highlanders of Scotland: With Details of the Military Service of the Highland Regiments* (March, 1822), by Colonel David Stewart, was reviewed in *BM* 11.387–96.

10.40 the Heavy Horseman Edward Quillinan published *Dunluce Castle: A Poem in Four Parts* (1814), styling himself 'of the Third Dragoon Guards': this was ridiculed by Thomas Hamilton as 'Poems by a Heavy Dragoon' in *BM* 4.574–9.

11.1 General Burgoyne General Sir John Burgoyne (1722–92) was also a dramatist: his 1786 comedy *The Heiress* was especially successful.

11.4 Southey's Robert Southey wrote a *History of the Peninsular War* (1823–32); Odoherty's 'Campaigns' are fictitious.

11.9 I intend contributing myself in 1824 Maginn was employed to edit a short-lived Wednesday edition of *John Bull* called the *John Bull Magazine*.

11.11 twenty guineas a-sheet £21 per printed sheet of sixteen double-column pages, or approximately 12,000 words.

11.14 John Home's Life *An Account of the Life and Writings of John Home* (March 1822) by Henry Mackenzie, whose novels all date from the 1770s.

11.19 Adam Blair ... Sir Andrew Wylie novels by Lockhart and John Galt, published in February and January 1822 respectively. The 'scene with old George', in which Wylie meets George III in Windsor Park without recognising him, is in Ch. 75.

11.21–7 Annals of the Parish ... the Provost two novels by Galt: *Annals of the Parish* was published in April 1821, *The Provost* in May 1822.

11.37 the New Forest a woodland and former royal hunting preserve in S Hampshire.

11.42 Lord Moira Francis Rawdon-Hastings, first Marquis of Hastings and second Earl of Moira, joined the Whigs in 1787. He was commander-in-chief of the forces in Scotland 1803–6 and visited Scotland again in 1823–4.

12.2 Sir Ronald Ferguson General Sir Ronald Craufurd Ferguson, a prominent liberal.

12.3 the Fox dinner the Fox dinners were held annually 1821–6 to celebrate the birthday on 24 January of the former Whig leader Charles James Fox (1749–1806), in opposition to the Pitt dinners held by the Tories in May.

12.9–10 the Thane of Fife William Tennant's poem was published in January 1822.

12.12–13 The Three Perils of Man Hogg's novel was published by Longman, Hurst, Rees, Orme and Brown in July 1822.

12.20–1 a capital manager about his farm this was unfortunately not so: when Hogg took on Mount Benger in 1820 in addition to Altrive his fortunes began to decline.

12.22–3 that article on his life   Wilson's savage review of Hogg's memoirs appeared in *BM* 10.43–52. To it was appended a mischievous note suggesting that Hogg himself might have written the review to arouse interest in his own works.

12.29 Kilmeny ... his dedication to Lady Anne Scott   'Kilmeny' is a ballad of the supernatural forming part of *The Queen's Wake: A Legendary Poem* (1813). The dedication of Hogg's novel *The Brownie of Bodsbeck* (1818) took the form of lines addressed 'To the Right Honourable Lady Anne Scott, of Buccleuch' (reprinted in *BM* 4.74–6).

12.31 Clare   John Clare, the English working-class rural poet.

12.33 I wish he would send me more articles   only one contribution from Hogg has been identified in *Blackwood's* in 1820 (March), none in 1821, and one in 1822 (December), though he was an active contributor before and after these years, which included a period of misunderstanding with Blackwood.

12.35 Dr Scott   James Scott, a Glasgow dentist. *The Odontist*, an imaginary publication, was advertised as a joke in *BM* 10.595.

12.39 the Bastile   the Bastille, Paris's fortress-prison, whose storming and demolition on 14 July 1789 marked the beginning of the French Revolution.

12.40 the Temple   the Inner and Middle Temple, two of the Inns of Court in London.

13.8 Wordsworth's Ballads   *Lyrical Ballads, With a Few Other Poems*, chiefly by Wordsworth but with a few poems by Coleridge, were published in 1798 and 1800.

13.10–11 Don Juan ... Christabel   Byron's satirical poem *Don Juan* (1819–24) and his dramatic poem *Manfred* (1817); Robert Southey's poem *Thalaba the Destroyer* (1801); Byron's poem *Childe Harold's Pilgrimage* (1812–18); 'The Pilgrimage to the Kirk of Shotts' was an article in the form of a letter from Hugh Mullion in 'The Tent' (*BM* 5.671–9) ridiculing the Whig contributors to the *Edinburgh Review* and the *Scotsman*; 'Christabel' is the poem by Coleridge, written in 1797–1801 but not published until 1816.

13.12 Essay on the Scope and Tendency of Bacon   Macvey Napier's *Remarks Illustrative of the Scope and Influence of the Philosophical Writings of Lord Bacon* [1818] emphasises the novelty and the importance for European thought of Bacon's advocacy of inductive method.

13.13 float   i.e. survive, for a century or more.

13.17–18 in my song ... what it was for   see the second and last lines of 'Lament of a Connaught Ranger', one of Maginn's 'Irish Melodies' (*BM* 10.618).

13.29 La Fontaine   Jean de La Fontaine (1621–95), author of verse fables.

13.32 Barry Cornwall   see note to 1.26. The *London Magazine*, to which Procter contributed, puffed his works, including his very successful tragedy *Mirandola* (1821: *London Magazine* 3 (January, February 1821), 66–7, 211–15). The Advertisement prefixed to *Mirandola* asserts that Mirandola is original, being unlike Othello or Polixenes (in *The Winter's Tale*).

13.34 Fogarty   Fogarty O'Fogarty was the pseudonym of Dr William Gosnell, an occasional contributor: for his views on personality see 9.377 and 10.439.

13.42   The glorious army   echoing 'The glorious army of martyrs' in the *Te Deum*.

14.11   Tom Thumb   in Henry Fielding's burlesque *Tom Thumb: A Tragedy* (1730).

14.13   Joseph Hume   (1777–1855), radical politician.

14.13   Edmund Burke   (1729–97), Tory statesman and writer.

14.14   the friend of Gerrald   Joseph Gerrald (1763–96) was a political reformer transported for sedition; his friend was the liberal lawyer Sir James Mackintosh (1765–1832).

14.14   Sir Philip Sidney   (1554–86), the model of Renaissance virtue.

14.17–18   Campbell ... Editorship ... Byron ... his   for Campbell's editing see note to 2.3. Leigh Hunt edited the four issues of *The Liberal* from Pisa October 1822 to July 1823: it had been conceived by Byron and encouraged by Shelley until his death in July 1822.

14.20–1   The Duke of Wellington ... corn-bills   in March 1822 proposals were being debated for the new Corn Law, passed in June, governing the importation of wheat. Arthur Wellesley, first Duke of Wellington, was not involved in the Corn Laws saga until later in the decade: the point is that his achievements as a soldier would not be enhanced by distinction in the political arena.

14.21–2   Hannibal ... Police   Hannibal (247–182 B.C.) led the Carthaginians against Rome, and after their defeat undertook the reorganisation of the corrupt government of his country.

14.25–8   On Linden ... rolling rapidly   the first four lines of Thomas Campbell's 'Hohenlinden' (1802).

14.31   This holy alliance of Pisa   see note to 14.17–18. The *Liberal*'s publisher in London was John Hunt, Leigh Hunt's older brother.

14.32   The Examiner   the radical Sunday journal edited by Leigh Hunt from its establishment in 1808 until his removal to Pisa: from 28 October 1821 it was probably edited by his nephew Henry Leigh Hunt.

14.37   Apt alliteration's artful aid   Charles Churchill, *The Prophecy of Famine* (1763), line 86.

14.41   Keats is dead   he had died in February 1821.

15.2   as Shelly says   notably in the 'Preface' to *Adonais* (1821).

15.5   Fudgiolo   a coinage on *fudge* ('nonsense'), Maga's nickname for Niccolò or Ugo Foscolo, a liberal Italian man of letters, who settled in London in 1816 and was welcomed by the Whigs.

15.8–21   Signor Le Hunto ... Glystero   this doggerel Italian sonnet may be 'translated': 'Mr Leigh Hunt, celebrated Cockney, who writes the poem Rimini [*The Story of Rimini* (1816)], which has every appearance, by jiminy, of having been sung on Ludgate Hill or Hampstead Heath, or on the edge of the Serpentine: how is Don John of Endymion [Keats], the great poet of ipecacuanha [an emetic]? You are the King of the Cockney Parnassus and he is the heir apparent; you are certainly a great jackass, and he is certainly a great jackass! You are the lord of the Examiner and he is the sweet lord of the clyster [enema, alluding to Keats's training as a surgeon].'

15.25–8   his Majesty's absence ... Prince John ... King George   Leigh Hunt set sail on 15 November 1821, arrived in Italy in July 1822 after a long delay due to storms, and stayed until 1825; his absence is here linked with that of George IV in Hanover (September to October 1821). 'Prince John' is John Hunt.

15.30–3 the Venus de Medicis and the Hermaphrodite ... Niobe and her Nine Daughters three celebrated classical statues or groups in the Royal and Imperial Gallery (now the Uffizi), Florence.

15.36 Dr Colquhoun P[atrick] Colquhoun, metropolitan police magistrate from 1792–1818, pointed out in his *A Treatise on the Police of the Metropolis* that 'above Fifty Thousand Females are supposed to live chiefly by Prostitution in this great Metropolis' (5th edn (1797), 421n).

15.39 The Fortunes of Nigel Scott's novel to be published in May 1822, set in London and featuring James VI and I and George Heriot.

15.41 the Pirate see note to 7.17–19.

16.6 he shews most in a bustle he is at his best when describing exciting activity.

16.7 the Monastery substantial parts of Scott's novel *The Monastery* (1820) are set in Glendearg near Melrose.

16.10 Sempstress Watts wrote (MS 4009, f. 260r) that John Hamilton Reynolds 'undertook to write a work for Constable called *Tales of the Seampstress*', but despite receiving £100 failed to write a word of it.

16.16–17 Tom Campbell ... book still the *New Monthly Magazine*, nominally edited by Thomas Campbell; the *London Magazine*, published by Taylor & Hessey. No *Aberdeen Review* is recorded before 1843, but there were two *Aberdeen Magazines* which ran from 1788–91 and 1796–8 respectively.

16.18 Steam-boats including an allusion to Galt's novel (or collection of short stories) *The Steam-Boat* (July 1822; originally published in *BM* February–December 1821).

16.19–22 Brighton ... in them all the *Brighton Magazine* ran from January to August 1822: none of its original literary material is likely to have been by Hogg. The *Newcastle Magazine* lasted from 1820 to 1831: it reviewed Hogg and referred to him in its early years, but it sems unlikely that Hogg actually contributed until 1825–7. *The Caledonian: A Quarterly Journal* was published at Dundee from June 1820 until October 1821: on internal evidence it is not impossible that some of its original literary material may be by Hogg. *The Caledonian Magazine and Review* was published at Dundee in 1822 and 1823, but its first issue is dated July 1822. No periodicals are recorded at Paisley at this date, and no titles including the word 'magazine' at Glasgow. *The Weavers' Magazine and Literary Companion* had appeared at Paisley in 1818–19, but it did not include anything of Hogg's. Glasgow produced *The Enquirer* in 1820–1: its few original literary contributions might possibly include material by Hogg. Maga may be encompassing Glasgow newspapers in its statement. *The Glasgow Sentinel* (10 October 1821–22 January 1823) claims an original contribution by Hogg, a 'Jacobite Song' (17 April 1822, 221): it reprints other Hogg compositions, and more of its original poems may possibly be his. *The Glasgow Herald*, launched in 1810, reprinted several of Hogg's poems; but none of the few poems in the *Glasgow Courier* or the many in the *Glasgow Chronicle* in 1820–2 is attributed to him.

16.26–7 Olive flag ... Blue *BM* had an olive cover; the *Edinburgh Review* sported the blue and buff colours of the Whigs, a frequent subject of allusion in Maga. In addition, the *Scots Magazine* had a blue cover and the *Scotsman* was distributed to country subscribers in a blue cover.

16.28–38   Fire upon ... Hazlitt   the contemporaneous Whigs and radicals referred to are: Francis Jeffrey; Sir James Mackintosh; Jeremy Bentham and his brother Sir Samuel; James Robert George Graham and at least one other unidentified Graham; Henry Grey Bennet; Joseph Hume; John George Lambton, first Earl of Durham; Henry Peter Brougham, Baron Brougham and Vaux; Henry Hallam; Peter Moore, the radical MP for Coventry, or the poet Thomas Moore; and William Hazlitt. The 'forgotten' last line is perhaps mildly obscene about somebody whose name rhymes with 'Moore', though it may be that Lockhart just ran out of ideas.

17.2   Willison Glass   a painter of W St Mary's Wynd referred to several times in Maga.

17.10–20.8   Dialogue   a parody of Coleridge's 'The Rime of the Ancient Mariner' (1798), with the prose gloss which first appeared in 1816.

17.11   Jeremy Bentham   the Utilitarian philosopher.

17 (gloss)   the sign of the Jolly Bacchus   if the sign denotes a specific tavern it has not been identified.

17.22   nappy ale   strong ale, with a *nap* or frothy head.

17 (gloss)   the young man of the west   James Grahame (1790–1842), an advocate who came of a Glasgow family, wrote *Defence of Usury Laws against the Arguments of Mr Bentham and the Edinburgh Reviewers* (1817).

17 (notes)   Essay on the Usury Laws ... Reform Catechism   Bentham's *Defence of Usury* (1787), and his Plan of Parliamentary Reform, in the Form of a Catechism (written 1809; published 1817).

18.3   the Quarterly bloodhounds   among those who attacked Bentham's views on a variety of subjects in the *Quarterly* were John Wilson Croker, the editor William Gifford, and Robert Southey.

18 (gloss)   nine pounders   guns firing shots of nine pounds weight.

18 (gloss)   a Berkeleian philosopher   an idealist philosopher following George Berkeley (1685–1753).

18.35   T.T. Walmsey, Esquire, Sec.   Tindal Thompson Walmsley, secretary to the Archbishop of Canterbury.

18 (notes)   Theorie de Legislation ... Church of Englandism   Bentham's *Theory of Legislation—Traités de législation civile et pénale*, ed. E. Dumont (Paris, 1802), and his *Church-of-Englandism and its Catechism Examined* (1818).

19.9   Your Panopticon roundabout   in 1791 Bentham had proposed a panopticon or form of prison of circular shape, having cells built round a central well.

19.15   Sir Richard of Bridge-street   Sir Richard Phillips (see note to 3.37), who had premises in New Bridge Street, Blackfriars, was known as Sir Pythagoras in allusion to his vegetarian principles.

19.16   Ensor   George Ensor, Irish radical political writer.

19.25   the ruin blue   (bad) gin.

19 (note)   Elements of Packing   Bentham's *The Elements of the Art of Packing, as applied to Special Juries* (1821).

20 (gloss)   Prince Charlie   Wilson calls Willison Glass's 'Prince Charlie' 'a
fine Jacobite strain': *BM* 5.677n. In Hogg's *The Jacobite Relics of Scotland*
(1819–21) this song ('Wae's me for Prince Charlie') is said to be by 'a Mr
William Glen, about Glasgow' (370): it was attributed as a joke to Glass.

20.14   Fleeting Impressions   alluding to the Fleet Prison: see note to 1.11.

20.26   The question, whether is Pope a poet?   this question was raised by
William Lisle Bowles in his 1806 edition of Pope and continued to be a subject
of furious controversy for many years.

**20.28–32   my tragedy of the Black Revenge ... The Decline and Fall of
Genius**   these works are presumably imaginary.

21.19   Adam Blair   Lockhart's novel *Adam Blair*: see note to 11.19.

21.27   meum and tuum   *Latin* mine and thine.

21.33   Coplestone   *An Enquiry into the Doctrines of Necessity and
Predestination* (1821), by Edward Copleston, Provost of Oriel College, Oxford,
was reviewed anonymously by Thomas Doubleday in *BM* 10.192–9, 376–82.

21.33–9   Cain ... Sardanapalus ... The Foscari   for *Cain* see note to 7.36;
Sardanapalus and *The Two Foscari* were published in one volume along with it
in December 1821.

21.41   Alfieri   Vittorio Alfieri (1749–1803), Italian poet and dramatist.

22.1–2   The Faustus of Goethe   the first part of Goethe's *Faust* (Tübingen,
1808) was first translated into English in its entirety by Lord F.L. Gower in
1823.

22.4   Pindarum quisquis   'Pindarum quisquis studet aemulari': 'Whoever
strives to rival Pindar [will fall like Icarus]' (Horace, *Odes*, 4.2.1).

22.5   Manfred   Byron's dramatic poem (1817).

22.5   Icarian   like Icarus who flew too near the sun so that the wax in his
artificial wings melted.

22.7–12   Nimrod and Semiramis ... the ancestors of Sardanapalus
Sardanapalus, 4.1.1–173 (compare 1.1.6).

22.13   Fingal   eponymous hero of the poem (1763) largely invented by James
Macpherson.

22.15   Norna   in Scott's novel *The Pirate*: see note to 7.17–19.

22.16–23   Mr David Lindsay ... Nereid's love   David Lyndsay's *Dramas of
the Ancient World*, dated 1822 but published by Blackwood in December 1821,
included *The Deluge* (Firaoun and the festival occur on pages 24–6), *The
Destiny of Cain*, and *The Nereid's Love*.

22.30   Ovid ... taste   among the moderns influenced by Ovid Keats would be
prominent.

22.36–23.10   An age hath been ... the reins   see Wordsworth, 'Ode to
Lycoris' (published 1820), lines 1–18.

23 (music)   There was a lady   the tune has not been identified, but its
feebleness suggests contemporaneous hack work, along the lines of an Irish
patter song, rather than a folk song.

25.10   rattles   rattles were introduced in 1789 originally to alert the
Edinburgh city guard, which was replaced in 1817 by a police force.

25.11   your crutch   Christopher North, 'the Editor', is habitually furnished
with a crutch in the *Noctes*.

25.12   Exeunt Ambo   *Latin* they both leave.

26.6 the Carlingford Mackenzie suggests that this was a Dublin hotel, but it has not been possible to confirm this: it does not appear in the list of such establishments in John James McGregor's *New Picture of Dublin* (Dublin, 1821).

26.9 the manos the waiter is made to use the Spanish 'manos' rather than the Italian 'mani', so that Odoherty can imagine he hears 'anus'.

27.5 Montifiascone Montefiascone, a town in N central Italy, gives its name to a white wine.

27.9 Lacryma Christi Lachryma Christi is (confusingly here) a strong sweet red wine from southern Italy.

27.11 Inishowen the northernmost peninsula in County Donegal: its whiskey 'is generally accounted the best potheen' (*BM* 16.346).

27.15 General Hart George Vaughan Hart, whose family seat was in County Donegal.

27.15–16 old Manners Thomas Manners-Sutton, first Baron Manners, Lord Chancellor of Ireland 1807–27.

27.20 twist off *probably* toss off, perhaps with an allusion to *twist*, 'a mixed drink'.

27.26 Hurlothrumbo *Hurlothrumbo; or, The Super-Natural*, a popular burlesque (1729) by Samuel Johnson (1691–1773), a Manchester dancing-master. At the beginning of the play (pages 6–7) Hurlothrumbo describes his highly athletic triumph over a lion in the imperial amphitheatre.

27.36 juniper gin gin flavoured with juniper: *juniper* on its own was slang for 'gin'.

28.8 Constantia a wine from the Constantia farm near Cape Town, South Africa.

28.15 the Coronation of George IV, 19 July 1821.

28.17 Appenine ... Grampian mountain ranges in central Italy and NE Scotland.

28.22–5 Jeffrey ... his book Jeffrey's book is presumably the *Edinburgh Review*.

28.33–4 Hunt ... called you "Dear Byron" ... in a dedication Hunt uses the expression twice in his dedication: *The Story of Rimini: A Poem* (1816), [v–vi]. For the *Examiner* see note to 14.32.

28.41 Hogg ... his last work *The Royal Jubilee: A Scottish Mask by the Ettrick Shepherd*, published in August 1822 to coincide with the King's Visit. Presumably it is 'quite a Chaldee' because it treats a contemporary subject in an archaic format, though since it is not satirical the effect is very different.

29.3 your good-humoured notice ironical: see note to 12.22–3.

29.6 poem ... on old Bam Rogers 'Question and Answer', written in 1818 against Samuel Rogers the banker poet, and sent in September 1820 after revision to John Murray for private distribution: *bam* means 'hoax'.

29.7 too much up to trap *perhaps* too prominent to be caught out.

29.9 Non mi ricordo *Italian* I do not remember. This had become a catch-phrase as a result of its frequent use by Italian witnesses at the enquiry into Queen Caroline's behaviour in Italy held in 1820.

29.9 civilation Maga's term for a state of intoxication (see also 11.viii and 18.160). 'As such an odiously long word [as *civilisation*] must ever be distressing to a gentleman taking his ease of an evening, unconsciously, perhaps, he [Maginn] abridged it always after 10 P.M. into *civilation*' ([Thomas De Quincey,] 'Sir William Hamilton', *Hogg's Instructor*, new series, 9 (1852), 273–4).

29.13 Ponder! The great god Pan! Laker, or Lake Poet; Pan was the Greek god of pastures, flocks, and woods: here the reference is to Wordsworth as the presiding genius of the natural world.

29.14 two octavos two volumes in octavo format, *Memorials of a Tour on the Continent, 1820* and *Ecclesiastical Sketches*, both published in March 1822.

29.16 so have I Byron did not publish any new works in the first half of 1822. The allusion is (depending on the sense of 'delivered') either to his two most recent octavo volumes, published in August and December 1821 respectively, *Don Juan*, 3–5 and *Sardanapalus ... The Two Foscari ... Cain*, or to the drama *Werner*, finished on 20 January 1822 and published in November, and *Don Juan*, 6–8, completed about the end of July 1822 and published a year later.

29.17 The Giants' Causeway the Giant's Causeway is a basalt rock formation on the N coast of Country Antrim, N. Ireland.

29.19–20 in the name of Nicholas a dismissive expression; compare *BM* 11.439: 'sends the concern right a-head to old Nicholas', i.e. to the Devil.

29.22 the Emperor of the West Murray: see note on 2.35–6.

29.26 what Jeffrey has said of you in his review of *Sardanapalus ... The Two Foscari ... Cain* Jeffrey deplored 'the ferocity of his attacks on Mr Southey': *Edinburgh Review*, 36 (February 1822), 452.

29.34 the holy bottle probably alluding to the Oracle of the Holy Bottle which advises Panurge to 'trinc' at the end of the Fifth Book of the story of Gargantua and Pantagruel. This book, doubtfully by the author of the rest of the story, François Rabelais, was originally published in French in 1564; the well-known translation by Peter Anthony Motteux appeared in 1693–4.

29.43 Sir Mungo Malagrowther a deformed and caustic character in Scott's novel *The Fortunes of Nigel* (1821). Murray's editor (of the *Quarterly Review*, which avoided reviewing *Don Juan*) was William Gifford, who was similarly sour and physically awkward.

30.7 the rock of Cashel a limestone outcrop and historical site in the town of Cashel, County Tipperary, Ireland.

30.8–9 Don Juan and Cain see notes to 7.36 and 13.10–11.

30.12–13 the war-hoop of ... Southey Robert Southey, the Poet Laureate, had attacked Byron and the 'Satanic School' in the *Courier*, 5 January 1822: his letter is reprinted in *BM* 11.93–4.

30.17–18 Dr Magnus Oglethorpe this 'itinerant lecturer on poetry, politics, oratory, and the belles lettres' appears in 'The Tent': *BM* 5.709–19.

30.27 all the Hannah Mores Hannah More (1745–1833) was an eminent literary bluestocking who wrote improving tracts.

30.36–8 a clever boy ... do think the source of the quotation has not been identified, but Southey makes similar points in similar (though more elegant) language in his *Letter to William Smith* (1817).

30.40 warmth of colouring pronounced sexual element.

30.41 Homer ... the cloud-scene in which Zeus and his wife Hera make love: *The Iliad*, 14.224–353.

30.41–2 Virgil ... the cave-scene in which Dido and Aeneas become lovers: *The Aeneid*, 4.160–72.

30.42 Milton ... the bower-scene Adam and Eve in *Paradise Lost*, 4.689–775; but Eve is not described as 'nothing loth' until after the Fall (9.1039).

31.7 Doctor Magee William Magee became Archbishop of Dublin in 1822.

31.12 Archbishop King William King, Archbishop of Dublin, published *De Origine Mali* [Of the Origin of Evil] in 1702. The work attempts, on a Lockean basis, to reconcile the existence of evil, and particularly of moral evil, with the idea of an omnipotent and beneficent deity.

31.18 Warburton ... Essay on Man William Warburton, Bishop of Gloucester 1759–79, published *A Vindication of Mr Pope's 'Essay on Man', from the Misrepresentations of Mr de Crousaz* in 1740.

31.23 Cumberland ... his Calvary Richard Cumberland published the poem *Calvary; or, The Death of Christ* in 1792.

31.30–1 the Prometheus of Æschylus Prometheus is the champion of mankind against Zeus in Aeschylus's drama *Prometheus Bound*.

31.34–6 the haughty speech of Satan ... the proud defiance of Moloch *Paradise Lost*, 5.772–802; 2.51–105.

31.40–2 Chief Baron O'Grady ... "there is no God" Standish O'Grady (1766–1840), first Viscount Guillamore, Lord Chief Baron of the Irish Exchequer 1805–31. The reference is to Psalm 14.1. The letter to Mr Gregory has not been identified.

32.1–2 Lord Eldon John Scott, first Earl of Eldon. For his treatment of *Cain* see note to 7.36.

32.8–9 Benbow ... the Chevalier de Faublas William Benbow, a notorious pirate publisher, was tried (and acquitted) on 11 July 1822, at the instigation of the Society for the Suppression of Vice, for publishing allegedly obscene material including a translation of *Le Chevalier de Faublas, comédie en un acte, en vers par M. W— d'A* [Jean Baptiste Louvet de Couvray]. In this year he also published an edition of Sir William Lawrence's materialist *Lectures on Physiology, Zoology, and the Natural History of Man*. No copies of the editions of Southey's or Thomas Paine's works published by Benbow appear to have survived.

32.25 three times three three sets of three cheers.

32.26 Bibunt ambo *Latin* they both drink.

32.32 Brutum Pecus *Latin* stupid herd.

32.39 the best book in the world ... Balaam referring to the story of Balaam in Numbers Chs 22–4, and *balaam* meaning 'trumpery paragraphs reserved to fill up columns'.

33.5–6 the Sporting Magazine this publication ran fom 1792 to 1870.

33.8 con amore *Italian* with affection.

33.9 Ebony *Blackwood's*: see note to 1.7.

33.18 Childe Harold Byron's *Childe Harold's Pilgrimage* was published in 1812–18.

33.25 Anastasius ... Hope see note to 4.40.

33.29 de re periodicali *Latin* of the periodical matter.

33.29 the Baron of Bradwardine a pedant in Walter Scott's first novel *Waverley* (1814).

33.33–4 Monthly ... Review the *Monthly Review* was founded by Ralph Griffiths in 1749; George Edward Griffiths took over the editorship in 1803.

34.4 Every fourth of a year the *Edinburgh Review* appeared quarterly from October 1802, with Jeffrey, Henry Brougham, Sydney Smith, and Francis Horner as its leading spirits.

34.11–12 Johnny Murray ... Billy Gifford see note to 29.43.

34.28 Cazzo *Italian* a meaningless exclamation along the lines of 'tush'.

34.37 too old a cat for that straw proverbial: see *ODEP*, 632, and Walter Scott, *Old Mortality* (*Tales of my Landlord*, Edinburgh, 1816), 4.246: 'I'm ower auld a cat to draw that strae before me.'

34.38 five or six good things the second and third items are properly 'McPherson's Farewell' and 'Orananaoig; or, The Song of Death' ('Farewell, thou fair day'). 'Mary's Dream' is actually the name of a song by John Lowe (1750–98); the only Burns poem to which it might conceivably refer is 'Afton Water' (published 1792).

35.3 Allan Cunningham the poet and miscellaneous writer who contributed to *Blackwood's* in 1819–21.

35.6–7 Jeffrey abused him ... praising the Cockneys in his review of R.H. Cromek's *Reliques of Robert Burns* Jeffrey, while recognising Burns's genius, criticised 'his contempt, or affectation of contempt, for prudence, decency and regularity': *Edinburgh Review*, 13 (January 1809), 253. He published generally favourable reviews of Leigh Hunt's *The Story of Rimini* (26 (June 1816), 476–91: probably a heavy revision of Hazlitt's original article), Hazlitt's *Characters of Shakespeare's Plays* (28 (August 1817), 472–88), Keats's *Endymion* and his *Lamia* volume (34 (August 1820), 203–13), and Barry Cornwall's *Marcian Colonna* (34 (November 1820), 449–60).

35.10 our Italian Improvisatores 'One of the greatest curiosities you meet with in Italy, is the Improvisatore: such is the name given to certain individuals, who have the surprising talent of reciting verses extempore, on any subject you propose': Tobias Smollett, *Travels through France and Italy* (originally published 1766), ed. Frank Felsenstein (1979), 231.

35.16–20 Ritson ... Old Still Joseph Ritson (1752–1803), the antiquary, published this song in his *A Select Collection of English Songs* (1783), 2.71–3. John Still (1543?–1608), Bishop of Bath and Wells, was long erroneously credited (but not by Ritson) with the authorship of the play *Gammer Gurton's Needle* (published 1575), in which a version of the song that follows occurs at the beginning of Act 2.

35.22 Cantat Dohertiades *Latin* Odoherty sings. The Latin version is remarkably close to the original.

36.31–2 Camillo Querno a Neopolitan poet (1470–*c*.1528), noted for extempore versifying.

36.35–6 Marsham of Serampore John Clark Marsham (1794–1877), historian of India.

36.37 A.W. Schlegel August Wilhelm von Schlegel, German Romantic philosophical critic.

37.12 the Falls of the Rhone a celebrated tourist attraction (since destroyed

by blasting and diversion) near Bellegarde, France, on the border with
Switzerland, where the Rhone plunged into underground caverns.

37.28   my Memoirs   *Memoirs of the Life and Writings of ... Lord Byron*,
published anonymously in June 1822 by John Watkins, compiler of *An
Universal Biographical and Historical Dictionary* (1800): in a letter to
Blackwood of 25 June 1823 (MS 4011, ff. 33v–34r) Maginn reports Colburn's
protestation that he had not engaged Watkins but bought these memoirs in good
faith. Byron gave his real memoirs to Thomas Moore in 1819, but they were
burned against Moore's wishes after Byron's death.

37.32   old Gropius   the origin of this name applied to Watkins has not been
traced. It may just be a general comic term for a blindly groping pedant.

38.1   from Burke to Jeremy Bentham   see notes to 14.13 and 17.11.

38.4   Day and Martin   see note to 1.31–2.

38.9–10   the Appendix to ... The Two Foscari   see note to 1.31–2.

38.17   Gouvernantes—Kings—laurel-crown'd Poets attacking   Byron attacks Empress Catherine of Russia in *Don Juan*, George III in 'The Vision of
Judgment', and the Poet Laureate Southey in both poems.

38.19   many more too long   the source of this quotation has not been traced.

38.21   the attack on Ebony   *BM* had published (5.512–22) an attack on the
first two cantos of *Don Juan*, probably by Lockhart; in March 1820 Byron sent
John Murray a long reply, 'Some Observations upon an Article in *Blackwood's
Magazine*', but it remained unpublished until 1830 when Thomas Moore
included extracts in his *Letters and Journals of Lord Byron*, 2.360–74.

38.26   the Irish Advent   see note to 3.23.

38.31   the Vampire affair   John William Polidori (1795–1821) wrote a tale
called *The Vampyre*, based on a ghost-story idea of Byron's dating from 1816.
The tale was first published in Colburn's *New Monthly Magazine* in April 1819
as Byron's (11.195–206): in his memoir of Byron (see note to 37.28), Watkins
censures the deception (320–3). *The Vampyre* was published as a separate
volume in 1819 by Sherwood, Neely, and Jones.

38.37   the Row   Paternoster Row, London, where Longmans and many other
publishers had their offices.

39.4   As for ... *****   the seven asterisks probably refer to Cyrus Redding
(Campbell's assistant), or to one of the following contributors in 1822: William
Hazlitt, Mary Russell Mitford, or Peter George Patmore. The five asterisks
probably refer to one or more of John Banim, Eyre Evans Crowe, Richard
Lalor, R.L. Shiel, Horace and James Smith, and Joseph Blanco White.

39.7   **** is a great officer   the owner of this four-letter surname has not
been identified. The main drama critic for the *New Monthly* was Thomas Noon
Talfourd.

39.10   Transeat   *Latin* let it pass.

39.13   Oxoniensis   see note to 8.39–40.

39.16–17   I remember ****   the young man in question has not been
identified.

39.17   n'importe   *French* it doesn't matter.

39.17   Covent-Garden   the second theatre on the site (1809–56) was devoted
mostly to drama rather than opera.

39.20   Rhedycina   Oxford. The Welsh name is Rhydhchen, from *rhyd* ('ford') and *ychen* ('oxen').

39.22   the first class   in honours examinations.

39.22   for Oriel   for a fellowship at Oriel College, Oxford.

39.25–6   When smitten … piles among   the source of this couplet has not been identified. Byron was at Cambridge, not Oxford.

39.31   the bog of Allen   a group of peat bogs in E central Ireland.

39.32   Clare poetizing for the London   John Clare contributed poems to the *London Magazine* between 1820 and 1824.

39.39   Quelle gloire!   *French* what glory!

39.39–40   like the clowns in Virgil   in Virgil's *Third Eclogue* the shepherds Damoetas and Menalcas engage in an amoebaean contest (singing alternately, responsively) with Palaemon as umpire.

40.1   Dedication to Mr Grieve   'To Mr John Grieve' appeared as a dedication in the first edition of Hogg's long poem *Mador of the Moor* (1816).

40.1–2   The flying tailor of Ettrick   'Further Extract from "The Recluse" A Poem: The Flying Taylor', one of Hogg's parodies of Wordsworth in *The Poetic Mirror; or, The Living Bards of Britain* (1816), 155–61.

40.10–13   the Quarterly hint … Van Diemen's Land … Botany   an anonymous review of George William Evans, *A Geographical, Historical, and Topographical Description of Van Diemen's Land, with Important Hints to Emigrants*, published in March 1822 (*Quarterly Review*, 27 (April 1822), 99–109) paints an attractive picture of Tasmania, for which Van Diemen's Land was the original European name. Botany Bay, New South Wales, was the traditional destination for criminals transported fom Britain. 'Shoulder of Mutton Bay' is probably imaginary, but 'Mutton' appears in various Australian place-names including Mutton Bird Island and Mutton Rocks in Tasmania; there is a Mutton Bay in Québec.

40.13–15   Taylor … Lives of the Poets   John Taylor edited the *London Magazine* from April 1820 to November(?) 1824: it was published by Taylor & Hessey from July 1821 to April 1825. The continuation of Samuel Johnson's *Lives of the Poets* in the *London* was in fact not by Taylor, but by Henry Francis Cary.

40.17   Chesterfield   Philip Dormer Stanhope, fourth Earl of Chesterfield, wrote a series of letters to his son from 1737 instructing him in good breeding; they were published in 1774.

40.21–2   Some new periodical … Proctor, the great tragedian   for Procter and his tragedy *Mirandola* (produced at Covent Garden in January 1821) see note to 13.32. The reference here would appear to be to a periodical beginning (or planned) in (or after) 1822 which has not been identified.

40.24–5   My Faliero … Elliston   *Marino Faliero* was produced (with little success) by Robert Elliston at Drury Lane Theatre in 1821, against Byron's wishes.

40.26   no making a silk purse … ear   proverbial (*ODEP*, 733).

40.27–8   My Grandmamma's Review, the British   this is Byron's description (*Don Juan*, 1.209.8) of the Evangelical *British Review*, whose editor William Roberts attacked him on moral grounds: 'merry and jocular' is ironic.

40.29–30   the British Critic is dying   in fact this Tory and Anglican publication continued until 1843, though its third series, begun in 1825, narrowed its scope. Apart from a gap in 1825 and 1826 (F.) C. and J. Rivington were its publishers (with variations in the partners) for most of its career.

40.30   the Monthly Literary Censor   the *Monthly Censor*, of which the Rivingtons were initially publishers, lasted for only one year (June 1822 to May 1823).

40.32   the Literary Gazette   this periodical (see note to 4.5) acknowledged Byron's talent, but objected to his freethinking.

40.35   Flebit et insignis tota cantabitur urbe   [whoever provokes me] will weep, and will be proclaimed as notorious throughout the whole city: Horace, *Satires*, 2.1.46. '*Flebit*' is italicised to emphasise its echoing of 'flea-bites'.

40.37   Valpy set up the Museum ... Dibdin   Abraham John Valpy was patron, printer, and publisher of *The Museum; or, Record of Literature etc.* which ran, with some variations in its title, from April 1822 to February 1824 (this was the last number in the British Library's unique set, destroyed by bombing: according to *The Dictionary of National Biography* the project lasted until December 1825). Valpy's collaborator was Thomas Frognall Dibdin, the fashionable bibliographer (hence *black-letter* or Gothic type); *fogrum* means 'old-fashioned'.

40.42–41.1   my Werner and my New Mystery ... in sheets   Murray had printed the tragedy *Werner* and the play *Heaven and Earth* as a single volume, but he took fright at the theological unorthodoxy of the latter and sacrificed the printing: it is imagined that Odoherty had seen the unsewn sheets. *Heaven and Earth* appeared in *The Liberal* (for which see note to 14.17–18), and Murray published *Werner* separately on 22 November 1822.

41.17–18   Doom'd ... engross   see Alexander Pope, 'Epistle to Dr Arbuthnot' (1735), lines 17–18.

41.28   Ismail Fitz-Adam   in 1818 Ismael Fitz-Adam (really John Macker) published a poem *The Hart of the Desert*, descriptive of the battle of Algiers, in which he had served as a common sailor in 1816; this was followed by *Lays on Land* (1821), which is actually in a variety of metres, not just *heroics* (iambic pentameters).

42.14–37   There's not a joy ... drunk with thee   a parody of Byron's 'Stanzas for Music' (1815).

42.12   grand march in Scipio   the triumphal march which opens Act 1 of Handel's opera *Scipione* (1726).

43.2   Apropos, de bottes   *French* turning to quite another subject.

43.3–7   Bowles ... rubbers   Byron defended Pope's poetry against Bowles's strictures (see note to 20.26). Bowles's pamphlet *Two Letters to the Right Honourable Lord Byron etc.* (1821) bore the motto, 'He that plays at Bowls, must expect rubbers. (Old Proverb)'.

43.9   Ali Pacha   Ali Pasha (1741–1822), originally a brigand, had become ruler of an extensive tract of the Ottoman empire, notably Albania. In *Childe Harold's Pilgrimage*, 2 (1812), 62 Byron writes: 'Yet in his lineaments ye cannot trace,/ While Gentleness her milder radiance throws/ Along that aged venerable face,/ The deeds that lurk beneath, and stain him with disgrace.' In a note to stanza 73 Byron praises Pasha's civility and hospitality to himself.

43.11 the great Ethic, the Bard of Twickenham   Pope lived at Twickenham, and his *Essay on Man* (1733–4) is subtitled 'The First Book of Ethic Epistles'.

43.12–14   Roscoe, the gillyflower of Liverpool ... Murray's editor   Watts explained (MS 4009, f. 213r–v) that Walter Scott had been approached by Murray to produce a new edition of Pope, but that he had declined when he heard that William Roscoe (who had an interest in botany, hence his appellation) was engaged on such an enterprise. Roscoe's edition was published in 1824 by a consortium headed by C. and J. Rivington, mainly composed of houses which had published Bowles's Pope of 1807.

43.14   His Western Majesty   Murray: see note to 2.35–6.

43.16–18   one of Murray's huff-caps ... in the Quarterly   Henry Matthews, reviewing anonymously the fourth edition of *The Sketch Book of Geoffrey Crayon, Gent.* in the *Quarterly Review*, 25 (April 1821), 50–67, refers (52) to Roscoe as 'the weakest of all political writers and speakers'. A *huff-cap* is a swashbuckler.

43.19   Joannes de Moravia   *Latin* John Murray.

43.21   Tickler   see Introduction, viii.

43.27   the expected turn-up ... Moore   *BM* 11 (January 1822) had begun with a 'Preface' in which Christopher North stated that he happened to know that Moore had written a satirical poem on the Magazine and its contributors, and recommended him not to publish it; adding that, if he did, North would republish it, so as to occupy the right-hand column of about a dozen pages of the Magazine, and would fill the left-hand columns with original verses in the same metre on Moore. To have fair play, he suggested that umpires be appointed from among the friends of the combatants: 'We appoint for ourselves Neat [the boxer] and the Rev. William Lisle Bowles—and we suggest to Mr Moore, in the true spirit of British courage, Gas [another boxer] and Mr Montgomery, the "Author of the World before the Flood."' (viii).

43.28   à la Pistol   in the bombastic manner of Pistol in *2 Henry IV*, *Henry V*, and *The Merry Wives of Windsor*.

43.29–30   gown and band ... shovel   clerical attire, including shovel-hat.

44.1   Hobhouse   for Hobhouse see note to 9.37–8. He laments the downtrodden state of modern Italy in *Historical Illustrations of the Fourth Canto of Childe Harold* (1818), 325–8.

44.2   Hobbio—mobbio   in 1820 Byron had written a 'New Song' ('How came you in Hob's pound to cool') accusing Hobhouse of supporting the mob, including the stanza: 'But never mind such petty things—/ My boy Hobbie O— / God save the people—damn all Kings—/ So let us crown the Mobby O!'   Murray allowed the poem to circulate in London, and a garbled version appeared in the *Morning Post* on 15 April 1820: this is alluded to in *BM* 7 (June 1820), 317.

44.2–3   the Austrian domination   at the Congress of Vienna in 1815 Lombardy-Venetia was incorporated into the Habsburg empire and remained Austrian until 1859 (Lombardy) and 1866 (Venetia).

45.5   Manet ... solus   *Latin* remains alone.

45.14–15   The King has left the Theatre   George IV attended a performance of Scott's *Rob Roy* adapted and produced by William Murray, on the evening of Tuesday 27 August, at the Theatre Royal which stood at the bottom of the North Bridge: it was demolished in 1859. The King left the theatre at about 11 pm.

**45.18	Seward, Buller**	the fictitious Oxonians Harry Seward of Christ Church and Buller of Brasenose, who first appear in 'The Twelfth of August' (*BM* 5.604), were probably 'embodiments ... of [Wilson's] old Oxford reminiscences' (Ferrier, 2.115n); Buller was probably based on John Hughes (1790–1857) of Oriel College.

**45.26	every inch a King**	*King Lear*, 4.6.107.

**45.27	A King of ... France**	the royal claim to France, long a formality, had been officially renounced as part of the Treaty of Amiens in 1802: its revival here is a piece of anti-Gallican bravado or jocular excess.

**45.30	Fame does no more than justice to his bow**	see, for example, Byron, *Don Juan*, 12.84.2–4: 'A Prince, the prince of princes at the time/ With fascination in his very bow/ And full of promise as the spring of prime'. North has two lines of blank verse here.

**45.35	the Duke of Argyll, or Lord Fife**	George William Campbell, sixth Duke of Argyll, succeeded 1806; James Duff, fourth Earl of Fife, succeeded 1811.

**46.13	coup d'œil**	*French* general view at a glance.

**46.16–18	the Scotch ... shop-keepers**	a remark believed to have been made by the King that the Scots were 'a nation of gentlemen' was reported in various forms; the English had been characterised as 'a nation of shopkeepers' from the mid-eighteenth century, most recently and disparagingly by Napoleon.

**46.30–2	the Thane ... Dalkeith**	the Earl of Fife, who had attended the King to his temporary residence at Dalkeith House, 11 km SE of Edinburgh. William Tennant's poem *The Thane of Fife* was published in January 1822.

**46.41	surgunt omnes**	*Latin* all rise.

**46.42	Conticuere omnes**	*Latin* all are silent.

**47.17	The "Scotsman in London"**	London papers taken by Maga to be of the same liberal persuasion as the *Scotsman*, e.g. the *Times* and *Morning Chronicle*.

**47.19–20	its hurdies like twa distant hills**	see Burns, 'To a Haggis' (1786), line 8: 'Your hurdies like a distant hill'. John Jamieson, *An Etymological Dictionary of the Scottish Language* (1808) defines *hurdies* as 'the hips, the buttocks'.

**47.30–1	Well done, old Mole ... Shakespeare**	see *Hamlet*, 1.5.162.

**47.35	Up with it**	come out with it, read it.

**47.37	Reikie**	Auld Reikie (Edinburgh).

**48.5	St Leonard's and Drumsheugh**	districts at the eastern and western extremities of early-19th-century Edinburgh.

**48.7	Heeland Dhuine Wassals**	clansmen of rank below the chief; gentlemen of secondary rank.

**48.13	the Celtic**	the fashionable Celtic Society was founded in 1820, its chief ostensible object being the promotion of Highland dress.

**48.18	Doctor Scott the Dentist**	see note to 12.35.

**48.19	Maccallum More**	the Duke of Argyll.

**48.27–30	Fat Teil ... Cherman**	what the devil: all of this speech is a conventional rendering of Highlanders speaking Scots. Highlanders acted as sedan chair porters, or *chairmen*, in Edinburgh.

**49.2	Glengarry**	Alexander Ranaldson Macdonell of Glengarry wrote two highflown letters to the *Edinburgh Observer* after the Royal Visit (2 and 5 September) attacking the Celtic Society as bogus. The first asserts: 'They neither speak the language, nor know how to put on correctly the garb of the "Gael;" and yet, *without possessing the blood, or the manly frame* of that interesting race, or any other ostensible cause whatever, they barefacedly *masked themselves* in the Highland garb …'. The second maintains, amongst other things, that the Society's members, being poor shots, offer no danger to the eagle.

49.2–3 the message … to the Chiefs on leaving Scotland the King caused to be sent for onward transmission by Scott a message praising the attendant Highlanders' 'ardent spirit of loyalty'.

49.12 Townsend John Townsend of Sussex undertook many pedestrian feats: for instance on 11 September 1822 he 'completed his task of walking 1000 miles in 18 days (one-half backwards)' at Cowgate, Newcastle (*Edinburgh Weekly Journal*, 18 September 1822, 301).

49.20 Article on the … Highlands of Scotland Blackwood's wish for such an article was not fulfilled.

49.22 Dog on it a vague imprecation.

49.40–50.4 Ossian … Wordsworth … Macpherson Ossian was a legendary Gaelic warrior and bard supposed to have lived in the 3rd century. In 1760–5 James Macpherson published a series of poems which he claimed were translations of Ossianic originals, but they were largely his own invention. Wordsworth attacked the Macpherson poems, in the terms indicated, in 'Essay, Supplementary to the Preface [to *Lyrical Ballads*]' (1815), lines 552–633.

50.11–12 He also says … cars 'Essay', lines 587–91.

50.20 Fingal see note to 22.13.

50.22 were not all the Highlands once called "Morven?" James Macpherson elevated Morven in this way, perhaps picking up a popular (but probably false) interpretation of the name as meaning *mòr-bheinn* ('great mountain') and extending that to *dùtheich nam mòr-bheann* ('land of the great mountains'), a description actually used of the Highlands in Gaelic.

50.24 the water-drinking laker Wordsworth had publicly proclaimed his teetotalism in *The Waggoner* (1819), lines 58–60: 'There, where the DOVE and OLIVE-BOUGH/ Once hung, a Poet harbours now,—/ A simple water-drinking Bard'.

50.27–8 Alice Fell … Malvina Wordsworth's ballad 'Alice Fell' was written in 1802 and published in 1807; Malvina is a character in James Macpherson's Ossianic poems.

50.28 Peter Bell … Abelard Wordsworth's long ballad 'Peter Bell' was written in 1798 and published after substantial revision in 1819; Pope's heroic epistle 'Eloisa to Abelard' was published in 1717.

50.39–40 O'Meara in the Edinburgh Barry E[dward] O'Meara's *Napoleon in Exile* (July 1822) was reviewed anonymously by Henry Brougham in the *Edinburgh Review*, 37 (June 1822), 164–204.

51.1 more lucrative the standard rate was ten guineas (£10.50) per sheet of 16 double-column (*c.* 850 words) pages, though special rates were often paid. Francis Jeffrey's basic rate for *Edinburgh Review* contributors (reckoned generous) was 16 guineas for a sheet of single-column (*c.* 450 words) pages.

51.10   Mr Bunting   apparently a fictitous figure: Crail, a burgh in Fife, did not have provosts, and the name Bunting does not appear in the council records of the period.

51.17–18   Mr Fox joining Lord North   Charles James Fox combined with his political enemy Frederick North, later second Earl of Guildford, in 1783 to overthrow Shelburne's ministry.

51.22   the seven young men   a band representing Christopher North's antagonists, the young Whig contributors to Constable's *Edinburgh Magazine*.

51.24–5   I respect him as the chief magistrate   the Edinburgh Tories attacked those Whigs who advocated paying respect to the King only as 'Chief Magistrate of the nation': see e.g. *Edinburgh Weekly Journal*, 21 August and 11 September 1822, 267, 292.

51.35   Mr Peel   Sir Robert Peel became Home Secretary in January 1822.

51.36   borough reform   Lord John Russell was to ask (unsuccessfully) for 100 new seats in the House of Commons on 25 April 1822.

51.38–40   Unless his Majesty's ministers ... modern Athens   in March 1822 more than three-quarters of the inhabitants of the Greek island of Chios were killed or taken into slavery by the Turks. Britain maintained a diplomatic neutrality.

52.19–21   I have just been perusing ... the Congress   Wellington did attend the final Congress of Allied Sovereigns in Verona in October and November 1822, where he unsuccessfully opposed plans for a reactionary invasion of Spain.

52.23   Benjamin Constant   French novelist, leader of the liberal opposition in France from 1818.

52.24   Madame de Stael   Anne-Louise-Germaine Neckar, Madame de Staël, French novelist and critic.

52.24   John Allan   John Allen, one of the Whig contributors to the *Edinburgh Review*.

52.24   Sir James Macintosh   Sir James Mackintosh, the liberal philosopher.

52.25   un homme bornè   *French* (*borné*) a man of limited intelligence, narrow, or short-sighted. Napoleon's low opinion of Wellington is implicitly endorsed by Henry Brougham in the course of his anonymous review of O'Meara: *Edinburgh Review*, 37 (June 1822), 182–4.

52.34   Soho   hey!

52.34–5   Man of the Mist   referring to the dense tobacco smoke, and perhaps alluding ironically to the term 'Children of the Mist' applied to the MacGregor clan in Scott's novel *A Legend of Montrose* (1819); compare *BM* 14.485: 'Sons of the Mist'.

53.4   Cape Clear   the southernmost point of Clear Island, SW Ireland.

53.11   Boreas   the north wind.

53.14   Miss Edina   Edinburgh.

53.21   First of all Minstrels   alluding to Scott's narrative poem *The Lay of the Last Minstrel* (1805).

53.29–37   Crabbe ... the Borough Bard   the English poet George Crabbe, author of *The Borough* (1810), was in Edinburgh during the King's Visit.

54.2–6   Croly ... Cataline   George Croly, Irish clergyman, poet, and journalist, contributed regularly to *BM* and published a tragedy *Catiline* in April 1822.

54.17 **Peveril** the novel *Peveril of the Peak*, dated 1822, published anonymously by Scott in January 1823.

54.25 **the Palmy Isle** John Wilson's poem *The Isle of Palms* was published in 1812.

54.26 **Valerius** a novel by Lockhart published in 1821.

54.36 **the Duke of Athol** John Murray (1755–1830) succeeded in 1774 as fourth Duke of Atholl.

54.36–7 **the Chain Pier** the chain pier at Newhaven was opened 14 October 1821.

55.1 **Tie my Barcelona round your neat neck** in the song 'A Sprig of Shillelah' by Henry Brereton Code, first published in his drama *The Russian Sacrifice; or, Burning of Moscow* (Dublin, 1813), an Irishman is described as wearing 'a new Barcelona tied round his neat neck': the *Barcelona* was a thick silk neckerchief, with bright colours, mustard being predominant.

55.10 **Palinurus** pilot, after the steersman in Virgil's *Aeneid,* 5 and 6.

55.20 **Brazen-nose** Brasenose College, Oxford.

55.20–1 **old Davis** Stephen Davis, an Oxford waterman and dauntingly spirited rowing tutor.

55.25 **Arthur's Ghost ... mountain-throne** alluding to the Edinburgh mountain Arthur's Seat.

55.27 **crown of gas-light** one of the chimneys of the Edinburgh Gas-Light Company (founded 1817), W of Canongate churchyard, was thus illuminated for the Royal Visit.

55.29 **Nelson's Pillar** or Nelson's Monument, a tower built 1807–15 to resemble an inverted telescope on Calton Hill in memory of Nelson: Archibald Alison had proposed its demolition in *BM* 5.386 and 6.146, but in the second noctes North argued, albeit less than wholeheartedly, for its retention (11.483–4).

55.32 **the Parthenon** the National Monument on Calton Hill, begun as an imitation of the Parthenon in 1822 but never completed, for lack of funds.

55.39–40 **my prize poem** *Parthenon*, the Oxford Prize Poem for 1811, was in fact by Richard Burdon of Oriel College.

56.4 **Parliamentary grants** a grant of £10,000 towards the National Monument was hoped for, but it was not forthcoming.

56.4–5 **a nation of Gentlemen** see note to 46.16–18.

56.8 **We call ourselves Athenians** Edinburgh had become accustomed to referring to itself as 'the modern Athens'.

56.17 **Mr Linning** Michael Linning, Secretary to the National Monument Committee.

56.20 **the Foundling Hospital, Dublin** an institution for deserted or exposed infants, founded in 1727.

56.26 **Sir William Curtis's yacht** the sumptuous yacht, *Die Jonge Vrow Rebecca Maria*, belonging to Sir William Curtis, a leading Tory and friend of George IV, was the subject of continuous Whig and radical mockery.

56.32 **Guildhall** the hall of the Corporation of the City of London.

56.32–3 **the Celtic Society** see note to 48.13.

56.42–3 **Davy's locker** the sea.

57.1 **Dog on it** a vague imprecation.

57.3   Newington   a new southern suburb of Edinburgh, where Blackwood had a house at 2 Salisbury Road.

57.3–4   My brother Thomas   Thomas Blackwood was a partner in T. and J. Blackwood, silk merchants.

57.21   the New Canal   the Union Canal joining Edinburgh to the Forth & Clyde Navigation was opened in May 1822.

57.22   called The Lady of the Lake   after Scott's narrative poem (1810), whose heroine Ellen, the Lady of the Lake, appears in a skiff on Loch Katrine.

57.23–4   lean, and lank … sea-sand   Coleridge, 'The Rime of the Ancient Mariner' (1798; revised up to 1816), lines 226–7.

57.32–3   six and eight pence   six shillings and eight pence (33.3p).

57.33   da capo   *Italian* from the beginning, repeat it.

58.3–4   the Surrey   the Old Surrey and Burstow Hunt, founded in the 18th century.

58.8   Temple Bar   the gateway between the City of London and the Strand.

58.12–13   the London or New Monthly   see notes to 3.32 and 2.3.

58.33   Colburn's   see note to 2.3.

58.35   he drags at each remove a heavier chain   see Oliver Goldsmith, *The Traveller; or, A Prospect of Society* (1764), line 10.

58.36   the pugilists   Jack the Butcher was decisively beaten by the great Jack Randall in Randall's first notable fight *c.* 1815; George Williams the swell (an amateur) challenged Joshua or Josh Hudson but was beaten in six rounds on 5 December 1820; the Birmingham Youth, Philip Sampson, suffered several defeats in 1820–1, but he was to stage a comeback in 1823. Messrs F., R., and T. are probably chosen for the combined effect of the initial letters rather than to indicate identifiable contributors.

59.1   Boxiana articles   see note to 6.21–2.

59.2–3   old —— in the "Fancy Gazette" … Josh. Hudson   the editor of *The Fancy; or, True Sportsman's Guide* was George Kent. Hudson, a promising young fighter, defeated Barlow, 'the Nottingham youth' with an exaggerated reputation, in five rounds on 10 (or perhaps 17) September 1822: the *Fancy* more or less admitted it had been wrong in its expectations (1.667: compare 644).

59.3   a rum one to go   see note to 6.37.

59.9–13   Dr Wodrow … Saunders Howie   the Rev. Donald Wodrow, DD (compare *BM* 11.602) is an imaginary figure, named after a prominent clerical family of the 17th and 18th centuries; his elder is probably also imaginary.

59.12   Christie's   John Christie, breeches-maker and glover, of 23 St Andrew Street.

59.13–14   old Tom Owen and Mendoza   the famous London boxer Daniel Mendoza (1764–1836) was unexpectedly beaten on his last appearance on 4 July 1820 by Tom Owen (b. 1768): a mock-Wordsworthian sonnet on the occasion by Maginn appeared in *BM* 8.63–4.

59.16   Covenanter   here used loosely and jocularly for 'Presbyterian'.

59.20–1   Randal … Macarthy … Jack Scroggins … Holt   Jack Randall (b. 1794), who is said to have approached pugilistic perfection, beat Dan M'Carthy at Tom Reynolds's Free and Easy Club, Drury Lane, on 6 April 1818; John Palmer (b. 1787), nicknamed Scroggins, the Kean of the prize-ring, beat Henry

Josiah Holt (b. 1792) in a hard-fought contest in May 1822.

59.24   Omnes   *Latin* all.

59.33   Salve, Pater!   *Latin* hail, Father!

59.34–5   little do you know ... crown   here and below North is parodying *2 Henry IV*, 3.1.4–31.

59.39   the gem   Blackwood's snuff-box is so described in the Chaldee Manuscript, 1.34.

59.40   Canning   George Canning succeeded Castlereagh as Foreign Secretary in September 1822 after the latter's suicide.

60.4   the blue devils   depression.

60.22   Mr Smith's Cutter, the Orion   possibly the Mr Smith referred to is the Leith shipmaster James Smith who moved in 1822 from 3 Commercial Place to 2 Old Bridge End.

60.33–4   Corney Macguire   the figure, if historical, has not been identified.

60.37   Ramsay-cut   it has not been possible to discover what this signifies.

60.40   miss stays   *nautical* fail in the attempt to go about.

61.2   her present interesting situation   pregnancy.

61.6   Alloa   a brewing town in Clackmannanshire (now Central Region).

61.9   eating him out of the wind   *nautical* stealing to windward of him.

61.13   O'Meara   for Napoleon's plans to invade Britain and reform British institutions on rational principles see Barry E[dward] O'Meara, *Napoleon in Exile* (1822), 1.349–55: Maga chooses to ignore O'Meara's rejoinders to Napoleon. For Napoleon's statement about Wellington's inability to retreat see 1.175.

61.15   laid his account with   reckoned upon.

61.29   a Liverpool barber   no more information about this barber or his Manchester rival has been found.

62.2   the Dollar Academy   the academy at Dollar, Clackmannanshire (now Central Region), was founded in 1818.

62.4   Anster Fair   a mock-heroic poem published in 1812 (2nd edn 1814) by William Tennant, teacher of classics and oriental languages at Dollar Academy.

62.5   the Zuyder Zee   the Zuiderzee, a former inlet of the North Sea in N Holland, divided in 1932 by a dam into the IJsselmeer and the Waddenzee.

62.6   Don Juan   Byron's poem.

62.12   Galt   John Galt died in 1839.

62.14   the Lairds of Grippy   subtitle of Galt's novel *The Entail* (December 1822).

62.23   the stars are paling their ineffectual fires   see *Hamlet*, 1.5.90.

62.26   Hopetoun House   seat of the Earl of Hopetoun, 5 km W of South Queensferry, at which the King was to breakfast on Thursday 29 August, the day of his departure.

62.37   Girnaway   the farm is apparently imaginary: its name derives from Scots *girn* ('complain', 'scold').

62.40   Reel of Tullochgorum   the words (by the Rev. John Skinner, first printed 1776) to this old reel (which first appeared in Alex Macglashan, *A Collection of Strathspey Reels* [1760], 4) include the lines (7–12): 'Let Whig and Tory all agree,/ To drop their Whig-mig-morum;/ To spend the night in mirth and glee,/ And cheerfu' sing alang wi' me/ The reel of Tullochgorum.'

63.10 fin' as gin feel as if.

63.14 a foursome reel a lively dance for two couples facing each other and describing a series of figures of eight.

63.15 I'll gang nae mair to yon town this tune was first printed in James Oswald, *Caledonian Pocket Companion*, Book 10 [*c.* 1756], 15. In Nathaniel Gow's *The Ancient Curious Collection of Scotland* [1823], 1–3 it has the subtitle 'King George the Fourth's Favorite'.

63.19 as wat's muck soaking wet.

63.31 just the age of the King George IV was sixty on 12 August 1822. The fictitious Christopher North is also a sexagenarian in *BM* 9.61.

63.41 on half pay on a reduced salary when not in actual service.

64.4 Maggy Lauder the tune to the comic ballad by Francis Semple of Beltrees (*c.* 1642) is by an unknown hand: it was first printed in Adam Craig, *A Collection of the Choicest Scots Tunes* [1730], 38.

64.9 The Bush aboon Traquair an old pastoral melody, sung to words by Robert Crawfurd (d. 1832): it was first printed in William Thomson, *Orpheus Caledonius* [1725], 3.

64.11 The Hen's March this tune, imitating the subject, was first printed in *A Collection of Airs & Marches* [1761], 64.

64.28–9 Mr Buller of Brazen-nose see note to 45.18.

64.36 a three-handed crack a conversation among three people.

65.2 the brass nose brass face, impudence. There is a play on 'Brasenose'.

65.7 gane fain on become fond of.

66.6 the Calton ... Holyrood the King was said to have been visibly moved on his progress from Leith as he looked up at Calton Hill, crowded with spectators, and down on Holyrood, his palace at the foot of the Royal Mile.

66.36 rudiments *probably* a malapropism for 'rheumatics': compare 126.1.

67.9 wi' the face of Geordie Buchanan on't the title-page and cover of each issue of *Blackwood's* bore a portrait of the Renaissance humanist George Buchanan (1506-82).

67.21–2 the opinion of the General Assembly the supreme court of the Church of Scotland, meeting annually in May. In spite of strong opposition, the 1822 Assembly agreed to include in the address to the King the following sentence: 'We have witnessed with deep concern the wicked and persevering efforts which in certain parts of the kingdom have recently been made to subvert the religious faith of your Majesty's people, especially in the humbler and more numerous classes of society, by means of publications replete with scepticism and blasphemy' (*Edinburgh Weekly Journal*, 19 June 1822, 198).

67.27 come mair speed have more success.

67.39 Antiburgher a member of the section of the Secession Church which separated in 1747 from the rest of that Church over the question of taking the burgess oath.

68.18 Torbolton Tarbolton is a village near Ayr, Ayrshire (now Strathclyde Region).

68.23 Oh! Beauty's tear is lovelier than her smile the source of this quotation has not been identified.

71.5–6 I'll gie him the floor I'll throw him to the floor.

71.7 Pate Muter a *muter* or *multure* is the duty, consisting of a proportion of the grain, exacted by the proprietor or tenant of a mill on all corn ground there.

71.8   Falkirk Tryst   the name given to sales of livestock held on Stenhousemuir near Falkirk on the second Tuesdays of August, September, and October.

71.10   Burniwin'   burn-the-wind; blacksmith.

71.28   the Book   the Bible, for family devotions.

72.17–18   our unconquered citadel … our ancient and holy temple   on Thursday 22 August the King was acclaimed standing in the rain on the battlements of Edinburgh Castle, which Prince Charles Edward Stewart had failed to take in 1745; and on Sunday 25th he attended morning service in the High Kirk of St Giles.

72.43–73.1   Wallace … Bruce   Sir William Wallace (1272?–1305), Scottish patriot; Robert de Bruce VIII (1274–1329), King of Scots.

73.16   the Ferry   Queensferry, the main crossing point for the Firth of Forth.

73.16–17   Lord Hopetoun   see note to 62.26. John Hope, fourth Earl of Hopetoun succeeded to the title in 1816.

73.26   close hauled   *nautical* with the sails hauled close, so as to sail as near to the wind as possible.

74.3–14   epigraph   the Greek couplet is by the 6th-century B.C. elegiac poet Phocylides (Phoc. ap. Ath.10.428b). A literal translation is: 'At a symposium, as the cups go round and round, one should drink one's wine while sitting chatting pleasantly.'   The selection and free translation of this motto are said to have been the work of Maginn.

74.15   Bathing-machines   wheeled vehicles designed to convey bathers into the water conveniently and with modesty.

74.15   Portobello   an eastern suburb of Edinburgh.

75.16   Inchkeith   an island in the Firth of Forth, 9 km north of Portobello.

75.20   Coromandel   the SE coast of India.

75.22   outower the lugs   over head and ears.

75.32   Lord Byron   Byron, who died in 1824, boasted of his prowess in swimming.

75.34   A Liverpool gentleman   this is probably a variant of the proposed feat recorded in the *Sporting Magazine*, 70 (July 1827), 240: 'A gentleman, resident in Manchester, has undertaken to swim from Liverpool to Runcorn, a distance of twenty-three or twenty-four miles, in one tide, on the 10th of July next.'

75.36   Saturn and Neptune   probably suggesting that Saturn (for slowness, as with the planet), and Neptune as god of the sea will defeat the Liverpool gentleman.

75.42   the great American serpent   reported sightings of a 'Great Sea Serpent' in America are discussed in *BM* 3.35–6, 206.

76.15   ninety   90 degrees fahrenheit (32.2 centigrade).

76.27   Arion   this semi-mythical poet was carried to land by a dolphin after being thrown overboard by sailors greedy for his treasure.

76.28–9   Byron … Grecian Isles   see *Childe Harold's Pilgrimage*, 4 (1818), 29.

77.7   Let him alane   trust him.

77.7–8   He's ca'd a fish in the Bible   see Jonah 1.17 etc.

77.8   Buffon   in Georges-Louis Leclerc, Comte de Buffon, *Buffon's Natural History* (1807–11) the whale is not included in the lists of animals.

77.17   Jonathan   a generic name for Americans.

77.25   Nae tricks upon travellers   proverbial (see *ODEP*, 657).

77.39–40   the James Watt steam-boat, Captain Bain   the *James Watt* was one of four boats operated by the London and Edinburgh Steam Packet Company: in 1827 it sailed from Edinburgh (Newhaven) and London on alternate Saturdays under its captain William Bain. During the King's Visit of 1822 the *James Watt* had towed the *Royal George* in the Firth of Forth.

78.14   a Nautilus   the paper nautilus, or argonaut, a mollusc formerly believed to sail on the surface of the sea.

78.22   the Forest   Ettrick Forest, including most of Selkirkshire and some adjacent areas (now mostly Borders Region).

78.22   David Ballantyne   (1787-1832), a member of the principal farming family in the Yarrow Valley, Selkirkshire (now Borders Region) farmed at Shaws, near Hermitage Castle, from 1818.

78.23   ower by yonner   over yonder.

78.23   Hermitage Castle   in Liddesdale, Roxburghshire (now Borders Region).

78.24–5   the Shepherd of the Sea   see 'Colin Clouts Come Home Againe' (1595), lines 66, 358, 428.

79.21   a white lace-veil, sic as Queen Mary's drawn in   for several examples see Lionel [Henry] Cust, *Notes on the Authentic Portraits of Mary Queen of Scots* (1903).

80.2–3   As when some shepherd … main!   see James Thomson, *The Castle of Indolence* (1748), 1.262–3 (stanza 30).

80.15   an Eolian harp   a stringed box-like instrument designed to be activated by the wind.

81.1   Venus and Adonis   referring to Shakespeare's poem, in which Venus woos Adonis aggressively.

81.36–9   Lord Wellington's amendment … M'Culloch   the Duke of Wellington's wrecking amendment in June 1827 was that 'no foreign corn in bond should be taken out of bond until the average price of corn should have reached 66*s*[hillings]', rather than the 60 shillings proposed in the bill. John Ramsay McCulloch, the Whig economist and contributor to the *Edinburgh Review*, was much criticised in *Blackwood's* under the name of the Stot.

82.2   Canning and Brougham   for Canning see note to 59.40. He had formed a centrist coalition administration in April 1827, which was supported by the leading Whig Henry Brougham; this survived Wellington's successful amendment, but Canning himself was to die on 8 August.

82.15   Bewick's birds   Thomas Bewick engraved the wooden blocks for *History of British Birds* (Newcastle, 1797–1804).

82.31   boxed the compass   recited the points of the compass in order.

82.38–9   the gallant Admiral   Rear-Admiral Sir Robert Waller Otway, commander-in-chief at Leith 1818–21. Bronte's father lived with him at Portobello (*BM* 21.912–13).

82.42   Bristol Hunt   Henry Hunt, radical politician.

82.42–3 Sir Thomas Lethbridge Tory MP for Somerset.

83.35–6 boatie rows—the boatie rows these words occur as a refrain in a song by John Ewen of Aberdeen (d. 1821).

83.40 the Odd Volume two volumes, consisting of miscellaneous tales including songs and other music, were published anonymously under this title by the sisters Grace and Walterina Corbett in July 1826 and 1827.

84.8 in or over *perhaps, either* more or less, *or* sinking below the water or swimming on top of it.

84.9 By the Nail six! variant of 'by the (sounding) lead six (fathoms)'.

85.3–14 epigraph see note to 74.3–14.

85.18 The three celebrated young Scottish Leanders this ensemble has not been identified.

85.19 Brose and Brochan and a' the song has not been identified: there was a Jacobite song 'Brose and Butter' with the refrain 'O gi'e my love brose, brose'.

85 (table-plan) Brown Soup *The Cook and Housewife's Manual* (1826), allegedly by Mrs Margaret Dods, landlady of the Cleikum Inn in Scott's novel *St Ronan's Well* (1824), but actually by Christian Isobel Johnstone, gives a recipe (73–4) for Scotch Brown Soup: its main feature is that pieces of browned beef steak are added to the basic stock.

85 (table-plan) White Soup a rich soup whose ingredients include white chicken and ground almond.

86.17–18 Saturn ... devourit his weans in classical legend Saturn, warned that one of his children would overthrow him, swallowed them at birth.

86.24–5 of imagination all compact *A Midsummer Night's Dream*, 5.1.8.

87.10 Kilmeny see note to 12.29.

87.13–14 the Forest see note to 78.22.

87.15–16 the Ettrick Shepherd the appellation commonly given to Hogg.

87.22–23 All Fool's Day 1 April.

87.26 the Border Club the St Ronan's Border Club was founded at Innerleithen in 1827 at Hogg's instigation, its principal achievement being the annual Border Games.

87.27 the late Dyuk o' Buccleuch Charles William Henry Scott (1772–1819), fourth Duke of Buccleuch.

87.29 Yarrow-Ford a hamlet on the lower part of Yarrow Water, Borders Region.

87.41 Allan Ramsay's ain Gentle Shepherd Ramsay's pastoral comedy (1725).

88.3–4 lichts and shadows ... expression the Shepherd is alluding to John Wilson's *Lights and Shadows of Scottish Life* (Edinburgh, 1822).

88.7 kittle dealin' troublesome to cope with.

88.10 the wrong side for a right-handed person to be able to draw a sword, it must be worn on the left side of the body.

88.24–5 worky-day *Antony and Cleopatra*, 1.2.50.

88.31 rather a wee owre slow a trifle too slowly.

88.42 He is a slave, the meanest we can meet Wordsworth, 'Personal Talk' (1807), line 28.

89.2 worms—and I wuss you muckle gude o' them compare the Clown, bringing the asps to Cleopatra: 'I wish you joy o' th' worm' (*Antony and Cleopatra*, 5.2.277).

89.9   Pan ... Cybele   for Pan see note to 29.13; Cybele was the Greek goddess of the powers of nature.

89.19   tak tent   be careful.

89.21   tremens   *Latin* trembling.

89.21   Tappytourie   this waiter's name means *inter alia* a knob of pastry over the central hole in a pie.

89.22–3   Moshy Shawbert   or Mosshy Shaubert (*BM* 22.122), a contemporary fire-eater (Ferrier).

89.25   the Standard   a Tory newspaper which began publication on 21 May 1827.

90.22   intus et in cute   *Latin* within and in the skin; thoroughly.

90.24   Confessions   De Quincey's *Confessions of an English Opium Eater*, published in the *London Magazine* in September and October 1821, and in book form in 1822.

90.26   a novel   De Quincey wrote to Wilson in January 1830 that the proposed work was to be called *New Canterbury Tales*, but if it was ever written it has disappeared. In 1832 De Quincey did eventually present Blackwood with a novel *Klosterheim; or, The Masque*.

90.36–7   the Exhibition ... at the Scottish Academy   the Scottish Academy (later the Royal Scottish Academy), founded in 1826, held its exhibitions at 24 Waterloo Place. Lists of some of the paintings exhibited may be found in Frank Rinder and W.D. McKay, *The Royal Scottish Academy 1826–1916* (1917).

90.41   the year   this year.

90.43   Mr Thomson of Duddingstone   John Thomson, minister of Duddingston, a noted landscape painter.

91.2   Williams   Hugh William Williams (1773–1829), known as 'Grecian' Williams.

91.21   Sir William Wallace   see note to 72.43–73.1.

91.30   William Simpson   William Simson specialised in Dutch landscapes.

91.33   Ewbank   John W. Ewbank specialised in Dutch shipping pieces. He had three moonlight scenes in the 1830 exhibition.

91.39   Fleming   John Fleming of Greenock, a landscape painter, had two paintings in the 1830 exhibition.

92.3   Pitches her tents before him   see Wordsworth's Prospectus (published 1814) to his uncompleted poem *The Recluse*, line 46.

92.4   Gibb   Robert Gibb (d. 1837), Edinburgh landscape painter.

92.15   Mrs Gentle   the widow Mrs Gentle and her daughter are fictitious characters in the *Noctes*.

92.21–4   O love! ... bizziness!   see the refrain of Hogg's song 'I lately liv'd in quiet case' to the tune 'Paddy's Wedding' in *The Forest Minstrel* (1810).

92.26–30   Nasmyth ... a noble picture of London   Alexander Nasmyth exhibited 'Part of London with Waterloo Bridge, from the Earl of Casillis' Privy Garden' at the Royal Institution, Edinburgh in 1827. The picture, which is now called 'England's Capital' and is on loan to the House of Lords from a private collection, is described and illustrated in J.C.B. Cooksey, *Alexander Nasmyth H.R.S.A. 1758–1840: A Man of the Scottish Renaissance* (Whittinghame House

Publishing, Scotland, 1991), 92–4. Nasmyth's artist son was Patrick, not Peter, and his artist daughters Jane, Barbara, Margaret, Elizabeth (who married Daniel Terry the actor), Anne, and Charlotte. The French *coup d'oeil* means 'general view at a glance'.

92.37   Colvin Smith   a painter of portraits in the Raeburn manner. Versions of his portrait of Jeffrey (no. 148 in the exhibition) are in the Scottish National Portrait Gallery, Edinburgh and the Kelvingrove Art Gallery, Glasgow.

92.38   armed at all points   see *Hamlet*, 1.2.200.

93.8   what you half-create and half-perceive   see Wordsworth, 'Lines Written a Few Miles above Tintern Abbey' (1798), lines 106–7.

93.16   Canning   see notes to 59.40 and 82.2.

93.18–19   as Burns said ... bright man   see 'Elegy on Capt[ain] M[atthew] H[enderson]' (published 1793), line 112.

94.1   the Schlegels   the German Romantic philosophical critics August Wilhelm von Schlegel and his brother Friedrich.

94.2   et id genus omne   *Latin* and everything of the kind; persons of this class.

94.9   genius loci   *Latin* spirit of the place.

94.12   soup maigre   soup made without using flesh.

94.21   John Watson's "Lord Dalhousie"   'The Earl of Dalhousie' (no. 116) by John Watson, known from 1826 as Watson-Gordon.

94.22   win upon you   gain your affection.

94.28   Duncan's "Braw Wooer"   a picture (no. 159) by Thomas Duncan based on Burns's song 'Last May a braw wooer cam down the lang glen' (written 1795, published 1799). The first stanza is quoted, with minor variants.

95.30–1   rigs o' barley   alluding to Burns's poem 'It was upon a Lammas night' (published 1786).

96.8   The Boatie Rows   see note to 83.35–6.

96.9   Picardy   Ambrose of Picardy Place.

96.13   the Great Deep   Isaiah 51.10.

97.3   Stentor   Greek warrior mentioned in Homer's *Iliad*, 5.785 (and hence a man generally) of powerful voice.

97.14   the noo   at present.

97.23   Linlithgow   from the loch at Linlithgow, 27 km W of Edinburgh.

97.34   ettlin ... at   trying for.

97.34   B flat ... A sharp   for most practical purposes these are the same note.

97.37   Bulls o' Bashan   see Psalm 22.12.

98.8   to airy nothing ... name   *A Midsummer Night's Dream*, 5.1.16–17.

98.23   Deathless Me—so Fichte and Schelling speak   the German Romantic philosopher Johann Gottlieb Fichte (1762–1814), leading proponent of the *Ichphilosophie* ('ego-philosophy'), and his follower in transcendental idealism Friedrich Wilhelm Joseph von Schelling (1775–1854).

98.24–5   the Bonassus   a *bonassus* is a bison. In Noctes 33 (21.914) the Shepherd tells of his purchasing the Bonassus.

98.34   wee Jamie   Hogg's son James was born in March 1821.

98.36   B sharp   usually termed C natural.

99.10   in puris naturalibus   *Latin* in a state of nudity.

99.38   Joachim Murat King o' Naples   one of Napoleon's marshals, a brilliant cavalry leader, and King of Naples from 1808 until his execution in 1815.

100.6–9   the Water-Kelpie on the Water-Horse ... a lurid cloud   this nocturnal kelpie is otherwise unrecorded, but a reference to similar activity in Ch. 6 of Scott's novel *The Monastery* (1820) may be the source; or both Wilson and Scott may be drawing independently on Border lore, and perhaps romanticising it.

100.17   Mazeppa   in Byron's poem of this name (1819), Mazeppa is bound naked to a wild horse's back and driven into the wilderness.

100.20   Loch Skene and the Grey Mare's Tail   a remote high loch and attendant waterfall in Dumfriesshire (now Dumfries and Galloway Region), 18 km NE of Moffat.

100.40   recoils into the wilderness   an echo of *Mazeppa*, line 850: 'Sent me forth to the wilderness'.

100.43   deserts idle   *Othello*, 1.3.140.

101.13   twice ten thousand horse   *Mazeppa*, line 411 has 'twice five thousand horse'.

101.26–8   Homer's description ... Achilles   *The Iliad*, 22.395–405.

102.26–7   witched the world with noble horsemanship   see *1 Henry IV*, 4.1.110.

102.33–4   Sol entering Taurus   the Sun enters the constellation of Taurus on or near 21 April.

102.39–40   the sign of the White Lion   no White Lion has been identified in the Moffat area. There may be a jocular allusion to the famous Black Bull in Moffat High Street.

103.9   Allan Kinninghame   see note to 35.3.

103.13   up the Yarrow frae Newark to Eltrive   up Yarrow Water, Selkirkshire (now Borders Region), to Altrive, a distance of some 13 km.

103.18–20   Noah ... Ararat   see Genesis 8.4.

103.25   Ens rationis   *Latin* an entity of reason, existing purely in the mind.

103.37–8   spare habit   lean constitution; abstemious disposition.

104.12   Emond ... Thurtell   Robert Emond was executed in Edinburgh on 17 March 1830 for a double murder; John Thurtell was executed on 9 January 1824 for a murder in Hertfordshire.

105.9   Rin ben   run into the inner part of the house.

105.26   Hey, Johnnie Cope, are you wauken yet?   an old tune 'Fye to the hills in the morning' was used for the song 'Hey, Johnnie Cope', written by Adam Skirving on the defeat of Sir John Cope by Prince Charles's forces at Prestonpans, 22 September 1745.

106.4–17   the Duke ... unprincipled ministry   Maga became increasingly unhappy with what it saw as the concessions by Wellington to liberals in the Tory government.

106.21   Say ... Ricardo   Jean-Baptiste Say (1767–1832), French economist, formulated the law of markets, which postulates that supply creates its own demand; David Ricardo was the author of *Principles of Political Economy and Taxation* (1817).

106.22   Cooke   James Cook (1728–79), the explorer, was killed by Hawaiians.

106.26–8   Columbus ... Solomon   Christopher Columbus (1451–1506) was the first European verifiably to visit the Caribbean; for Solomon's richly laden ships see Chronicles 9.21.

106.30   Smith and MacCulloch   John Ramsay McCulloch (see note to 81.36–9) published *The Principles of Political Economy* in 1825, and edited and revised Adam Smith's classic *The Wealth of Nations* in 1827.

106.32   the Jew   Ricardo.

106.35   a priori   *Latin* from general principle.

106.43–107.2   Vents ... lums   the Shepherd takes *vents* to mean 'chimneys' rather than 'market outlets'.

107.9   Seth   son of Adam (Genesis 5.3).

107.10   the Stot   Maga's name for McCulloch: his 'doctrine about Absentees' was that the non-residence of the Irish proprietors could not injure the general prosperity of Ireland.

107.12   nati consumere fruges   *Latin* born to eat [earth's] fruits: see Horace, *Epistles*, 1.2.27.

107.27   The Reliquiæ Danaum   Trojan remnant: see Virgil's *Aeneid*, 1.30.

108.12–13   The verra Deevil ... Rab Montgomery   Robert Montgomery in his poem *Satan* (February 1830).

108.23–4   goin' bodily about ... devour   see 1 Peter 5.8.

108.26   atween and the sky   between this place (i.e. the earth) and the sky.

108.43   Pollok ... the Course of Time   Robert Pollok wrote *The Course of Time: A Poem, in Ten Books* (1827), an enormously popular blank verse survey of human history.

109.10–14   Blanco White's London Review ... prize poem   Joseph Blanco White of Oriel College, Oxford edited the *London Review*, which actually lasted for two numbers (unusually thick with 594 pages in all), in 1828. Richard Whately was Professor of Political Economy at Oxford University 1829–31 and a friend of White's. The review of Pollok's poem (1.233–51) is sometimes minutely critical.

109.15   Mount-Benger   see note to 12.20–1.

109.19   drab-and-ditch-delivered   see *Macbeth*, 4.1.31.

109.42   the new editor   Macvey Napier succeeded Francis Jeffrey as editor of the *Edinburgh Review* in October 1829.

110.15   Wash him in the Sky-blue Pool   to change the *Edinburgh Review*'s blue and yellow/buff Whig colours to Tory true-blue. Maga frequently referred to the *Edinburgh* as 'the Ram': see also note to 112.28.

110.18–26   Southey's Colloquies ... young Macauley ... Macqueen   Thomas Babington Macaulay was the son of Zachary Macaulay. He reviewed Robert Southey's *Sir Thomas More; or, Colloquies on the Progress and Prospects of Society* (1829), anonymously, in the *Edinburgh Review*, 50 (January 1830), 528–65. The passages quoted are found (not always in the order given) on 528–30, 532, and 537; there is only one serious inaccuracy: on 532 Macaulay writes 'Almost all', not 'All' of Southey's heroes. Zachary Macaulay was prominent among campaigners for British action against the slave trade (popularly known as 'Saints'), whereas James MacQueen argued that the evil could only be rooted out by the extension of civilisation within Africa itself: his views were conveyed (under the pseudonym 'Colonist') in his series of letters

H

to the *Glasgow Courier* published at Glasgow in 1816 as *The Edinburgh Review and the West Indies; with Observations on the Pamphlets of Messrs. Stephen, Macaulay, &c.* In 1793–9 Zachary Macaulay had been Governor of Sierra Leone, a colony for emancipated slaves.

110.27–9   Charles M'Kenzie ... Notes on Hayti   Charles [Kenneth] Mackenzie, FRS, *Notes on Haiti, Made During a Residence in that Republic* (published by H. Colburn and R. Bentley, 1830). Mackenzie was Consul General of Haiti in 1825–8. From 20 February 1830 to November 1834 he acted as the British commissioner of arbitration to the mixed (British-Spanish) commission in Havana set up to supervise the application of restrictions on vessels engaged in the slave trade as originally agreed in a treaty of 1817.

111.13   the Laureate   Southey was appointed Poet Laureate in 1813.

111.14   A Lilliputian atween the spauls o' Gulliver   the Lilliputians are tiny people encountered by Gulliver in the first book of *Gulliver's Travels* (1726) by Jonathan Swift.

111.22–3   and some odds   and a bit.

111.36   Pye ... Cibber   Henry James Pye, Poet Laureate 1790–1813; Colley Cibber, Poet Laureate 1730–57.

112.1–4   the love of Thalaba ... bridal chamber   in Southey's poem *Thalaba the Destroyer* (1801), Books 7 and 8.

112.9–10   a perfect chrysolite   an uncomprehending reference to *Othello*, 5.2.148.

112.18   what for   why.

112.28   Aries—a sign into which the sun never enters   'the Ram' is Maga's name for the *Edinburgh Review*, which it sees as unenlightened, unlike the constellation Aries into which the sun enters on 21 March.

112.41–2   the following insulting sentence   *Sir Thomas More*, 2.407–8; Montesinos's reply is on 408–11 and incorporates extracts from De Quincey's anonymous translation of Kant's 'Idea of a Universal History on a Cosmo-Political Plan' which had appeared in the *London Magazine,* 10 (October 1824), 385–93. For the *London Magazine* see note on 3.32. Among the contributors were W.H. Reynolds and Richard Ayton (1786–1823), whose *Essays and Sketches of Character* were published posthumously in 1825.

114.13–14   myriad-minded   recalling Coleridge's application of this term to Shakespeare at the beginning of Ch. 15 of *Biographia Literaria* (1817).

115.2   the shelf Cæsar   the books in the celebrated library of Sir Robert Bruce Cotton (1571–1631), now in the British Library, were arranged in fourteen presses, each of which was surmounted by a bust of one of the twelve Roman emperors, together with Cleopatra and Faustina, and each press was named after one of these personages.

115.4   Henderson   Henderson, Bisset, and Co., bookbinders, Mound Place.

115.9–116.17   In the Colloquy entitled—Walla-Crag ... conduct   Colloquy 6: 'the progress ... harden the heart' occurs (a little different from Maga's quotation) on 1.128, and the remaining passages are found (sometimes also with slight variations) on 128–31.

115.15   Utopian   Sir Thomas More published *Utopia* in 1516.

115.21   John Fox   John Fox(e) (1516–87) wrote to Queen Elizabeth in June 1575: 'such is my disposition ... that I can scarce pass the shambles where

beasts are slaughtered, but that my mind secretly recoils with a feeling of pain' :
J.F. Mozley, *John Foxe and his Book* (1940), 87.
116.9–10 Dr Beddoes Thomas Beddoes, M.D. (1760–1808), whom
Southey had greatly admired.
117.9–10 Cockneyism ... Little Britain referring to Maga's early
campaign against 'The Cockney School of Poetry', embracing Hunt, Keats,
Barry Cornwall etc. Little Britain is a street in the City of London used by
Blackwood's as a symbol of Cockneyism.
117.20 the Auld Man o' the Mountain the 12th-century Syrian grand
master Rashid ad Dīn as-Sinān, the legendary *shaykh al-jabal* (Arabic
'mountain-chief', mistranslated by Crusaders as 'Old Man of the Mountain').
117.21 a Sant a Saint: see note to 110.18–26.
117.24 the Ram the *Edinburgh Review*: see 110.15.
117.26 δι περι Ambrose *Greek* Ambrose and his colleagues.
117.27 Ggemm! and Fools! game and fowls (being the fourth course).
117 (table-plan) Cock of the Wood capercailzie.
118.21 Sotheby has published three Specimens William Sotheby
published *The First Book of the Iliad; the Parting of Hector and Andromache;
and the Shield of Achilles: Specimens of a New Version of Homer* (March
1830). Pope translated Homer's *Iliad* (1715–20) and *Odyssey* (in collaboration,
1725–6).
118.29 Sotheby's Georgics *The Georgics of Virgil Translated ... by W.
Sotheby* (1800).
118.31–3 I have read his Specimens ... sift them Wilson wrote five
articles on Sotheby's *Georgics* translation in *BM* 29–31.
118.34 Pope, Hobbes, Chapman, Cowper Homer had been translated by
Pope in couplets (1715–26), by Thomas Hobbes in quatrains (*Homer's Odysses*,
1675), by George Chapman in fourteen-syllable lines (*The whole Works of
Homer; Prince of Poetts*, [1612]), and by William Cowper in blank verse (*The
Iliad and Odyssey*, 1791).
118.37 a rump and dozen a rump of beef and a dozen bottles of claret.
118.38–119.10 Tales in Verse ... The Brothers 'The Brothers' is one of
the *Tales in Verse, Illustrative of the Several Petitions of the Lord's Prayer* by
Henry Francis Lyte (first published 1826; 2nd edn 1829).
119.2 Goldsmith ... Crabbe Oliver Goldsmith (1730–74) and George
Crabbe (1754–1832).
119.7–8 The harvest ... its own heart see Wordsworth, 'A Poet's Epitaph'
(published 1800), line 51.
119.12–13 Mrs Norton, that wrote the Sorrows o' Rosalie *The Sorrows
of Rosalie ... With Other Poems* (1829) by Caroline Elizabeth Sarah Norton,
daughter of the minor poet Thomas (or Tom) Sheridan, granddaughter of the
dramatist Richard Brinsley Sheridan, great-granddaughter of the dramatist
Thomas Sheridan, and great-great-granddaughter of the classical scholar
Thomas Sheridan.
119.33 A tale of tears—a mortal story Wordsworth, *The White Doe of
Rylstone* (published 1815), line 336. This poem describes the sufferings of a
family called Norton during the Reformation.
119.37 a wee thocht ower doun-lookin' a trifle too sullen.

120.2–3   The Undying One   *The Undying One, and Other Poems* (early 1830).

120.8   Benlomond   Ben Lomond is a mountain in Stirlingshire (now Central Region), on the E side of Loch Lomond.

120.8–9   Gabrielle ... Cyrus Redding   *Gabrielle: A Tale of the Swiss Mountains* (1829), by Cyrus Redding, in verse. For Thomas Campbell and the *New Monthly Magazine* see note to 2.19-22.

120.16–18   Mr Ball ... The Creation   *Creation: A Poem* (April 1830), by William Ball.

120.21   Descent into Hell   *The Descent into Hell: A Poem* (February 1830), by John Abraham Heraud.

120.22–3   Mooshy Shawbert   see note to 89.22–3.

120.25   Pollok   see note to 108.43.

120.43   Jock Linton   the individual has not been identified, but there were Lintons around in Ettrick and Yarrow during this period.

120.43   Fahope's   Robert Ballantyne Junior (1778–1835), known as 'Phawhope' from his ownership of Over Phawhope at the head of the Ettrick valley, was also a tenant of Dryhope, with land touching the shore of St Mary's Loch. It was from Dryhope that the ducks had stravaiged to the Loch. Robert was the elder brother of the David referred to in the note to 78.22.

121.8   as Homer—that's Pop—says ... bow   see Pope's translation of Homer's *Iliad* 1.590 (published 1715).

121.9   dilution of trashiness   the source of this quotation has not been identified.

121.11   The Exclusives   this novel (dated 1830, but published towards the end of 1829) was actually written by Lady Charlotte Susan Maria Bury.

121.24   Richelieu and Darnley—by Mr James   *Richelieu: A Tale of France* (1829) and *Darnley; or, The Field of the Cloth of Gold* (January 1830), by George Payne Rainsford James.

121.33   St Giles's   a district in the West End of London notorious for fashionable dissipation.

121.39   the Bench   the King's Bench, the Supreme Court of Common Law in England.

121.39–40   returned and received for a rotten borough   sent to Parliament and received there as members of parliament for a borough without a proper constituency.

121.41   upon town   in the swing of fashionable life or dissipation.

121.43   Jack Thurtell   see note to 104.12.

122.7   Lord Normanby, Mr Lister, and Mr Bulwer   Constantine Henry Phipps, first Marquis of Normanby, novelist; Thomas Henry Lister, poet and novelist; Edward George Earle Lytton Bulwer-Lytton, novelist.

122.10   cacoethes scribendi   *Latin* itch for scribbling.

122.12   Murray's Family Library   this series of works on a variety of subjects, published by John Murray, was begun in April 1829.

122.13–14   Allan Cunningham's Lives of the Painters   *The Lives of the Most Eminent British Painters, Sculptors, and Architects* (published by John Murray, 1829–33).

122.19   Stebbings' History of Chivalry and the Crusades   this work by Henry Stebbing appeared in February 1830.

122.20–1 Constable's Miscellany *Constable's Miscellany of Original and Selected Publications in the Various Departments of Literature, the Sciences and the Arts*, 82 vols (published by Archibald Constable, Edinburgh and London, in 1826–35).

122.25 the Collegians a novel (1829), by G[erald] G[riffin].

122.26 Leitch Ritchie author of historical fiction and travel literature.

122.26 Picken's Dominie's Legacy Andrew Picken published *The Dominie's Legacy* anonymously in three volumes early in 1830: 'Mary Ogilvie: A Tale of the Squire's Experience' begins the second volume.

122.32 that letter ... in the Examiner an unsigned letter appeared in the *Examiner* of 28 February 1830 (133-4), attacking a 'PROVINCIAL SCOTSMAN' for his book *A Glance at London, Brussels, and Paris* (1829), and taking the opportunity to assert that the Scots were inferior to the English in every field. On 11 March two letters were published in reply (165–6) from 'A British Subject' and 'N.' of Edinburgh. A brief rejoinder by the author of the original letter appeared on 4 April (213), now signed 'G.P.' of Birmingham.

122.35 the Standard see note to 89.25.

122.38 Thrice is he armed ... just *2 Henry VI*, 3.2.233.

122.39 at odds at a disadvantage.

122.39–40 cunning of fence see *Twelfth Night*, 3.4.271.

123.9–10 a galloping consumption a tubercular disease that makes rapid progress.

123.18 articulate presumably a misuse by the Shepherd, meaning 'hear'.

123.20 disallow to disapprove of.

123.25 certain sneering uses o' the word "Scotch" perhaps Wilson is recalling in particular De Quincey's sketch of Wilson himself, in which he writes: 'The Scotch ... know just as much about what they call "Moral Philosophy" and Metaphysics as the English do, viz. exactly nothing at all' (*Edinburgh Literary Gazette*, 1:9 (11 July 1829), 131).

123.33 Stagyrite Aristotle was a Stagirite, i.e. a native of Stagira, a city of Macedonia, Greece.

124.6 the esse sunk in the posse the actual existence sunk in the potentiality.

124.10 Job ... Diogenes Job in the Book of Job is a proverbial figure of patience; Diogenes was a 4th-century B.C. Greek cynic philosopher of unsociable disposition, who is said to have lived in a large earthenware jar.

124.16 A true bill a true statement.

124.17 Scotland thorough throughout Scotland.

124.31 Dr Chawmers for Thomas Chalmers see note to 4.29.

124.31–2 Dr Thamson Andrew Mitchell Thomson, DD (1779–1831).

124.32 Dr Gordon Robert Gordon, DD (1786–1853).

124.34 like a' the ither lakers like the Lake poets Wordsworth, Coleridge, and Southey.

125.8–9 that inward eye ... solitude see Wordsworth's 'I wandered lonely as a Cloud' (published 1807), lines 15–16.

125.15–16 Southside ... Northside the areas of Edinburgh immediately S and N of the Old Town.

125.17 every inch a king *King Lear*, 4.6.107.

125.32   its stature reached the sky   see *Paradise Lost*, 4.988.

126.1   rudiments   *probably* a malapropism for 'rheumatics' (compare 66.36).

126.39   Lambert   Daniel Lambert (1770–1809) of Stamford, Lincolnshire is officially recorded as having weighed 52 stone 11 lb (835kg).

127.36   are of men the chief   see Thomas Campbell, *Gertrude of Wyoming* (1809), 1.6.7.

127.38–9   Are sprung ... manifold   Wordsworth, 'It is not to be thought of' (a sonnet published 1803), lines 13–14.

127.41–128.1   Spenser ... Newton, Bacon   the poet Edmund Spenser (1552?–99), the scientist Sir Isaac Newton (1642–1727), and the miscellaneous writer Francis Bacon (1561–1626).

128.4   rutili spatia ampla diei   *Latin* the broad expanse of the golden day. The source has not been identified.

128.7–8   a glorious train attending   see Milton, *Paradise Lost*, 7.574: 'The glorious train ascending'.

128.11   Science has frowned not on her humble birth   see Thomas Gray, *Elegy Written in a Country Churchyard* (1751), line 119.

128.17–18   Comparative Estimate of the English and Scotch Character   this did not appear.

128.23–4   Gibson ... Campbell ... Scoular ... Steele   the sculptor John Gibson, who lived in Rome from 1817, was actually Welsh. Thomas Campbell (1790–1858) was in Rome from 1818 to 1830;   William Scoular studied in Edinburgh and was in Rome for some years from 1825; John Steell, best known for his statue of Scott for the Scott Monument, Edinburgh, also spent several years in Rome around this time.

128.25   Fletcher   Angus Fletcher was born in Edinburgh.

128.25–31   Lawrence Macdonald ... Achilles   Lawrence Macdonald was born at Gask, Perthshire. His *Ajax and Patroclus* was exhibited at the Royal Institution in the autumn of 1829. His *Thetis and Achilles* was exhibited along with *Ajax* in London in March 1831. A copy of *Ajax* was at one stage at Powerscourt, Co. Wicklow, but its present location and that of *Thetis* are unknown.

128.27   boys and virgins   see *Troilus and Cressida*, 2.2.104.

128.38–9   Thom and Greenshields ... the Jolly Beggars   James Thom, a self-taught Ayrshire sculptor, became famous in 1829 for his statues of Tam o' Shanter and Souter Johnny, now in the garden of the Burns Monument, Alloway. A version of John Greenshields of Lanark's group of the Jolly Beggars was presented to the Hunterian Museum, University of Glasgow, in 1875, but its present location is unknown.

129.8–9   Kings ... straw   notably, King Lear.

129.9–14   the Prince ... English nobles   Prince Hal: see *2 Henry IV*, Induction, lines 26–7 and *1 Henry IV*, 5.4.102–10.

129.15–17   that son ... hideous   see *Hamlet*, 1.4.53–4.

129.22   Galt's Lowrie Todd   *Lawrie Todd; or, The Settlers in the Woods* (January 1830).

129.25–33   the Editor of the Monthly Review ... Lord Hill's Father   the new editor was Michael Joseph Quin (1796–1843). Lord Hill is Rowland, first

Viscount Hill, son of John Hill, third Baronet, whose family seat at Hawkstone, Shropshire, had been developed by his elder brother Sir Richard Hill (1732–1808) into a moralised landscape with a famous grotto. Mackenzie notes that the estate is said to have employed several hermits, but Quin could hardly have found time to be one of them in the course of a short and busy life. In the *Monthly Review*, 3rd series, 13 (January 1830), 2–20 there is an anonymous review of Scott's *History of Scotland* (1830) which is found 'dry, meagre, and lifeless' (2) and typical of Scott in its 'great want of accuracy' (3); the term 'feeble' is actually applied to William Robertson (12) but Scott's narrative is 'tame' (5); the savage review (March, 408–17) of John Bowring's *Poetry of the Magyars* does accuse that author of quackery (408), but not specifically of linguistic incompetence; the remarks on Galt and *Blackwood's* occur in a review of new novels (March, 466), but they are inaccurately reported here.

129.38   Giordano Bruno   (1548–1600), Italian philosopher and astronomer, a model of constancy under pressure: accused of heresy, he said that he had nothing to retract and did not even know what he was expected to retract.

129.41   Knowles's Lectures on Dramatic Poetry   James Sheridan Knowles's lectures, which he began to give during his residence in Glasgow in the 1820s, were eventually published in 1873.

130.4–5   The Gloomy Nicht is gatherin' fast   Burns's words, first published in 1787 to the tune 'Roslin Castle', were set to another tune by Allan Masterton in 1790 and called 'The Bonnie Banks of Ayr'.

131.8   Chaldean   skilled in occult learning. There is also an allusion to the Chaldee Manuscript (see Introduction, ix).

131.12   bis   *Latin* twice: a direction to repeat the last line.

131.28   Parr   Samuel Parr (1747–1825), a noted Latin scholar.

132.3–4   The French Institute ... one Scotchman more   in 1823 the botanist Robert Brown and the mathematician John Leslie were Scottish corresponding members of the relevant section of the Institut de France, the Académie des Sciences.

132.6   Supplement Napier   Macvey Napier edited a supplement to the sixth edition of the *Encyclopaedia Britannica* 1814–24.

132.8   Altrive   Hogg lived permanently at Altrive from his marriage in April 1820.

132.15   Ettrick   Hogg's birthplace.

132.17   Mullion   see Introduction, viii.

132.36   at livery   kept for the owner, fed and groomed at a fixed charge.

132.37   John Watson   see note to 94.21.

133.3   Francis Maximus Macnab's Theory of the Universe   *A Theory of the Moral and Physical System of the Universe* (1817), a work of demented systematisation based on 'the original system of universal science, or harmony of the spheres or the analogy of nature & providence being the same with typical Christianity or natural religion which was perverted by the first idolators'.

133.5   the Scotsman   the Edinburgh liberal newspaper founded in 1817.

133.9   Polito   Polito's famous menagerie had first taken the road in 1758. *BM* 5.291–8 had an article headed and signed 'Polito' (probably by Thomas Gillespie) giving a sketch of the monster Giant Whig.

133.13   Mungo Park   (1771–1806), African explorer.

133.13–14   Sir Hector Munro   (1726–1805), a Scottish general distinguished for his services in India: he was not devoured by a tiger.

133.20–1   a new edition of my Confessions   second and third editions of *Confessions of an English Opium Eater* were published in 1823, and a fourth edition in 1826.

133.27   Deevil ... nane   no fear, Mullion will not die at all.

133.28   the morn   tomorrow.

133.28–9   a shave o' the red roun'   i.e. a slice of beef.

133.29   luking fra him   gazing around.

133.34   siccan a like   such a.

133.38   Phin's   William Phin had a fishing-tackle shop at 40 North Bridge: it is described in detail in *BM* 20.327–8.

134.1   Kirby   'The early Fellows of the Royal Society, who attended to all the useful and common arts, even improved fish hooks; and Prince Rupert, an active member of that illustrious body, taught the art of tempering hooks to a person of the name of Kirby; under whose name for more than a century, very good hooks were sold.' [Humphry Davy,] *Salmonia; or, Days of Fly Fishing* by an Angler (1828), 144.

134.5   argand lamp   a ring-shaped gas burner, working on a principle established by Aimé Argand *c*. 1782.

134.6   Barry Cornwall   see note to 1.26.

134.17   through alang   along through.

134.18   ettling ... at   making for.

134.19   Fahope's house   see note to 120.43.

134.20   give him the butt   turn the bottom of the rod towards him so as to get a more rigid hold upon the line.

134.26–7   Fair as a star ... sky   Wordsworth, 'Song: She dwelt among th' untrodden ways' (published 1800), lines 7–8.

134.28   Isaac Walton   Izaak Walton, author of *The Compleat Angler* (1653).

134.37   Liston   Robert Liston, an Edinburgh surgeon.

135.15   the Theatre   see note to 45.14–15.

135.17   Vandenhoff   the actor John M. Vandenhoff visited Edinburgh several times; in the spring of 1824 he played a number of Shakespearean roles, and was a great success as Count Procida in Felicia Dorothea Hemans's new tragedy *The Vespers of Palermo* on 5 and 7 April.

135.27   Allons   *French* let us go.

135.38   thrones, and dominations, and principles, and powers   see Colossians 1.16: 'thrones, or dominions, or principalities, or powers'.

136.11 In defence   the Latin motto 'In defens' appears on the arms of Scotland.

136.12–19   Faster ... stranding!   a variant of Scott's 'Pibroch of Donuil Dhu' (1816), stanza 4.

136.30–9   A convent ... place   Wordsworth, 'Glen-Almain' (published 1807), lines 23–32.

137.3   you and Byron   in fact Hogg and Byron never met.

137.5   as thick as weavers   extremely intimate.   Proverbial, especially in the form 'as thick as inkle-weavers', inkle-looms for making linen tape being so narrow and close together.

137.6 tway three two or three.

137.6–7 Wulson and Soothey John Wilson had a country house near Ambleside in the English Lake District, and Robert Southey was a permanent resident at Keswick in the same area.

137.8 John Grieve Grieve was a minor poet and businessman who befriended Hogg in Edinburgh *c*. 1810–12 and who retired to Ettrick because of ill health in 1818.

137.9 glowring frae me staring in front of me.

137.10 an be not an it be not, except.

137.13 a thocht a little, somewhat.

137.16 hold ourselves acquaintance make each other's acquaintance.

137.20–1 Don Juan Byron's unfinished poem was published 1819–24.

137.26 Wordsworth's way wi' me Hogg gives his own version of the anecdote, which he maintains was really 'no joke', in 'Reminiscences of Former Days', *Altrive Tales* (London, 1832), cxxiv–cxxx.

137.34 Godswhittle the individual referred to has not been identified.

137.35 the day today.

137.39 deil mean him! the devil take him!

138.1 his sister Dorothy Wordsworth.

138.8–9 Wordsworth's first meeting with Byron in 1834 the poet Samuel Rogers recollected that he had arranged for Wordsworth and Byron to meet for dinner in 1812, but Wordsworth 'tried to talk his best and talked too much' (*Henry Crabb Robinson on Books and their Writers*, ed. Edith J. Morley (1938), 1.436).

138.12–16 Rydallwood … Grasmere Rydal Mount, Wordsworth's home from 1813; and Grasmere, the lake and village a little to the north, where he had lived previously.

138.17 the Director-General's 'the Director General of the Fine Arts in Scotland', according to Maga (5.672/3), was David Bridges Junior, of the Bank Street cloth merchants David Bridges and Son, Treasurer of the Dilettanti Society of Edinburgh.

138.27 Duddingston Loch a small loch to the S of Arthur's Seat.

138.27–8 the great day on Saturday 14 January 1826 the Duddingston Curling Society and the [Edinburgh] Skating Club were active on the loch: 'The bands of the 6th Dragoon Guards and the 17th Regiment played at intervals during the day, and were surrounded by crowds of well dressed persons. A military friend informs us, that as nearly as he could calculate, there were upwards of eight thousand persons on the Loch at one time' (*Edinburgh Evening Courant*, 16 January 1826).

139.6 the Club-house the Skating Club did not have a club-house as such. On 14 January 1826 the members met at Mrs Frazer's Hotel, Duddingston (National Library of Scotland MS 24641, f. 39v).

139.8–9 Mr Tory o' Prince's Street Archibald Torry, cloth and wine merchant at 32 Princes Street.

139.10–11 Henry Cowburn Henry Thomas Cockburn, the prominent Whig lawyer, later a lord of session and of justiciary.

139.11 a sticket minister a person intended for the ministry but unable, for whatever reason, to pursue that career.

139.15   Jemmy Simpson   James Simpson, Whig lawyer, and author of *A Visit to Flanders, in July, 1815, Being Chiefly an Account of the Field of Waterloo* (Edinburgh, 1815).

139.20   an offisher   the *Scotsman* suggested that this officer, mentioned in several of the Edinburgh papers, belonged to the 17th Regiment.

139.27   The curlers quat their roaring play   Burns, 'The Vision' (published 1786), line 2.

139.30–2   the 47th Proposition of Euclid ... the Pons assinorum   two propositions in the first book of the pioneering Greek geometrical treatise (*c.* 300 B.C.). The fifth proposition of the first book was known as the 'bridge of asses' (translated from the Latin 'pons asinorum') because of the difficulty beginners have in mastering and proceding beyond it, and also because its shape was conceived of as resembling a bridge.

139.33   Mr Editor   earlier in this noctes the Shepherd has playfully told Tickler in confidence that he is 'noo the Yeditor o' Blackwood's Magazine'.

139.39–40   feats celebrated in all the newspapers   the two Whigs are praised only in the *Scotsman* of 18 January and the *Edinburgh and Leith Advertiser* of 21 January. The other papers omit mention of Cockburn, or of both gentlemen.

140.7   Mrs Fergusson's, High Street   probably the establishment run by Mrs Ferguson, vintner, in Sellar's Close, Lawnmarket from 1806.

140.9   Meg Dods   in the June 1826 number of Maga from which this extract is taken Wilson reviewed (19.651–60) *The Cook and Housewife's Manual* (see note to [85 (table plan)]).

140.9–10   The Director General   see note to 138.17.

140.14   auld Mr Laidlaw   James Laidlaw, tenant in Blackhouse, Yarrow, and father of Scott's steward William Laidlaw.

140.15–21   Robert Burns's description ... the great chieftain o' the Pudding race   'To a Haggis' (1786), lines 2, 8.

140.30–1   Shooshy Dagleish ... Tommy Potts   perhaps not real people, but alluding to a ballad or folk nexus: the ballad 'Tommy Potts' (Child no. 109) tells the story of a serving man who marries a noble bride. Tommy Potts is one of the partly autobiographical Cochrane's physical opponents in Hogg's 'Love Adventures of Mr George Cochrane' (1810: expanded 1820).

140.40   lay my lugs   wager.

141.3   Theocritus has been blamed   the 3rd-century B.C. Greek poet of Sicilian pastoral was criticised on these grounds, notably by Alexander Pope in 'A Discourse on Pastoral Poetry' (1717), lines 92–5.

141.4   Allan Ramsay   alluding to Ramsay's pastoral drama *The Gentle Shepherd* (1725).

141.25–7   Mount Benger ... Yarrow   in 1820 Hogg took a lease on the large farm of Mount Benger, adjoining his own at Altrive, Yarrow.

142.12   the Guse-dubs o' Glasgow   Gusedubs Lane formerly ran between Stockwell Street and Bridgegate Street. Maga's reference recalls its mockery of the 'Glasgow Gander' John Douglas, the Whig writer and editor.

142.38   Salvator   Salvator Rosa (1615–73), Italian painter noted for his wild, sublime landscapes, often featuring banditti.

143.2   fash his thoomb   be put out.

143.17 Bell-meadow bleachfield this bleaching works was situated at Kirkintilloch, Dunbartonshire (now Strathclyde Region).

143.19 Kingswell Kingswell, or Kingswells, at Fenwick, a toll-post on the Glasgow-Kilmarnock road 7 km N of Kilmarnock.

143.22–3 this plan ... fish the noctes goes on to identify a Mr Denovan as the author of a prospectus proposing to sell perfectly fresh fish for the first time in Edinburgh.

143.27 Nereids sea-nymphs.

143.40 Leith Walk the road linking Leith and Edinburgh.

144.3–4 St George's Kirk the Church of Scotland place of worship in Charlotte Square, now West Register House.

144.8 the Martello tower built during the Napoleonic wars on a rock near the E pier-head at Leith; it was absorbed by the expansion of Leith docks in the late 1960s.

144.23 Rodney ... Langara George Brydges Rodney, first Baron Rodney, defeated a Spanish squadron under Don Juan de Langara in 1780 to relieve Gibraltar.

144.37 Richmond and Molineaux Tom Molineux (1784–1818) and Bill Richmond (b. 1763), two celebrated black American pugilists.

145.21 a natural philosopher a physicist.

145.29 Lewis Mackenzie this would appear to be a semi-fictionalised episode based on the military executions of mutineers at Musselburgh and nearby Gullane on 20 January and 10 July 1795. One of those executed in July was called Macintosh, and the description of his behaviour in the *Edinburgh Advertiser* for 17–21 July corresponds closely to that in this extract.

146.24 sin syne ago.

146.25 the Grass-Market an open area immediately S of Edinburgh Castle.

146.32 Holyrood see note to 66.7.

147.3 Sarah Sarah Siddons gave her farewell performance as Lady Macbeth in London in 1812, but she came out of retirement occasionally, and on 19 November 1815 she played the same part at the Theatre Royal Edinburgh with Daniel Terry as Macbeth.

147.32 John Kemble John Philip Kemble (1757–1823), the celebrated actor.

147.40 purging the soul ... wi' pity and wi' terror in accordance with Aristotle's theory of tragic catharsis.

148.6–7 No ae ... ony ae not a single ... a single.

148.16 the late Lord Melville Henry Dundas (1742–1811), first Viscount Melville: his statue surmounts a column in St Andrew Square.

149.7 Mr Phin see note to 133.38.

149.10 out o' sicht out o' mind proverbial (*ODEP*, 602).

149.17–19 thae Annuals ... Wunter-Wreaths *Forget Me Not* (1823–47); *The Amulet ... A Christian and Literary Remembrancer* (1826–36); *The Keepsake* (1826–57); *The Bijou; or, Annual of Literature and the Arts* (1828–30); *The Gem: A Literary Annual* (1829–32); *The Anniversary* (1829); *Literary Souvenir; or, Cabinet of Poetry and Romance* (1825–37); *Friendship's Offering; or, The Annual Remembrancer* (1824–44); and *The Winter's Wreath: A Collection of Original Contributions in Prose and Verse* (1828–32).

149.24–5 King Pepin ... Sir David Gam *Pepin* is Scots for 'prosperous'. Gam is the name given to a Welsh waiter because of 'a slight limp in his left leg' (*BM* 24.676): David Gam was a famous Welsh warrior who fell at Agincourt in 1415.

149.26 a la Meg Dods for Meg Dods see note to 85 (table plan). Her recipe for boiled tripe is on pages 16–17 of *The Cook and Housewife's Manual*.

149.26 Tapitourie see note to 89.21.

150.3 the croon-head o' the roun' the best of the round of beef.

150.4 the fire-drum a public alarm was sounded by beating a drum through the streets, 'three quavers, a crotchet, and a rest' (*BM* 16.701).

150.28 passing through Natur' to Eternity *Hamlet*, 1.2.73.

150.29 Clarence's dream see *Richard III*, 1.4.9–63.

150.36–7 the pious Æneas ... Troy see Virgil's *Aeneid*, 2.705–51.

151.5 Horrible! most horrible! *Hamlet*, 1.5.80.

151.10 Nine times nine i.e. cheers.

151.15 High Jinks frolics indulged in at Scottish drinking parties.

151.22 a traveller in the soft line a commercial traveller in soft goods.

151.22 the day today.

151.23 blude meer mare of good pedigree.

151.28 Castor in classical mythology, the twin brother of Pollux, famous for his skill in horse-training.

151.32 on shank's naiggie on Shanks's mare; on foot.

152.35–7 Traquair ... Peebles Traquair is a village 10 km SE of Peebles, a royal burgh 37 km S of Edinburgh.

152.39 ettled at aimed to have; desired.

152.40 Eddlestone Eddleston is a village 7 km N of Peebles.

153.1 Mazeppa see note to 100.17.

153.3 the wildest o' the desert-born the wild 'noble steed,/ A Tartar of the Ukraine breed' which carries Mazeppa is described in Byron's poem as 'desert-born' (*Mazeppa*, lines 359–69).

153.6 Spinoza Baruch or Benedict de Spinoza (1632–77), the Dutch rationalist philosopher and religious thinker.

153.20 a king's plate at Doncaster the King's Plate for four year olds over four miles for 100 guineas was first run at Doncaster, Yorkshire (now South Yorkshire Region), in September 1803.

153.28 the Pentland Hills a range of hills to the SW of Edinburgh.

153.37–9 the muir o' Rannoch ... Loch Ericht ... Glenorchy on the borders of Tayside, Highland, and Strathclyde regions.

155.27 even on the wound himself has made the source of the quotation has not been identified.

155.35–6 Arcades ambo ... parati *Latin* both arcadians, both ready to sing in even contest, both ready to make reply (Virgil, *Eclogue* 7, lines 4–5).

155.39 Aristæus in Virgil's fourth Georgic, Aristaeus is a bee-keeper.

156.14 O'Bronte the son of North's (and Wilson's) dog Bronte, who was believed to have been poisoned by some of Dr Robert Knox's students in revenge for the exposure in Noctes 41 of his methods of obtaining bodies for dissection. Cyprus is the corresponding 'unique male tortoise-shell cat' (*BM* 27.929).

156.18 yokin' to attacking.

156.22   stoop and roop   completely.

156.24–5   Sir Walter's Ayrshire Tragedy   Scott, *Auchindrane; or, The Ayrshire Tragedy* (1830); the catastrophe involves the coming ashore of the bodies of two people murdered at sea.

156.25   Mr Murray   William Henry Murray, manager of the Theatre Royal, Edinburgh 1815–48.

156.29–30   gaiety of nations be eclipsed   Samuel Johnson wrote in his life of Edmund Smith that the actor David Garrick's death 'has eclipsed the gaiety of nations' (*Lives of the English Poets*, ed. George Birkbeck Hill (1905), 2.21). The allusion here is probably also to the exchange between Johnson and Boswell in Boswell's *Life of Johnson* where Johnson says: 'nations may be said—if we allow the Scotch to be a nation, and to have gaiety,—which they have not' (ed. George Birkbeck Hill, revised L.F. Powell (1934–50), 3.387).

156.31   Nox   *Latin* night.

156.36–7   have slain your dozens and your tens of dozens   alluding to 1 Samuel, 18.7: 'Saul hath slain his thousands, and David his ten thousands.'

157.11   Southside   Mr Timothy Tickler of Southside.

157.41–2   The Owther o' the Queen's Wake   see note to 12.29.

157.42–3   John Watson Gordon   see note to 94.21.

158.1   wee Jamie   see note to 98.34.

158.8–9   Sure such a pair ... nature!   the source of the quotation has not been identified.

158.11   O'Bronte ... still under the influence of opium   earlier in this noctes the English Opium-Eater, desirous of forming the friendship of O'Bronte, gives him a box of opium (*BM* 27.927): O'Bronte rushes around and upsets, *inter alia*, the beehive.

158.37   Mr Wordsworth's auld leech-gatherer   in 'Resolution and Independence' (published 1807).

159.4–5   A louse ... sharp   alluding to *Romeo and Juliet*, 2.2.43–4 ('That which we call a rose/ By any other name would smell as sweet'), and possibly also generally to Burns's 'To a Louse' (1786).

159.6   the Excursion   Wordsworth's long philosophical poem published in 1814.

159.27   The Fable o' the Bees   alluding to Bernard de Mandeville's satirical collection, *The Fable of the Bees; or, Private Vices, Publick Benefits* (1714–28).

160.9   Johnny Ballantyne   John Ballantyne (1774–1821), manager of Scott's publishing firm.

160.19   Canters and Covenanters   ostentatious evangelicals and staunch Presbyterians.

160.26   Sandy   Alexander Ballantyne (1776–1847), a noted musician, was the younger brother of James and John, Scott's publishing partners.

161.4   richt doon   quite.

161.14   domiciliuncula   *Latin* little houses.

161.15   Captain Macraw ... Captain Maclaver   the names are probably intended to suggest noise rather than to allude to actual gentlemen.

161.23   etcetera, etceterorum   *Latin*   and so on and so forth (humorously pedantic).

161.29   double X   medium quality ale.

161.30 Cape sherry   sherry from Cape Colony, South Africa.

161.30 of the earth earthy   1 Corinthians 15.47.

161.37 Schiedam Hollands   gin distilled at Schiedam in Holland

162.2 Bell's ale   beer brewed by Bell, Keir & Co., Pleasance, Edinburgh.

162.2 heavy wet   a drink of strong ale or ale and porter mixed.

162.2 blue ruin   (bad) gin.

162.7 milk punch   a drink made of milk, rum or whisky, sugar, and nutmeg.

162.11 Oh! horrible—most horrible   see note to 151.5.

162.26 the Reform Bill   the first or great Reform Bill eventually received the royal assent on 7 June 1832, the previous bills having been thrown out by the House of Lords in October 1831 and May 1832.

162.31 The wine of life is on the lees   a combination of *Macbeth*, 2.3.93 and Isaiah 25.6.

162.38 hic jacet   *Latin* here lies.

162.40 Cowper   the poet William Cowper (1731–1800).

163.10 Alfred Tennyson   the poems referred to are 'Recollections of the Arabian Nights' (whose refrain runs 'golden prime/ Of good Haroun Alraschid'), and 'The Ballad of Oriana'; they were both published in *Poems, Chiefly Lyrical* (June 1830).

163.11 the cockneys   Maga's attack on the London poetic clique continues: see note to 117.9–10.

164.4 for bread ... give them a stone   see Matthew 7.9 and Luke 11.11.

164.10 Cobbett ... Paine   the radical writers William Cobbett (1762–1835) and Thomas Paine (1737–1809).

164.16 devils get into the swine   see Matthew 8.28–32, Mark 5.1–13, and Luke 8.26–33.

164.22 the cant of "free trade"   the landed interests opposed the repeal of the Corn Laws in favour of free trade, and although they had been eased in 1828 as a concession to advocates of free trade they were not finally repealed until 1846.

164.28 Greeks ... Turks   believing that the newly independent Greece, emancipated from Turkish rule in February 1830, would come under Russian influence, the western powers made it as small as possible.

164.33 saintly Macauleys, and some other Macs   for the Macaulays see note to 110.18–26. The 'other Macs' might include the Whig reformer Sir James Mackintosh, who was to die in May 1832, and the Whig economist John Ramsay McCulloch, for whom see note to 81.36–9.

165.3 Sierra Leone   see note to 110.18–26.

165.14 the Regicide Bill   i.e. the Reform Bill.

165.20 Lord Chancellors   the Lord Chancellor, Henry Peter Brougham, Baron Brougham and Vaux, ended his marathon and increasingly drunken speech commending the Reform Bill to the House of Lords on 7 October 1831 by falling to his knees in supplication. In spite of this, twenty-one bishops ensured the defeat of the bill by voting against it. In general, however, Brougham as Lord Chancellor proved more deferential to the bishops than people had expected.

165.33–166.2 Brummagem ... "National Guards"   in 1831 the council of the Birmingham Political Union discussed the formation of a national guard to further the reform movement.

166.8 La Fayette the Marquis de Lafayette had been an active supporter of American independence in 1777–81; in 1830 he was instrumental in bringing to the French throne Louis Philippe, the 'Citizen King', in reaction against the reactionary rule of the Bourbons.

166.10 Burdett the prominent parliamentary reformer Sir Francis Burdett.

166.16 insult ... a Queen Queen Adelaide's Lord Chamberlain, Lord Howe, had been dismissed for agitating against reform: the Queen shared his aversion.

166.22–6 Shiel ... O'Connell ... Catholic rent the prominent Irish nationalist leaders Richard Lalor Sheil and Daniel O'Connell founded the Catholic Association of Ireland in 1823, and in 1824 O'Connell introduced associate membership at the rate of one penny a month. This subscripton was known as the 'Catholic Rent' and turned the Association into a mass movement pressing for Emancipation, parliamentary reform, and the repeal of the 1801 Act of Union.

167.11 that in Glasgow the old Theatre Royal in Queen Street, built in 1805 and burnt down in 1829, seated nearly 1500.

167.11–12 Covent-Garden see note to 39.17.

168.3–6 Inchkeith ... North Berwick Law ... the Bass for Inchkeith see note to 75.16; North Berwick Law is a hill near the coast 37 km E of Edinburgh; the Bass Rock is an island 5 km NE of the Law.

168.9 Under the opening eyelids of the morn Milton, 'Lycidas' (1638), line 26.

168.27–8 Crust and broon aside the Roon' bread and brown ale beside the round of beef.

168.30 hooly—hooly—hooly *hooly* or *huilie* means 'wait a moment'; the triple occurrence punningly recalls Isaiah's vision of God ('Holy, holy, holy': Isaiah 6.3).

169.7–12 O Gurney! ... fit home for Thee! see Wordsworth, 'To the Cuckoo' (published 1807), lines 3–4, 29–32. For Gurney see Introduction, vii.

169.18 Loch Aven Loch A'an or Avon, a small loch in the heart of the Cairngorm mountains, Banffshire (now Grampian Region).

170.1–2 a richt gude wullie-waught Burns, 'Auld Lang Syne' (written or arranged *c.* 1788, published 1796), line 23.

171.14 the Mountain Bard Hogg's volume of poetry with this title was published in 1807.

171.33 procreant cradle *Macbeth*, 1.6.8.

172.8 Lunardi in 1784 Vincenzo Lunardi made a balloon flight from Chelsea nearly three weeks after the first such flight in Britain, made from Edinburgh by James Tytler on 27 August.

GLOSSARY

This selective glossary includes single English words likely to present difficulties for modern readers, and all but the most common single Scots words. Phrases are glossed in the notes.

abstersive purgative
accoucheur male midwife
affront confront, face
aiblins perhaps
airt direction, way, point of the compass
amabean amoebaean, answering alternatively as in pastoral poetry
animalcula small animal, invertebrate
Antiburgher *see note to 67.39*
apropos by the way
ashet oval serving dish
aum measure (*c*. 40 gallons) of Rhenish wine
ava, ava' at all
awee a little while
  backside fields adjoining house
bagman commercial traveller
bailie town magistrate
bakie square wooden container for ashes, coal, rubbish etc.
balaam trumpery paragraphs reserved to fill up columns
balaam-box receptacle for the preceding
bam *noun and verb* hoax
bang surpass
bantling child, brat
barcelona neckerchief of soft silk
barken'd encrusted
barmy frothy
barn-balk barn-rafter
bashaw pasha, grandee, haughty man
basket overhanging back compartment
bate bet
bear rough mat for wiping boots on

bearings line of flotation
beat make way against the wind
Bedlamite mad creature
ben in
besom *curling* broom
bick bitch
big build
big-wig officiously important person
billiard-marker person who marks the score in billiards
birk birch
birr momentum
birse bristle
bit sweet, dear, little, bit of
bite deception
blacking boot-polish
blanks blank verse
blarney speak flatteringly
blash heavy shower
blate modest, diffident
blaze be fired up
blin-worm blind-worm
blink brief gleam or glance
bobbery noisy disturbance
bock retch
bodle small copper coin, something of little value
bog-trotter *generally* one accustomed to making way across bogs, Irishman
boiled fired up
bonspiel curling match
bookseller publisher
boot-hook hook for pulling on boots
booty unfairly
borachio wineskin
bother give oneself trouble
bottle-holder boxer's attendant
bottom staying-power

bouk, bowk size, bulk
box-coat heavy overcoat for driving
brace-piece mantelpiece
braird first shoots of grass or corn
bravo bravado
brawly well
break go bankrupt
breether brothers
brent steep
brimmer brimming cup
brose oat- or pease-meal mixed with
 boiling water or milk, with salt,
 butter etc. added
bruising boxing
bullaboo *ironic* fine fellow
bumper *verb and noun* (drink) a full
 cup
bumping huge, great
bunker chest, often used as seat
burst energy
bustle frame or pad to make skirt
 hang out behind
butter unctuous flattery
buzz busy rumour, ferment
 callan, callant youth
can cup
canny lucky, of good omen
cantrip magic, a spell
canty cheerful
capellaire capillaire, syrup flavoured
 with orange-flower water
capper-plate copper-plate print
cast swarm
catastrophe denouement, final event
catsup ketchup
cattle (tow-)horses
caudle warm drink sweetened and
 spiced given to the sick
cauk provide a pointed piece of iron
 for a horse-shoe to prevent
 slipping
cauker, caulker dram of liquor
cauld-rifed cold
caulker *see* cauker
causeway road paved with stones
cave toss
cayawne cayenne pepper
centaur mythical monster, half man,
 half horse
chafts cheeks, jaws
chairman one of the two men
 carrying a sedan-chair
chaise light open carriage for one or
 two people
Chaldean *see note to 131.8*
change-house inn, alehouse
chaw-bacon country bumpkin
cheerer cheering cup
chevalier gallant
chiel fellow
chitter shiver
chowk jaw
chuckleheaded stupid
chucky-stane pebble
cipher nonentity
civilation *see note to 29.9*
clack continuous chatter
claes clothes
clampering clumping, noise of
 heavy walking
clart mud
clarty dirty, muddy
claut scratch, scrape
clavers nonsense, prating
cleik hold with a hook
cloot hoof
clour blow
cock upward turn
cock-laird small landowner farming
 his own land
combine form a political union
coof fool
corkish somewhat corked, tasting of
 cork
correlate a person or thing
 correspondingly related to another
 person or thing
cover table utensils for one person
cowp overbalance, toss
cramp cramped
cranreuch hoar-frost
crater large wine goblet or bowl
 (ancient Greek in origin)
creenkle *see* crinkle
creeshy greasy, dirty
crinkle emit sharp, thin sounds

cross cheat
croupier assistant chairman at the lower end of the table
crousely boldly
crunkle crinkle
cut up review severely
cutty mischievous girl
   daedal manifold, variegated
daffin' fun, foolish behaviour
daidle potter about
dang *euphemism for* damn
dauner'd stupid
days-darg day's work
dead-thraw death-throe
defunckin' dying
delve plunge into water
depend hang down
devil printer's errand-boy
ding (dung) knock(ed), beat(en)
dinnle vibrate, tingle with pain
dirl vibrate
dirty-like mean
discuss consume, try the quality of
distillery-whusky cheap whisky made from distillery refuse
dog-days midsummer, specifically 3 July to 11 August
dominie schoolmaster
donneration stupefaction
doobler blow that doubles up a person
dooken, dookin', dooking, douking bathing
dooms very
doondracht heavy load
douking *see* dooken
doup buttocks
dressing castigation
drookit, droukit drenched
dub muddy pool
dun plague for money or an article
Dunlop sweet-milk cheese
dunsh thump
dwam, dwawm swoon, stupor
   eau-medicinale medicinal water
ee-bree eyebrow
eerie weird, gloomy
electuary medicine mixed with

honey or the like
emprise undertaking
ethic (author) dealing with moral questions
ettle *see notes to 97.34 and 152.39*
ettling conjecture, notion
evendoun downright, complete
   facer blow in the face
facete elegant, polished, witty, gay, jocular
fancy-plan favourite plan, ornamental design
fankle ensnare, entangle
fanners grain-sifter, winnowing-machine
far-retiring disappearing into the distance
farden farthing
feather turn oar sideways as it leaves water to cut air edgeways
feck number
feckless ineffective, incompetent
fickle puzzle
figured adorned with patterns
fin feel
finger-neb fingertip
Finnan, Finzean haddock cured with the smoke of green wood
fire-balloon balloon with combustible material at its mouth
fistic pugilistic
flaff flap, flutter
flaffer blow with a gust of wind
flag-staff-lieutenant flag-lieutenant, officer acting as aide-de-camp to admiral
flash superficial brilliancy, ostentation
fleech cajole, flatter
flesh-blind *perhaps* temporarily, superficially blind
flip mixed beer and spirit with sugar, heated with a hot iron
flummery nonsense
flunkey footman
flyte altercate
foam-bell bubble of foam
forfeuchen exhausted

fou' drunk
foulzie, fulzie filth, garbage, excrement
freeze made of frieze or coarse woollen cloth
frith firth
frush rotten, frail
fud tail
fudge nonsense
fuizenless *see* fushionless
fulzie *see* foulzie
funk restive kick
furbelow pleated border of a gown
fushionless, fusionless, fuizenless insipid, spiritless
  gaily fairly
gambooshe bright yellow, gamboge-yellow
gamut full range of notes
gar make
gasconize boast
gash grim, solemn
gate distance, way
gawpus fool
gay very
gean wild cherry
gemman gentleman
geyan rather, very
ggegg trick
gill .11 litre, vessel holding this amount
gillyflower clove-scented flower
gin if
glaff moment
glamour alluring charm, magic
glaur mud
glee'd squinting, one-eyed
Glenlevit, Glenlivet, Glenlivit whisky from Glenlivet, Speyside
glint dart, flash
glower *noun and verb* intent gaze, gaze intently
good-fellow agreeable companion, convivial person
goose-winged with the middle part of the sail furled
gouvernante female ruler
gowany covered with daisies

gowk fool
gowmeril fool
gowpen fill of the two hands
gree live together as friends, get on
Greenlandman boat involved in Greenland whaling
greet (grat) weep (wept)
grips embrace
grog spirits and water
groset gooseberry
grue shudder
gudeman husband
guller gurgling noise
gulleral gullery
gulley large knife
gummy puffed, swollen
gushet gusset, clock or ornamental pattern on side of stocking
gut fishing line
gutle guzzle
  haar east coast sea-fog
hack horse
hag hillock of firmer ground in a bog
hantle great deal
happer hopper, funnel for receiving grain
harl drag, haul
harn hempen
harn-pan skull
hash slash
haver speak nonsense
havers nonsense
heartsome cheerful
heavy *adj.* sluggish
heavy *noun* stage goods wagon
hebetate make dull, blunt
heckle *fishing* artificial fly
hell gambling-house
heroics iambic pentameters
high extreme, risqué
hirdum dirdum noisy revelry
hirple limp, hobble
hizzie housewife
hoghead cask
Hollands Dutch gin
honey term of affection applicable to friends of either sex
hooly be careful! wait a moment!

host army
hot-press'd smoothed to fine quality in a hot press
hotch-potch mutton broth with many kinds of vegetables
how-towdie large pot chicken
howe hollow, hollow space
howk dig out, hew
howlet owl(et)
huff-cap swashbuckler
humbug *verb and noun* (practise) hoax or (piece of) nonsense
hurdies buttocks
 impress characteristic mark
inexpugnable invincible
ingan onion
ingle hearth
instanter immediately
instinct moved, animated
 jack machine for turning spit when roasting meat
jade woman
jalap purgative root
jalouse suspect
jaw scold
jimp slender, graceful
jobbery turning public service or trust to private gain or party advantage
jockteleg clasp-knife
Johannisberg fine white Rhenish wine
jorum bowl of punch
jug *noun* drinking vessel, drink
jug *verb* jog
 keckle express unrestrained delight
keek glance, peep
kelpie water demon
kerne vagabond
key-bugle bugle fitted with keys to increase number of sounds
Kilmarnock broad flat woollen bonnet
kintra country
kirn uproar
kitly tickly
kittle *adj.* tricky, troublesome
kittle *verb* tickle

knowe knoll
kye cattle
kyloe one of a breed of small Highland cattle
kythe show itself
 laconics brief sentences
lacryma lachryma Christi, strong sweet red wine of southern Italy
laigh low
lair place where animals have lain down
laker English Lake poet
Lammas 1 August, a Scottish quarter day
land-louper vagabond
lantern-jaws long thin jaws
lardner store-room for meat etc.
lave remainder
laverock skylark
lay line, tack
leal loyal, faithful, true
lean-hurdied with lean buttocks
leech apply leeches to draw blood
leman sweetheart
leuch laughed
lift air, sky
limmer term of abuse for woman, whore
linn waterfall
lintwhite linnet
lister spear
loun rascally servant
loun, lown calm, sheltered, restrained
loup leap
lown *see* loun
lozen pane of glass
lubberly stupid
lug ear
lum chimney
lumpish heavy, unwieldy, dull
Lundy-Foot a kind of snuff
lunelle lunel, sweet muscat wine
luxurious lascivious
 mailin' tenant-farm
maist almost
mauley fist
mault-worme one who loves liquor

maun must
mawsey amply-proportioned, motherly-looking woman
max gin
mew gull
midden dunghill
minimeter apparatus for measuring small quantities
miniver fur lining
misty tipsy
mitre hat
mobbery matters concerning the mob, the general lower populace
molliculi moleculae, small particles
mouls the earth of the grave
mount put on
muckle much, big, great
mum not a word!
mumper mumbler
mutch cap
mutchkin .43 litre
mystery mystery-play
nane not at all
nankeen cotton cloth
nappy having a nap, shaggy
natatory of swimming
nautilus *see note to 78.14*
neb spout
neif-fu fistful
neive, nieve fist
nibbler carper
opossum possum, small American marsupial mammal
or before
ordination ordering
orrery clockwork mechanism representing motions of planets, here illuminated by gas
Otaheitish from Tahiti
outower over to the other side of
oxter armpit, under part of upper arm
pabble bubble
palates ox palates
park set
patron pattern
paunin' dredging, scooping
peck small quantity of something edible
peg hammer
pellock porpoise
pepper beat, do for
perry drink made from fermented pear juice
personality disparaging references to individuals
petrology science of rocks
philabeg kilt
piperly beggarly
pirn reel
plat (vegetable) plot
plaudite appeal for applause at end of performance
played went
plotty mulled wine
plouter splash aimlessly, wade, fiddle
porpus porpoise
porringer small basin
porter dark-brown, bitter beer
pour pouring stream
pouzzolanum pozzolana, pozzuolana (volcanic ash)
pow head
powldoody Irish oyster
pree taste
preen pin
preserves woods or other grounds for the rearing and preservation of game
prie-my-mou kiss me (try my mouth)
prig entreat
prin pin
proctor collector of tithes
prog food
puff *verb and noun* praise extravagantly (often with ulterior motives), extravagant praise
pugilist boxer
puling weakly querulous
punch-royal strong or first-rate punch
purchase means of exerting force
purl ale warmed and spiced
pyrite fire-stone

quack impostor
quackery charlatanry
quadrille square dance
quaich drinking-cup
quarter rear upper part of ship's side
quate quiet
quean lass
queue pigtail
quiz *noun* odd or eccentric person
quiz *verb* make fun of
ramping unrestrained, romping
rattling lively in manners or speech
rax hand
reek smoke
reest stop and refuse to move, jib
rep man or woman of loose
character
repeater watch which could be made
to repeat the striking of the
previous hour
ribroasting thrashing
ridicule reticule, lady's small bag
rig arable ridge
rizzar redcurrant
rizzard dried
roarer *horse-racing* horse with
disease of the wind
roaring noisily riotous in behaviour
roose praise
rouchness roughness
roué roué, debauchee, rake
rouse *see* roose
rout *noun* fashionable assembly
rout *verb* roar, bawl
rowan berry of mountain ash
rubber decisive game
rug tug, drag
rum odd customer
rumble-te-thumps mashed potatoes
either with milk, butter, and
seasoning, or with cabbage or
turnip
rumbo strong punch, made chiefly
of rum
sabbase surbase; border or
moulding immediately above the
base or lower panelling of a
wainscoted room

sabretache leather satchel suspended
from cavalry officer's belt
saloon-library drawingroom library
saloop drink made of powdered
sassafras with milk and sugar
sark shift
sarsnet sarcenet, fine silk
Sassenach English-speaker,
lowlander
schist a crystalline rock
schorl the mineral tourmaline
science trained skill
sclutter mass of dirty semi-liquid
scolloped baked in a scallop shell
scoriae masses of cooled lava
scunner shrink back, feel disgust,
nauseate
sea-mew common gull
seidlitz artificial aperient water
self-sufficient overweening
sempstress seamstress
sereawtim seriatim, one after
another
shackle-bane wrist-bone
shambles slaughter-house
shandry-dan chaise with hood
shaver fellow
shillala Irish cudgel
shop printing-house
shouther-bun' stiff in shoulders or
arms
shovel-hat hat with shovel-like
curves in front and behind, worn
by some ecclesiastics
siccan such
sidelins obliquely
skaith harm
skelp smack somebody's bottom
skirl scream
skraigh screech
slap-bang immediately
slick smartly, completely, cleanly
sliddery slippery
slobbery of a soft yielding texture,
slimy
slop weak or insipid liquor or semi-
liquid food
slum nonsensical writing, blarney

sly roguish, waggish

smack taste

smacking exceptionally, tasting

smeddum spirit

smeek suffocate with smoke

snaffle simple bridle-bit

sneezable contemptible

sneeze snuff

snoke poke

snood ribbon worn round brow by young unmarried women

snore roar, drone, snort

snove, snuve glide

snuff-olive brownish-olive coloured jacket

snuggery bar-parlour

snuve *see* snove

soho hey!

somerset somersault

soom swim

soop sweep

sough, sugh rustling sound, sound of the wind, breath

sourocks sulks

soy soya

spang bound

spar crystalline mineral

spavin horse tumour

spawl shoulder

speldrin split and dried (or smoked) fish

spence inner apartment

spirituous spiritual

spleuchan pouch for money or tobacco

spoon ninny

sport play at being, emulate

spring dance tune

squabash crush, demolish

squash impact (or sound) of soft heavy body falling on surface

stack-yard rick-yard

staingalt stringhalt, disease of horse's hind legs causing muscular spasms

staring glaringly conspicuous

stave verse

steadins farmhouse (and outbuildings)

steek shut

steer bustle

stey steep

stingo strong ale or beer

store abundance

strath broad river-valley

stravaig stray

streck hook

streek, strieck stretch

stretch make one's way rapidly or with effort

stuff nonsense

stumble trip up

sub sub-editor

succinct girded up

sugh *see* sough

sumph simpleton

swankie smart, active, strapping young man

swarf swoon

swash swaggerer

swell highly distinguished, accomplished, or fashionable person

swelter flounder

synthetical involving combination rather than analysis

tail retinue

tap-room room in tavern where liquors are kept on tap

tappin' crest

tapsalteerie topsy-turvy

tattle chatter

tauted shaggy

tawpy slovenly

tawty shaggy

tax-cart two-wheeled open cart drawn by one horse

tea-and-turn-out tea and something with it

tearer swaggerer

tearing roistering, boisterous

teetotum dice designed to be spun like a top

Templar barrister at the Inner or Middle Temple, London inns of court

ten-penny token of Bank of Ireland for ten pence (4.2p), issued 1805, 1806, 1813

tent care

tenuity thinness

tester sixpence

teuch tough

Thebans stupid and sluggish people

thingumbob what-you-may-call-it

thir this

thirlage obligation on tenants of estate to use a particular mill and pay duty

thole endure, tolerate

thrang crowded, busy

thrapple throat

thumping huge

thunder-plump sudden heavy thunder-shower

tickle divert, puzzle

tint lost

tip let have

tod fox

toddy whisky, or other spirit, with hot water and sugar

tokay sweet Hungarian wine

ton wine-cask

top-boot long-legged boot with showy band of leather round the top

touchant touching

towzy-headed with dishevelled head

track-boat towed boat

train line of gunpowder

trance alley

trap deception

tree-dropped sprinkled or dotted with trees

tua two

turn-up boxing contest

turnspit dog kept to turn roasting-spit by means of treadmill

twist drink made by mixing two liquors

unco extremely

uncognoscible incapable of being known

underscrub undergrown,
insignificant fellow

until into

valley-de-sham valet de chambre

vapour show off, especially linguistically

vent market outlet

vice voice

volant active, nimble

wallop *noun* floundering movement, leap

wallop *verb* leap about, dance

wauf feeble-minded, shoddy

wean child

wear turn head away from wind

wecht weight

weel-faured well-favoured, good-looking

wersh insipid

wet drink

whalp term of abuse for a person

whammle roll

wherry light rowing-boat to convey passengers and goods on rivers

whiff small amount

whiles sometimes

whirligig top

whist hush, be quiet

whistling enticing, intoxicating

whitesmith tinsmith

whustle throat

wing *angling* imitation wing on fly

wirewoven resembling fine paper

wrap additional outer garment for travelling

wud, wudd mad

wudness madness

wullie-waught hearty swig

wunnock window

wus wish

yill ale

yokin' rough handling

youf bark

younker young man

zeolite any of a large group of alumino-silicates

INDEX

This is an index to the main text. It includes actual but not fictitious items, though in the *Noctes* the distinction cannot always be made with certainty. Except in the cases of Burns, Byron, Hogg, Scott, Shakespeare, and Wordsworth, published works are covered by the names of their authors.